THE LANDSCAPE OF THE CHANNEL ISLANDS

La Seigneurie, Sark. Victorian wing and medieval chapel.

The LANDSCAPE
of the
CHANNEL ISLANDS

Nigel Jee

Phillimore

1982
Published by
PHILLIMORE & CO. LTD.,
London and Chichester

Head Office: Shopwyke Hall,
Chichester, Sussex, England

ISBN 0 85033 458 6

Printed and bound in Great Britain by
BILLING & SONS LIMITED
Guildford, London, Oxford, Worcester

CONTENTS

LIST OF HALF-TONE PLATES

Frontispiece: La Seigneurie, Sark

LIST OF COLOUR PLATES

(*between pages 86 and 87*)

LIST OF MAPS

SOURCES OF ILLUSTRATIONS

Monochrome illustrations: Frontispiece and Plates 2-7, 9, 10, 13-15, 17-20, 23-36, 38, 39, 41, 42, 44, 46, 47, 49-51 are by Carel Toms; Plates 1, 8, 11, 21, 22, 37, 40, 43, 48 are from the collection of the Société Jersiaise, by whose permission they are reproduced.

The colour photographs are by the author and the maps were drawn by Alan Middleton.

ACKNOWLEDGEMENTS

I am most grateful to Alan Middleton for drawing the maps, and to 'Burble' Carey for typing the manuscript.

I acknowledge with gratitude the help I have received from Joan Stevens and Frances Le Sueur of Jersey, who with unfailing courtesy have answered innumerable questions about the history and natural history of their island. Any errors are, however, entirely my own.

DEDICATION

*To the Island Development Committees of Jersey
and Guernsey, with a mixture of admiration and
exasperation, this book is respectfully dedicated*

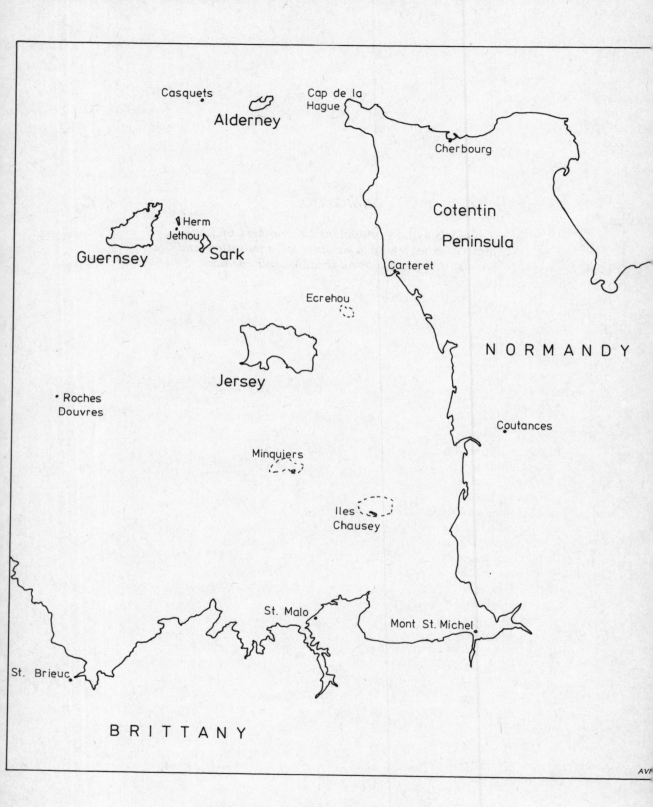

Map 1. The Norman Archipelago

INTRODUCTION

The archipelago known to the English as the Channel Islands and to the French as the Norman isles lies in the Gulf of St. Malo, tucked into the angle between the provinces of Normandy and Brittany. Alderney, the most northerly of the islands, is a mere eight miles from Cap de la Hague, the rugged and beautiful promontory that forms the north-west corner of the Cherbourg Peninsula. Lying 30 miles to the south is Jersey, the largest of the islands and the most southerly except for two groups of rocks and islets, the Minquiers and the Chausey Islands, belonging respectively to Great Britain and France. From Jersey, Normandy lies 15 miles to the east, Brittany 35 miles to the South, and Portland Bill 100 miles to the north. Roughly mid-way between Alderney and Jersey, but further to the west, lies Guernsey, with Herm and Sark sheltering on its eastern side.

The total land area of the archipelago is roughly 75 square miles—about half the size of the Isle of Wight. Crammed into this area is a population of about 127,000 souls, compared with the Isle of Wight's 109,000.

In terms of human history the Channel Islands have enjoyed an importance out of all proportion to their size. Their significance in Neolithic times, when the first seafaring traders ventured round the Iberian Peninsula from the Mediterranean, is demonstrated by abundant megalithic remains. There is evidence, too, of a good deal of activity during the Bronze and Early Iron Ages, and the position of the islands in the south-west approaches to the Channel has ensured that down the centuries they have maintained their importance both as havens of refuge and as hazards to navigation.

Very little is known about early Christian times in the islands; the Dark Ages here are particularly obscure. In about the year 933 the Channel Islands became part of the Duchy of Normandy, and after the Conquest of Britain in 1066 they lay for a time at the centre of a unified empire. The strategic importance of the islands dates from the year 1204, when King John of England lost continental Normandy to Philip II of France. He retained the Channel Islands, which despite brief periods of foreign domination have remained attached to the British Crown ever since. Their position as British islands on the French side of the Channel has ensured for them a turbulent history. The islands were of particular value to the British in the 13th and 14th centuries, when England still held possessions in southern France. A glance at an atlas will show that a ship from Gascony, having rounded Ushant and heading up the Channel for Southampton or London, will pass close to Guernsey and Alderney, and it was important that the islands should be friendly. The first expansion of St. Peter Port as a commercial centre dates

1

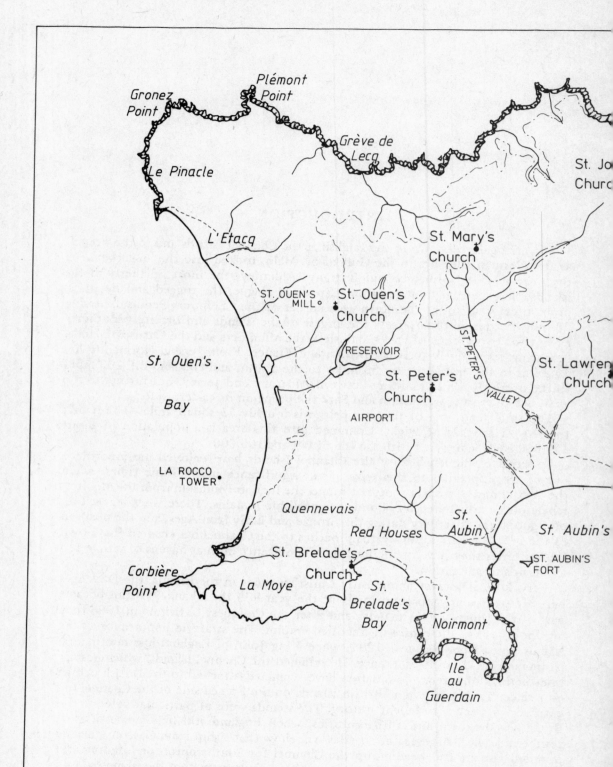

Map

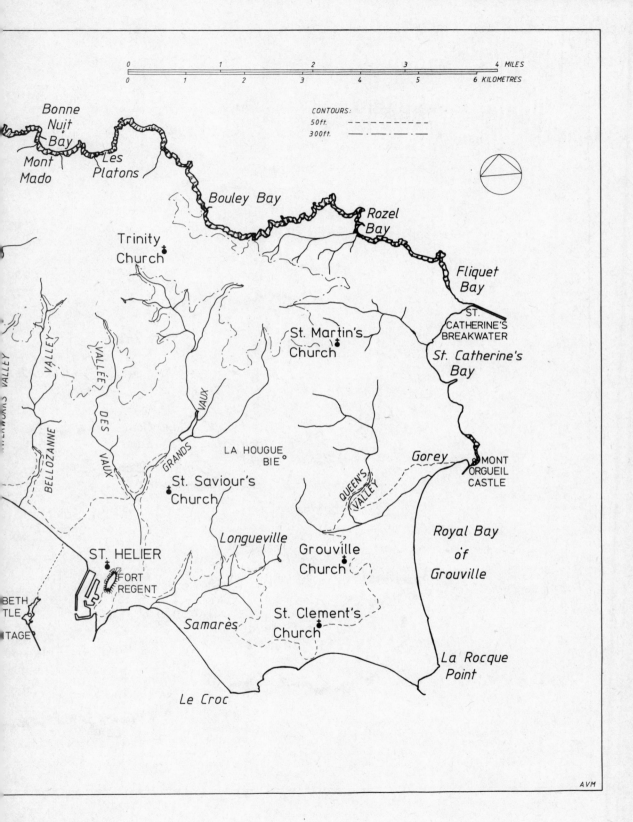

Jersey

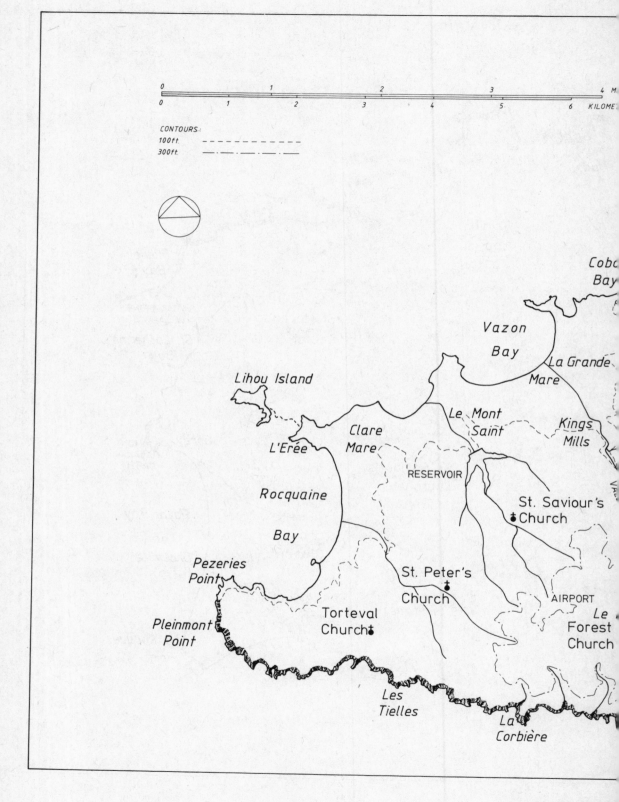

CONTOURS:
100ft. ------
300ft. -·-·-·-·-

0   1   2   3   4 Mi.
0   1   2   3   4   5   6 KILOME...

Cob[ ] Bay
Vazon Bay
La Grande Mare
Lihou Island
Clare Mare
Le Mont Saint
Kings Mills
L'Erée
RESERVOIR
St. Saviour's Church
Rocquaine
Bay
Pezeries Point
St. Peter's Church
AIRPORT
Le Forest Church
Pleinmont Point
Torteval Church
Les Tielles
La Corbière

Map 3.

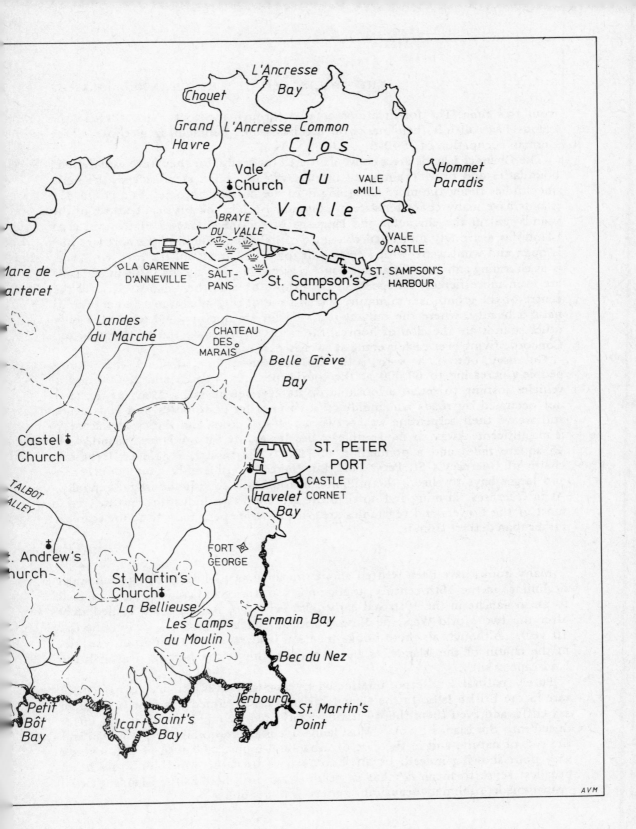

Guernsey

from this time. The fortifications erected through the centuries to defend the islands have all left their marks on the landscape, culminating in those of the German occupation of 1940–5.

The Channel Islands are a convenient area for study, for they have well-defined boundaries and provide abundant interest within a small area. Indeed, the more one studies them, the more absorbing does the interest become. As a group, the islands have many characteristics in common, both in the physical features of the islands and in the character and language of the inhabitants. Despite this, each island has a strongly individual character of its own. Alderney, the northern isle, is open and windswept, with a feeling of space and freedom. Its town, St. Anne, is as charming and unspoilt as one could reasonably wish, and its 1,700 inhabitants are even more fiercely independent than those of the other islands. Sark, at the centre of the group, is a miniature feudal state of 500 inhabitants and enormous natural beauty, where the only motor vehicles are tractors, and where the only other sounds are the clop of hooves, the rattle of cycles on the dusty roads, and Concorde flying over each evening at twenty past nine.

Guernsey, out to the west, is the most densely populated island with 54,000 people (increasing to 69,000 at the tourist peak in August) and 29,000 motor vehicles jostling to retain a foothold on its 24½ square miles. Much of the land not occupied by roads and buildings is covered by glasshouses, but leafy lanes still weave their serpentine way between fields of cows, and the coastal scenery is magnificent. Away to the south-east lies Jersey, by far the largest island, with 45 square miles and a population of 73,000. Its capital, St. Helier, lacks the charm of Guernsey's St. Peter Port, but there is considerably more countryside and larger bays to absorb the million-odd tourists who visit the island annually. As in Guernsey, farming and horticulture are important industries, but in Jersey most of the flowers and vegetables are grown in the open, and add to the scenery rather than detract from it.

*   *   *   *   *   *

Many books have been written about the Channel Islands. Starting with small beginnings in the 16th century, topographies, histories and guide-books increased to an avalanche in the 19th and early 20th centuries. Between and immediately after the two World Wars the flow subsided, to revive strongly within the last 10 years. Although all these books mention landscape as an important element in the charm of the islands, as far as I know this is the first to deal with the landscape as such.

Purely natural landscape, unaffected by man's restless activity, is extremely rare in the British Isles. In the Channel Islands it is confined to a few inaccessible sea cliffs, and even there the vegetation is affected by rabbits, which were introduced into the islands by man. Most landscape is a compromise between man and the rest of nature, and in the case of urban and industrial landscape nature has a very poor showing indeed. In this book I have used the word landscape in its broadest sense to mean *all* that is visible from anywhere in the islands; natural or man-made, sublimely beautiful or grievous to behold.

Any writer on landscape since 1955 must acknowledge the debt he owes to Professor W. G. Hoskins, whose book, *The Making of the English Landscape*, pioneered a completely new approach to the subject. As he described in his introduction, what he did in 1955 was

> to take the landscape of England as it appears today, and to explain as far as I am able how it came to assume its present form, how the details came to be inserted, and when.

I have presumed to attempt to do the same for the Channel Islands. My book contains no new discoveries, no facts that were not already known to specialists in the various subjects that must be covered in a work of this kind. But if it enables visitors to look at the islands with renewed interest, and more particularly if it help islanders to understand and appreciate what they hold in trust, it will have served its purpose.

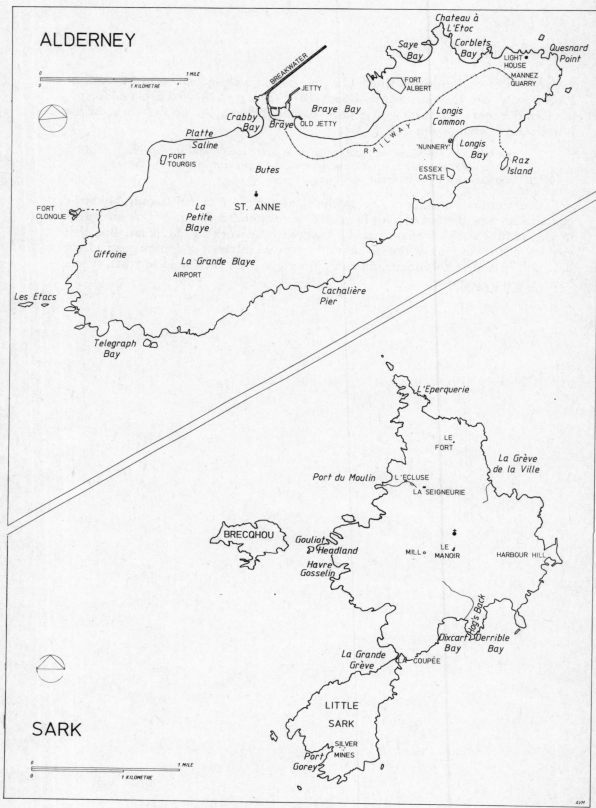

Map 4. Alderney and Sark

Chapter One

THE NAKED LANDSCAPE

The impression left on the visitor is that wherever he goes he meets granite, sometimes red, sometimes blue, sometimes grey, sometimes purple—granite cliffs, granite castles, granite churches, granite farms, granite piers and pavements.—G. R. Balleine, 1951.

A FAVOURITE STOPPING PLACE for holidaymakers in Guernsey, and for local people on their leisurely Sunday afternoon drives, is the car park on the cliff-top a little to the west of Icart Point. It is reached by squeezing through the lanes of St. Martin's towards Saints Bay and then turning right to follow a road which eventually emerges on the open plateau of the Icart peninsula. It is one of the few places on Guernsey's wild and rugged south coast where cars can be driven right to the brink of the cliff, and the cliff-top for a few yards in each direction thus receives more than its fair share of wear and tear. The view is magnificent. To the west, farmland extends to the edge of the plateau. The fields, quite large by Guernsey standards, are separated by earth banks which give some protection to the cattle grazing in them. A stone wall, encrusted with orange and grey lichens and with cushions of campion and thrift, forms a boundary between the farmland and the cliffs, which plunge 300 feet to the sea. The upper part of the cliffs are covered in some places by gorse, in others by broom or heather. Rockery-like outcrops in the more exposed places have stonecrop and autumn squill; in sheltered parts where some soil has accumulated there is bracken, with bluebells in April and May. At intervals a trickle of water descending the cliff has carved a little valley whose sides are occupied by a tangle of blackthorn.

The view to the west is bounded by Pointe de la Moye, a mere mile and a quarter distant as the raven flies, but double that distance if one follows the cliff path round the bays and headlands in between. The path runs the whole length of Guernsey's south coast from Pleinmont to Jerbourg, and then turns north to follow the more sheltered eastern cliffs until they descend to the town. It plunges through woods and over streams, descends steps and ascends more steps, but as it passes the car park at Icart it is in its typical position at the top of the cliff, with the stone boundary wall on one side and the sea far below on the other.

Turning to the south-east from the car park, it is a few minutes walk to Icart Point. The walk is well worth the effort, for on rounding the point another fine view opens up, this time across Moulin Huet Bay to the Jerbourg peninsula. Surmounting the neck of the peninsula is the needle-like monument commemorating General Sir John Doyle, Lieut-Governor from 1803–16, who did a great deal for the island, in particular by improving the roads. The original Doyle

Column, a larger monument with steps and a lookout gallery at the top, was destroyed by the Germans during their occupation, and replaced by the present more modest affair after the war. Below the monument a precipitous flight of steps leads down to the sands of Petit Port. The southern extremity of the Jerbourg peninsula appears to crumble into a series of great rocks—les Tas de Pois d'Amont—the Pea Stacks. The third stack from the end, which resembles an elderly monk, is Le Petit Bonhomme Andriou.

The Precambrian Foundations

The cliffs on either side of Icart Point are composed of one of the oldest rocks known anywhere in western Europe. It is a coarse-grained, granite-like rock containing in particular large crystals of feldspar which gives it a reddish-brown colour. It forms the main part of the plateau of southern Guernsey, covering some 12 square miles and forming the cliffs along most of the south coast, and the eastern cliffs from Soldier's Bay to Bec du Nez. Inland exposures are rare, but it can be seen in walls and old houses throughout St. Martin's and the Forest. Because of its flaky structure it is not a granite in the restricted sense of the word used by geologists, but is called the Icart gneiss. It is a metamorphic rock; that is, it has been transformed from its original structure by intense heat and pressure deep within the earth's crust. This is not surprising for the Icart gneiss is at least 2,500 million years old. Nor is it surprising that opinions differ as to how the rock was formed. It is possible that some, at least, of the gneiss was originally sedimentary rock, deposited at the bottom of some primeval sea. But the most likely origin of the main body of the gneiss that now forms the foundation of southern Guernsey is a mass of molten rock which very slowly cooled and crystallised to form granite. After perhaps hundreds of millions of years the granite was altered and partly re-crystallised by the enormous heat and pressure generated by movements within the earth's crust.[1] And so it remained for millions of years, penetrated by veins and dykes of other rocks during later earth movements, until finally it was left at the surface by the erosion of the rocks above.

The Channel Islands form part of the Armorican Massif, the complex of hard, ancient rocks that make up Brittany and the western part of Normandy. The general distribution of the various rocks in the islands was well known by 1900; indeed, the subject of the very first paper in the first volume of the Transactions of the Geological Society, published in 1811, was an 'Account of Guernsey and the other Channel Islands', by Dr. John MacCulloch. As he sadly explained when he delivered his paper, he had mislaid the specimens he had collected in the islands, and had to confine himself to a verbal description of the Channel Islands and their rocks. And if the title of his lecture seems to lay undue emphasis on Guernsey, this is because Dr. MacCulloch was a Guernseyman.

If much was known about the distribution of the rocks, the history of their formation had received little study. It was known that some of the rocks were sedimentary, having been deposited at the bottom of the sea; many were plutonic, having solidified, like granite, from the molten state, while yet others were metamorphic. Since the sedimentary rocks contained no obvious fossils it was assumed that they were Precambrian, or contemporaneous with the oldest era of British rocks. But Precambrian was an immensely long period—longer, in fact, than all the subsequent eras put together. By using the sophisticated dating techniques now available, and by regarding the islands as part of Armorica, much progress has been made within the last decade. It is reasonable, therefore, to use the terms used by geologists in Armorica.

The name given to the earliest period, when the Icart gneiss was formed, is Pentevrian, after the ancient province of Penthièvre in northern Brittany. It is applied to all Armorican rocks that are more than 1,000 million years old.

The Icart gneiss has been widely exploited as a building material, and many of the old houses and cottages in the southern valleys of the island have an overgrown quarry immediately behind or beside them, which provided the stone for the house. But the gneiss is only suitable for the rubble, or uncut, part of the building. Its foliated, flaky structure makes it unsuitable for cornices or lintels. Cornices in the humbler houses are often of brick, while lintels are usually cut either from 'pink' Cobo granite or 'blue' diorite from the north of the island.

Another metamorphic rock of Pentevrian age is the schist which outcrops here and there on the cliffs between Jerbourg Point and Fort George, where it forms grey bands of varying width within the gneiss. It can be seen particularly well immediately south of Divette. Schists were originally sedimentary rocks, in this case sandstone and silt, deposited at the bottom of an ancient sea. Later they were metamorphosed, like gneiss, by heat and pressure. They have a finer flaky structure than gneiss, and the folds into which the bedding planes have been thrown can be made out. Dr. R. A. Roach[2] considers the schists to be the oldest of all the Guernsey rocks, having been laid down in a Precambrian sea over 2,600 million years ago. But it depends whether you count the age of the rock from the time the sediment was laid down, or from the period when it was transformed into schist. Re-cycling is no new phenomenon. The materials of the earth have been used over and over again; indeed, the sediments deposited in the Precambrian sea were themselves eroded from an even more ancient land-mass.

A good exposure of schist may be seen at the extreme western tip of Lihou Island, where it gleams with tiny silvery crystals of mica.

The rock-mass that forms the core of the western part of Alderney is also of Pentevrian age. It is an igneous rock—that is, it was formed, like granite, by a gradual cooling of a molten mass deep in the earth. It is a dark grey, coarse-grained rock which, though altered in places, is not a true gneiss. It is usually described as a granodiorite. The magnificent coastal scenery of Alderney, from Fort Tourgis round the west and south coasts to a point just west of Cachalière Pier, owes its existence to this rock. It outcrops all along the cliffs, for instance at Telegraph Bay and opposite Fort Clonque, and it forms outlying stacks such as Les Etacs, where the gannets breed.

The granodiorite cliffs are seamed by numerous dykes—more or less vertical bands of several other types of rock, injected in molten form into cracks in the granodiorite during the various upheavals in the earth's crust that have occurred since the basement rocks of the Channel Islands were laid down. In particular, the Alderney cliffs exhibit swarms of dykes of felsite, a fine-grained and particularly hard rock that varies in colour from pink to purple. Several such dykes can be seen beside the causeway leading to Fort Clonque, and some of the sharper-looking stacks further to the south are also of felsite.

On the plateau of Alderney the granodiorite is overlain by a horizontal layer of felsite, which some geologists[3] have interpreted as a sill; a horizontal seam injected in molten form into the granodiorite mass. The granodiorite that once lay over it has nearly all been eroded away, but the harder felsite has resisted erosion and given rise to the plateau.

The plateaux of Alderney and Guernsey are the isolated remnants of a great mass of Pentevrian rock which by about 1,000 million years ago covered much of Armorica, including the area now occupied by the Channel Islands.

The era that succeeded the Pentevrian has been named the Brioverian, after the Norman town of St. Lô, whose Roman name was Briovera. During this time, which lasted some 300 million years, part of our area was elevated as dry land, while other parts were under the sea. Material eroded from the land was deposited in the sea, where it accumulated to form various sedimentary rocks. In the Channel Islands these marine sediments survive mainly in Jersey. The western part of Jersey, west of a line from the town to Bonne Nuit Bay, consists of a broad central belt of Brioverian shale sandwiched between more recent granitic masses to the north and south. Inland the shale is overlain by deposits of a much more recent date, but a fine expanse of shale is exposed at low tide in St. Ouen's Bay, for instance near La Rocco Tower at the southern end of the bay, and again near La Saline slipway at the north end. South of Mont du Feu and north of Le Pulec the sedimentary rocks give way to granite.

Fossils are extremely rare in the Channel Islands, since most of the rocks are igneous and the sedimentary rocks are so ancient and altered that any trace of primitive life that they may once have contained has been obliterated. Indeed, until recently it was believed that life had hardly begun so early in the earth's history. But traces of worm burrows have lately been found in Jersey's Brioverian sediments.

Towards the end of the Brioverian period volcanic activity began to dominate the scene. There were probably several volcanoes in the Armorican area, and at least one grew out of the sea somewhere near Jersey, giving rise to the volcanic rocks that make up most of the north-eastern part of that island. On the north coast, lava flows can be made out at Bonne Nuit Bay, Giffard Bay and Bouley Bay, and volcanic rocks outcrop on the east coast for a short distance south of Archirondel. In Havre de Fer a flow of lava has fractured into hexagonal prisms not unlike those of the Giant's Causeway in Antrim.

The Brioverian period ended 700 millions year ago, when a series of earth movements began which convulsed the Armorican area. During this mountain-building period, named the Cadomian after the Norman city of Caen, the rocks laid down during the previous eras were compressed between two great plates of the earth's crust—one might call them continents—which were moving slowly but relentlessly together. Some folds of rock were doubtless forced upwards to form mountains, but the rocks that have survived are those that were forced downwards, were melted by heat and pressure, and then forced their way to the surface again where they crystallised out to form various igneous rocks; granites, gabbros and diorites. In Guernsey the rocks exposed at low tide at L'Erée and part of the way across the causeway to Lihou Island consist of a granite intruded at this time, later partly transformed to Gneiss. It is a greyish rock, with large pink crystals of feldspar. Much of Great Sark owes its magnificent cliff scenery to granites that were intruded at about the same time, and again transformed later into various kinds of gneiss.

At a later stage in the Cadomian upheavals more molten rock-masses mixed and acted upon each other to give the diorite which forms the central part of Alderney, much of northern Guernsey, and parts of the north-west and south-east of Jersey.

Diorite is very variable; generally it is a dark grey, medium-grained rock containing black crystals of hornblende which, with the light crystals of feldspar and quartz, give it a speckled appearance when examined closely. It has been extensively quarried in all the islands, and is usually referred to as 'blue' or 'grey granite'. It is an excellent building stone and is also used as road-metal, but its principal use today is for crushing to make aggregate for concrete. In Alderney the diorite forms a central triangle bounded by Fort Doyle, Corblets Bay and Cachalière. The rocks exposed at low tide in Braye Bay are diorite, and it forms Roselle Point below Fort Albert and the cliffs around Cachalière Pier. York Hill Quarry, now a power station, Battery Quarry, now used for water storage, and l'Etoc Quarry are all legacies from the extraction of diorite. In the south of the triangle the diorite is particularly hard and in the early years of this century thousands of tons were shipped as building stone from the quarry at Cachalière, from the jetty built for the purpose.

In Guernsey the diorite forms the basic skeleton of the parishes of St. Sampson and the Vale; among the disused quarries are the huge hole at Bordeaux at present being filled with refuse, and the quarry at Beaucette now used as a yacht marina.

Between St. Sampson's Harbour and St. Peter Port the rock is a related igneous type called gabbro. This is perhaps the hardest and most durable of all the Channel Islands rocks, and huge quantities were exported from the quarry near St. Sampson's church, now used for water storage. The gabbro is a speckled grey rock of two types. That known to quarrymen as 'long-grain' has elongated, sickle-shaped, dark brown or black crystals of hornblende, which give the rock a definite grain. 'Bird's-eye' has rounded hornblende crystals.

In Jersey gabbro can be seen at Sorel Point on the north coast, while diorite outcrops on the cliffs nearby. In the south-east of the island diorite is the under-lying rock in the Samarès area, and forms the reefs exposed at low tide between Havre des Pas and Le Nez Point.

Not all the granitic intrusions were intermixed and altered to diorite or gabbro. The islands of Herm and Jethou owe their existence to a granite intruded during the late Cadomian; Little Sark and the western part of Brecqhou are granite, and in Great Sark l'Eperquerie Common and the stacks that form the northern tip of the island are of a similar rock. Bosses of granite are responsible for some of the most striking geographical features of Jersey and Guernsey. The Town Hill from whose summit Fort Regent commands St. Helier Harbour, and the Isiet of St. Helier on which Elizabeth Castle is built are composed of a fine-grained dull red granite, easily distinguished from the other Channel island rocks, that was intruded into the surrounding diorite. Dr. A. E. Mourant has described how this Fort Regent granite was used in many of the megalithic monuments of Jersey.[4] Another boss of granite is responsible for the magnificent site of Gorey Castle, and in the south-east corner of the island vast areas of granite are exposed at low water in St. Clement's Bay and at La Rocque.

In the south-west of Jersey the headlands of Noirmont and La Moye are composed of a hard and slightly older granite which affords some beautiful cliff scenery and also some excellent building stone; the granite of the Thames Embankment comes from La Moye. Finally, in the north-west of the island a broad band of newer granitic rock stretches from Grosnez Point to St. John's Bay, forming the rugged northern cliffs and extending inland to meet the central belt of Brioverian shale. As is to be expected over such a large area the type of granite varies from place to place. At the St. John's Bay and the Mont Mado quarry, now filled in, used to produce Jersey's most prized building stone: a fine-grained, pale pink granite flecked with grey and black. A little further west at La Perruque the stone is similar, but with fewer pink and more black crystals, while in the extreme south of the granite area Gigoulande Quarry, which is still working, has a coarse-grained granite containing large, pink crystals of feldspar. This range of colour, particularly of reds and oranges, contributes much to the landscape and is often remarked upon by visitors.

In Guernsey, an attractive red granite outcrops on the west coast from Vazon Bay to Port Soif. It forms the headlands of Fort Hommet and Grandes Rocques and acres of it are exposed at low tide at Cobo. This part of the coast is particularly beautiful in the evening, when the rocks glow red in the light from the sun as it sets into the sea. The hillock of Le Guet, once bare except for its watch-house, but now planted with pines, is composed of this Cobo granite. There are several overgrown quarries among the trees, but by far the largest is the one on the coast road immediately below the watch-house, which provided 'pink' granite for many of the houses and fortifications in the west of the island.

Cobo granite is still much in demand as a building stone, but the quarries are no longer worked and, as with Jersey's Mont Mado granite, the chief source of supply is demolished buildings.

Palaeozoic and Mesozoic Rocks

The close of the Cadomian marked the end of the immensely long period that the early geologists lumped together as the Precambrian; in the next era, the Palaeozoic, most of the remaining Channel Island rocks were laid down. The

Cadomian upheavals had left a range of mountains somewhere in Armorica. Judging by the distribution of the debris that was washed from them, the mountains must have been somewhere not far from Jersey—perhaps to the south, since we know that Alderney at this time was under the sea. The north-eastern corner of Jersey, between Bouley Bay and Archirondel, is composed of conglomerate, a highly characteristic rock that resembles badly-made concrete. Small, angular stones, larger stones and massive boulders are cemented together in a finer-grained background material. Since one of the best exposures is in Rozel Bay, it is known as the Rozel conglomerate. Another impressive exposure is in the Neolithic gallery grave of Le Couperon, just to the east of Rozel, which is entirely composed of boulders of this rock, dragged up from the beach nearby. The conglomerate can also be seen in numerous walls and buildings in the area.

The angular nature of the stones in the conglomerate suggests that they were washed by violent storms from an arid mountain range, and the large size of some of the boulders suggests that Jersey must have lain very close to the mountains, perhaps in the foothills.[5] The smaller particles were carried further by the rivers, much of the sand being deposited on a large delta which seems to have included the site of present-day Alderney. This is the origin of the sandstone which forms the eastern part of Alderney and the whole of Burhou, a small island a mile to the north-west. The hard, gritty sandstone that forms the Casquets, the notorious reef of rocks eight miles west of Alderney, was laid down at the same time.

The eastern end of Alderney is entirely composed of this hard sandstone. It outcrops all round the coast from Corblets Bay to L'Etac de la Quoire, forming cliffs some 200 feet high to the south of Essex Castle. On Longy Common the Palaeozoic sandstone is covered by much more recent wind-blown sand, but extensive areas of sandstone are exposed at low tide in Longy Bay.

The Alderney sandstone is an excellent building stone, being hard and durable but more easily worked than the igneous rocks. The Breakwater and most of the forts were built of it, and it can be seen in many of the houses and in the road-setts of St. Anne. The breakwater consumed such vast quantities of sandstone that a railway was built, connecting it with Mannez Quarry; it is still used occasionally to haul some of the remaining stock of stone from the quarry to the breakwater, where it is tipped over the edge to break the force of the waves. When the sandstone has been pulverised by the waves the sand is washed by the tide to Platte Saline, where it is collected and used, among other things, for bird-cages—another example of re-cycling.

At Cachalière the pebbly base of the sandstone can be seen resting on the diorite. This lower sandstone was deposited when the nearby mountain range was young and erosion violent. With the passing of time the mountains wore down and the particles became finer, so that the upper beds of sandstone are fairly fine-grained. The island of Burhou is composed of this finer, upper sandstone.

As the Palaeozoic era wore on the Cadomian mountain range was eroded down to its roots and the Channel Islands area became part of a vast plain. No rocks from this time survive in the islands, but there is some evidence that towards the end of the era a new range of mountains arose either on or close to the site of the present islands, only to be eroded away over millions of years, this time supplying debris to the area that is now southern England.

During the next era, the Mesozoic, the American continent began its long drift away from Europe and Africa. As the Atlantic opened, considerable faulting occurred around the edges of Armorica, creating submerged basins in which sedimentary rocks were laid down. A particularly deep trough to the north and west of our area created the western part of the English Channel. Towards the end of the Mesozoic era chalk was deposited in a tropical sea which approached to within a few miles of Alderney and Guernsey. But throughout the era Armorica, with its firm Precambrian base, remained intact while the seas ebbed and flowed and the land writhed around it.

The Tertiary Plateaux and Cliffs

By the beginning of the Tertiary era, some 65 million years ago, the basic form of the future Channel Islands could have been made out—sometimes as peaks rising from a dry plain; at other times with only their summits rising above the waves; the summits had yet to be planed down to today's plateau levels. Although the islands themselves contain no limestone, a considerable thickness of this rock was deposited in the warm Tertiary seas nearby. At times the limestone sea encroached between the present islands; soft Tertiary limestone has been found in deep water immediately to the north of Jersey.

A chronology for the various changes in sea level in Tertiary times has yet to be worked out; at some stage, when the sea was considerably higher in relation to the land than it is at present, the summits were planed down in stages to give the various plateaux that are such an important element in the landscape of all the main islands.

From within the islands the plateaux are not always obvious; the three airports make full use of them, but elsewhere the tableland is interrupted by housing and hedges, and dissected by tree-lined valleys. But when the islands are viewed from a distance their flat tops are most striking. From the sea some distance to the west of St. Ouen's Bay, for instance, the island of Jersey appears to have been planed level by some gigantic tool, as indeed it has.

On a rocky shore the waves tend to cut a platform at the lowest level of the tide. If the sea remains at about the same level for long enough, the platform may extend for a considerable distance. Such a wave-cut plain, still in the process of formation, can be seen in the reefs and islets of Les Minquiers, between Jersey and St. Malo, whose area at low water is greater than that of Jersey. Another example is the treacherous expanse of rocks around Les Hanois lighthouse, off the south-west corner of Guernsey.

To produce the summit plateau of northern Jersey would require a sea-level nearly 400 feet higher than it is at present, and it must have remained at this level long enough for the waves to cut a platform right across the summit of the island. The lower plateau levels of Jersey and of the other islands would have been cut at different times, perhaps as the sea-level fell towards the end of the Tertiary.

A study of a relief map of Guernsey shows that the southern plateau has two levels, connected by a gentle slope. The upper level, covering much of St. Martin's and the Forest, is at an altitude of approximately 300 feet, rising to 340 feet near the airport. The lower level, at slightly over 200 feet, extends further to the north and west and covers much of the parishes of St. Andrew's, St. Saviour's and St. Peter's. This lower plateau ends abruptly in an ancient cliff that plunges between the 200 feet and 100 feet contours to the lower-lying parts of the island. Though softened now by erosion, this inland cliff must have formed a shore-line at some stage, either towards the end of the Tertiary or early in the following era, when the sea was about 100 feet above its present level. The main Cobo road runs along the foot of the cliff from the bottom of the Rohais to La Haye du Puits; Rectory Hill climbs the cliff to the Castel church, built on the brink of the plateau. The cliff is interrupted by the Talbot Valley, but reappears behind King's Mills and the road again follows its foot from here to Mont Saint. In Rocquaine Bay the ancient sea cliff runs parallel to the coast, but a quarter of a mile or more inland. It can be seen from the coast road, across a strip of reclaimed marshland. At last it meets the present sea cliff at Pleinmont Point, but even at La Table des Pions there is a level, grassy strip between the cliff and the present shore.

In Jersey a similar fossil cliff has been left stranded in several places in the west, south and east, where the sea has been pushed back by comparatively recent accumulations of blown sand. In St. Ouen's Bay the cliff hangs steeply over the low-lying dunes from Le Pulec to the airport, before being smothered further south by the lofty dunes of Les Quennevais. Le Mont Matthieu climbs the cliff to St. Ouen's church on the plateau above; a mile further south a delightful miniature valley, Le Mont du Jubilé, cuts up through the cliff towards the church of St. Peter. In St. Brelade's Bay the cliff line can be seen some distance inland from the coastal road. In St. Aubin's Bay the cliff again leaves the coast to form an amphitheatre around Beaumont and Bel Royal, and in the south-east of Jersey it runs far inland from the reclaimed marshland and dunes of St. Clement and Grouville, rejoining the coast at Gorey.

In Alderney the cliff begins to leave the coast east of Fort Clonque, where the path runs along a narrow strip of land at its foot. Between Fort Tourgis and the town it runs further inland around the shingle and sand deposits of Platte Saline, and again it overlooks the dunes of Braye Bay. As one stands on Butes, admiring the view of the harbour and the small craft butting through the Swinge, with the islet of Burhou crouching beyond, one is standing on the brink of the Tertiary cliff.

It is not surprising that the same stranded cliff occurs in places on the French coast adjacent to the islands. The tiny harbour of Goury, immediately south of Cap de la Hague and nine miles from Alderney, is in a cove extremely reminiscent of Guernsey's Rocquaine, with the same sweep of cliffs separated from the sea by a strip of low-lying fields.

Sark is entirely cliff-girt, the whole of its cliff-line still resisting the onslaught of the waves, as it has periodically since Tertiary times. The table-land of Sark, like the higher plateau of Guernsey, must have been planed by a sea just over 300 feet above its present level, while the Alderney plateau is just below this height. Herm and Jethou, like the lower Guernsey plateau, are nearer 200 feet. Despite the slight difference in altitude, as one looks east from a vantage point such as Castle Cornet, it is very striking how the summits of Herm, Jethou and Sark appear to have been levelled by the same tool. Looking in the opposite direction from, say, La Coupée, the higher parishes of Guernsey are seen to be part of the same wave-cut plain.

The windswept plateaux of the Channel Islands are one of the most characteristic features of the landscape; they are also the most vulnerable to unsympathetically planned development. Every building that does not take shelter, as the older ones all do, in a hollow, will make a stark break in the skyline that will be visible from every direction.

The Ice Age

The Tertiary era was succeeded (between one and three million years ago, according to which authority you consult) by the Quaternary. This has often been called the Ice Age, although in fact it consisted of several intensely cold periods, or glaciations, alternating with interglacial periods when the climate was mostly milder than it is today. During the glaciations an immense ice-cap built up over northern Europe. It did not reach quite as far south as the Channel Islands, but they lay near enough to it to be included in the tundra zone. As more and more water became locked up in the ice-cap the level of the oceans fell. In our area the shoreline retreated far to the west, leaving the islands standing as a fragmented plateau in a vast plain stretching from Brittany to Normandy. Immediately to the north of Alderney a great river flowed westward to the sea.

The lack of vegetation in the extreme conditions at the height of the glaciations, and the repeated freezing and thawing of the soil and surface rock, caused rapid erosion. Pieces of rock and soil, loosened by frost and rain, slumped down the slopes and accumulated to a depth of many feet in hollows and valley bottoms. This deposit, which is known as 'head' may be seen exposed in the more sheltered parts of the coast in all the islands. It often forms a low cliff, perhaps four or five feet deep, at the top of the beach, composed of an ill-assorted mixture of boulders, angular rock fragments and silt. In these conditions the streams, rushing from the plateaux to the plain below, carved out valleys far more rapidly than would be possible under milder conditions such as we enjoy today, when the valley sides are protected by vegetation. This explains the deep, steep-sided valleys such as those leading down to Grève de Lecq in Jersey, or Petit Bôt in Guernsey, which it seems could never have been carved by the tiny streams they contain today.

All the plateaux are dissected by these miniature valleys, which have an importance in the landscape out of all proportion to their size. In their shelter woodland can develop, which in turn encourages shade-loving flowers and ferns, in contrast with the windswept plateau above. In Alderney Le Val de la Bonne Terre, carrying the mill-stream surreptitiously down to Platte Saline, provides a complete contrast with the open fields of the Blaye. The mysterious valley is made doubly attractive by the fact that the only thoroughfare it contains is an overgrown footpath. In Sark the road leading up from the harbour makes use of a steep-sided valley, and the Dixcart Valley shelters an unexpected ash wood.

At times during the glacial periods, a strong and persistent dry east wind blew across our area, bringing with it vast quantities of dust from the plains of central Europe. This covered the land with a silt-like deposit known as loess. The loess deposited during the last glaciation accumulated to a depth of several feet and forms the basis of the most fertile soils in the islands.

With the melting of the ice-cap during the mild interglacials, the sea level rose and the islands were once more isolated. At times the sea was higher than its present level, and when it remained at a particular height for long enough it cut a platform and deposited beach pebbles. Traces of these 'raised beaches' remain, sometimes far inland, in all the islands. Although a whole section of the beach is seldom exposed, a raised beach usually consists of a wave-cut platform, sloping up from the low-water mark of the time and supporting an accumulation of pebbles and gravel, sometimes cemented together to form a conglomerate. If the shoreline is formed by a cliff, this may have a groove cut into it, corresponding to the high-water level of the time.

Throughout the Quaternary the sea level was constantly moving up and down, and raised beaches have been found at many different levels. Broadly, however, they represent three shorelines at heights above the present mean tide level of approximately 25 feet, 60 feet and 120 feet.

The 120-foot shoreline seems to be the oldest, and few traces of it remain. The best exposure is at the top of South Hill in Jersey, where there is a sloping platform, a notch in the cliff, and a deposit of pebbles. Near St. Clement's church there is a platform at a slightly lower level, with pebbles covered by head. In Guernsey deposits from this shoreline have been found in two quarries; at St. Germain, in the Castel parish, beach sand was found at 110 feet, and in Les Vardes Quarry, near Port Grat, pebbles and beach sand were exposed at the same height. The presence of dune sand lying immediately over the beach deposit at Les Vardes suggests that the sea did not rise further than 100 feet before retreating again.[6] A small cave high in the cliff at Les Tielles, on Guernsey's south coast, may belong to the same shoreline.[7]

Fragments of the 60-foot beach are more numerous. In Jersey it has been found in two places on the east side of the Town Hill, on which Fort Regent stands, and notches at this height occur in several of the Jersey cliffs. One such site is La Cotte à la Chèvre, a narrow cave, later occupied by Palaeolithic man, whose floor is 56½ feet above the waves at the extremity of a rocky headland near Grosnez Point.[8] There are several exposures of beach pebbles at this height far inland in Guernsey, for instance in the hedge at the corner of a lane at Pleinheaume, in Noirmont Quarry, and at Anneville. In Alderney a good example is to be seen near the pond in Mannez Quarry, where pebbles and sand are overlain by loess and head.

The age of these two upper shorelines is still subject to debate, though they are both at least 100,000 years old. The 25-foot level is more recent and can be ascribed with certainty to the last interglacial period. Numerous exposures are to be seen in all the islands, in rocky coves and at the foot of cliffs. Present-day high spring tides just reach the wave-cut platform at the base of this 25-foot beach. Resting on the platform is a conglomerate of cemented beach pebbles, and this is often overlain by a crumbling cliff of head. In Jersey excellent exposures of the 25-foot beach may be seen in Portelet Bay and in Belcroute Bay, just south of St. Aubin's harbour, and there is a good example of a broad wave-cut platform with a notch in the foot of the cliff just east of Belle Hougue Point, on the north coast. In the beach conglomerate in the cave nearby, the bones were found of a tiny race of red deer which had evolved while isolated in Jersey during the last interglacial period.[9]

In Guernsey the 25-foot beach may be seen on all the western headlands, and the wave-cut platform is particularly impressive on the east coast at Bec du Nez and Divette, and also on each side of Fermain Bay. Evidence of the 25-foot beach is widespread in Alderney; a particularly good exposure may be seen in the rubbly cliffs to the south of the causeway to Fort Clonque.[10]

Many people who have sat on one of the pebble beaches of the Channel Islands will have noticed that some of the pebbles are not of local origin. Chief among these are nodules of flint, their black core usually covered by a white crust or patina which indicates that they are derived from chalk. As there is no chalk in the islands, the presence of the flints poses something of a problem. Some, if not all, have been eroded out of the 25-foot beach, which can still be seen to contain flints. The proportion of flint in the 25-foot beach increases from just over one per cent. at Bouilly Port in the south of Jersey to 38 per cent. at Hommet Herbé in Alderney.[11] This clearly indicates a northern origin, and there is indeed chalk in the sea bed quite close to Alderney. With the lowering of the sea levels in the glacials, the flints may have been eroded from the chalk and then washed up by the rising sea to be incorporated in the 25-foot beach. But this does not account for the presence of the other foreign pebbles. One ingenious theory is that they were carried by icebergs which broke from the northern ice-cap during the penultimate glaciation and were stranded on the depressed shoreline down the continental slope from the Channel Islands. With the rising of the sea-level in the last interglacial the foreign pebbles were, according to this theory, washed up the slope to be incorporated in the 25-foot beach.

The Last 10,000 Years

Between the end of the last glaciation and the present day some 10,000 years have elapsed—a tiny fragment of the geological time-scale. The first 3,000 years of this post-glacial period, when the climate slowly improved and the sea began to return from its low glacial level, appear to have left no trace in the Channel

Islands. But there is considerable evidence that in the warm and wet Atlantic Phase which began 7,000 years ago, an extensive forest of oak, hazel and alder not only covered much of the area of the islands, but extended beyond the present shoreline, perhaps as far as France.

Deposits of peat containing stumps of oak, acorns, hazel nuts and the pollen of several other forest trees, are known to exist under the sand and shingle in many of the bays of Jersey and Guernsey. Occasionally the peat is exposed when an exceptionally heavy storm scours away the overlying sand. In 1902 the sand was swept from St. Ouen's Bay to reveal some 500 tree stumps extending from the high-tide level halfway to the low-water line. Stumps are still occasionally exposed, for instance at the top of the beach near Kempt Tower and opposite St. Ouen's Pond, but sometimes years elapse between exposures. The peat extends inland for some distance under the dunes.[12, 13] It has been seen in St. Brelade's Bay, right across St. Aubin's Bay, and even at Grève de Lecq on the north coast. In Guernsey the forest bed has been exposed from time to time at Vazon and L'Ancresse, and revealed by excavation in several other places.

Excavations for buildings in the coastal plain of St. Helier, and dredgings in the harbour, have established that there are two distinct layers of organic material: a lower, black peat containing the pollen of oak and hazel, and an upper, brown layer consisting of a mat of sedges, rushes and reeds. The two are separated by gravel and shell deposits which indicate a temporary inundation by the sea. The lower peat is clearly part of the forest bed mentioned above. The upper bed of marsh plants indicates swampy conditions. A similar bed has been found extensively around lowland Guernsey, where it has been suggested that it is 3,500 years old, or less.[14]

Investigations at Vazon have indicated what the west coast of Guernsey would probably have been like at this time. The sea was by now close to its present level, and the shoreline much as it is today. A bar of shingle and sand across Vazon Bay impeded draining from the land, and a lagoon of fresh water formed behind it— La Grande Mare—in which silt and the remains of marsh plants accumulated. Borings have shown that the peat and other material in the Grande Mare were deposited in a V-shaped valley, perhaps a continuation of the Talbot Valley, cut at a time when the sea level was low.[15] The pebble barrier, along which the coast road runs today, was pushed back with a rise in sea level to dam the outlet from the Grande Mare and cause the stagnant conditions in which the valley bottom was silted up.

Similar ponds formerly existed behind many of the western bays of Guernsey; often the only indication today is the word Mare in the place-name. La Mare de Carteret is the site of a school. La Grande Mare, La Claire Mare and La Mare Hailla are used for agriculture when the level of the water-table permits. Only La Rousse Mare at L'Erée remains in its original state, though it is perhaps untypical as the water is brackish. The coast road running north-east from L'Erée Headland passes between a tall shingle bank on the seaward side and a flat, low-lying area, formerly an aerodrome, on the landward side. La Rousse Mare is the lowest part of this area, immediately by the road. In it such salt-marsh plants as glasswort, which have died out in other parts of the island, maintain a slender hold.

In Jersey, too, there were once extensive marshes behind the dunes and shingle-banks of the low-lying parts of the island. La Mare au Seigneur (St. Ouen's Pond), now a nature reserve, survives, and at the eastern end of St. Brelade's Bay there is still a marsh on Ouaisné Common, but the broad marshy areas that once existed inland from St. Aubin's Bay have been drained. In the south-east Grouville Marsh is the remains of a formerly extensive swampy area, and near Samarès Manor, as the name suggests, there was once a salt-marsh—a *salse marais*—which was only drained in the last century.

In Alderney La Mare Roe or Longy Pond is the remnant, now nearly overgrown with reeds, of a marsh behind Longy Bay.

The youngest geological feature of the islands is the deposit of blown sand which accounts for a considerable area of every island except Sark. Fragments of fossil dunes have been found in one or two places associated with raised beaches, but the present dunes are post-glacial and many of them have accumulated within the last 2,000 years. The most extensive sandy area is in the west of Jersey, where the long sweep of St. Ouen's Bay is backed by a belt of dunes half a mile or more wide. Over most of this area the sand has been fixed by vegetation to form a low-lying, undulating plain, dry and free-draining except for the hollow occupied by St. Ouen's Pond, and its surrounding reed-beds. South of the airport the belt of sand extends further inland and climbs a steep scarp to the lofty dunes of Les Quennevais, which reach a height of 259 feet above sea level. Here the sand is far less stable. On the summit of the Quennevais the covering vegetation has been breached in many places by rabbits and by human disturbance, resulting in 'blow-outs' of bare sand, interspersed with tussocks of marram grass. The St. Ouen's dunes are of widely different ages. Archaeological discoveries have proved some of them to be at least 3,000 years old, but some at least of the Quennevais dunes seem to have formed in medieval times. There is a folk-memory in Jersey that this area, formerly fertile land, was overwhelmed by sand during a single storm. According to one account[16] the storm was on St. Catherine's Day, 1495, when no fewer than five Spanish ships were wrecked on the rocks of La Corbière; the sandstorm which destroyed the fertility of the Quennevais was attributed to Divine retribution against the wrecking activities of the inhabitants. In fact, the advance of the dunes is more likely to have taken place in stages, a process that continued at least until the late 17th century. The present fragile cover has established itself within the last 100 years for Ansted, writing in 1862, described the Quennevais as 'a bare desert'.[17]

Another sandy area is in the south-east of Jersey, in the coastal parts of St. Clement and Grouville; the dunes of Grouville are used as a golf course.

In Guernsey, the remains of sandy, coastal plains or *meilles* survive in a few places on the west coast, for instance at Port Soif and Portinfer, but the only extensive dune area is L'Ancresse Common. This is a rolling expanse of dune turf, interspersed with rocky outcrops or *hougues*. The Common forms the western and northern fringe of the Clos du Valle, formerly an island separated from the rest of Guernsey at high tide. The presence on the common of megalithic remains shows that the dunes existed in Neolithic times, and the well-established turf is encouraged by fertilisers applied by the Royal Guernsey Golf Club.

Herm Common owes its existence entirely to blown sand. It consists of a low-lying, sandy plain from which rise two hillocks, Le Grand and Le Petit Monceau. The plain is protected from the sea on three sides by a chain of mobile dunes. In Alderney there are dunes at Braye and around Saye Bay, and a large area of dune turf at Longy. Here, as at St. Ouen, there is a folk-memory of a medieval sandstorm. The original town of Alderney is said to have been at Longy; its inhabitants were forced to retreat to St. Anne when the old town was over-whelmed by sand. There is no archaeological evidence of a medieval town at Longy, but in 1968 the remains of an Iron Age pot factory of about 500 B.C. were found on the golf course.[18] The site was covered by 18 inches of blown sand, and had the appearance of having been evacuated in a hurry.

Chapter Two

CLOTHING THE LANDSCAPE

Nowhere else, that I ever saw or heard of, is there such a sea for
background to such shores—or such land for background to such seas.—
Algernon Charles Swinburne, 1837–1909.

EXCEPT FOR THE WAVE-WASHED intertidal rocks and the more precipitous parts of the cliffs, the geological skeleton of the landscape is hidden from view by a covering of soil and vegetation. The soil and the plants rooted in it have been built up together over thousands of years, and neither could exist without the other. Besides influencing each other, the types of soil and vegetation that have built up have been determined chiefly by the underlying rock, by the climate and by the activities of animals, particularly man and the animals he has introduced. The influence on the landscape of man's agriculture, horticulture and building will be considered in subsequent chapters; in this chapter we shall consider the climate, soils, flora and fauna of the islands, and the main natural and semi-natural habitats that between them they have produced.

Climate

We have seen how widely the climate has fluctuated during the last million years. The present climate is similar to that of the coastal parts of southern England and the adjacent French coasts, but as is to be expected there is a stronger oceanic influence. Strong, salt-laden winds blow for much of the year, extremes of temperature are rare, severe frosts are uncommon, and snow seldom lies on the ground for long. The prevailing winds, from the west and south-west, blow with such persistence and force that the growth of trees is prevented in exposed places, and on the coasts and plateaux any shoot that ventures above the level of the crouching vegetation is ruthlessly cut back. Many of the Atlantic depressions that afflict the British Isles also affect the Channel Islands, though some pass them by to the north. The prevailing winds also bring with them an extremely high humidity—the average minimum daily temperature is only just above the dew point and heavy dews are frequent. Long periods of cold northerly and easterly winds also occur, particularly in the spring and early summer; apart from these dry periods the annual rainfall of some 30 to 40 inches is well distributed throughout the year.

The part of the British Isles with the most similar climate to the Channel Islands is perhaps the Isles of Scilly. The rainfall, indeed, is practically identical, Jersey having an average of 33.07 inches, and Scilly, 32.71 inches. These figures are very low when compared with south-west England, but are near the average of 32.67 inches for the whole of England. But Channel Island summers tend to be slightly sunnier, warmer and drier than the Isles of Scilly, while winters in the Channel Islands are not quite so mild and frosts, though rare, are more frequent than in Scilly.

Within the Channel Islands the sunniest island is Jersey: between 1959 and 1976 it was top of the British sunshine league on 11 occasions. Jersey's sunny, warm summers are usually attributed to the fact that it is the most southerly island and, in contrast to Guernsey, has its highest land in the north, so that much of Jersey is tilted towards the sun. More significant, however, is the fact that it is tucked further into the Gulf of St. Malo and is more influenced by the continental climate than are the other islands. Jersey is slightly drier than the other islands, the temperature range is greater and it is more liable to frosts. At Jersey airport the average daily minumum temperature in February (the coldest month) is 3.2 deg. C., and the average daily maximum is 7.7 deg. C. In August, the warmest month, the average daily minimum and maximum are 13.7 deg. C. and 19.2 deg. C.

The sunniest months are June and July, with an average of eight hours' sunshine a day; the least sunny month, December, has an average of 1.72 hours' sunshine per day. Significant falls of rain occur on 180 days of the year. Some snow falls on an average of 13 days, though it very rarely settles on the ground; air frosts occur on 13.8 days.

According to Dury[1] the rainfall varies significantly in different parts of Jersey, averaging over 40 inches on the highest ground in the north, and less than 30 inches on the south-east lowlands.

The figures issued by the States of Guernsey Meteorological Office are difficult to compare with those of Jersey, since the years used in compiling the averages do not coincide, but at Guernsey airport the average temperature in July and August appears to be a degree lower than in Jersey, the average winter temperatures are a degree or so higher, and the annual sunshine is a few hours less. Dury claims that in Guernsey the rainfall increases from west to east, the rainiest area being the elevated south-eastern corner of the island.

The climate of the smaller islands is very similar to that of Guernsey, though Alderney is particularly renowned for its bracing air. This is perhaps because much of the island is bare and open, with few trees to break the force of the wind.

Soils

Soil is formed partly by the weathering of the underlying rock and partly by the plants, animals and micro-organisms that live on and in it. But the fertile soils of the Channel Islands owe their existence also to the farmyard manure and *vraic* (seaweed) that have been added to it over the centuries. There is no chalk or limestone in any of the islands, and the soils that have formed on the ancient, hard rocks all tend to be acid. The only soils to be naturally alkaline are on the sands, particularly the dunes of St. Ouen, L'Ancresse, and Herm Common, where the sand contains a high proportion of fragmented sea shells.

In each island the pattern of soils is basically the same. The heaviest land is on the plateau, where a layer of *loess* three feet or more thick is underlain in places by a deposit of head. The *loess* was blown here by persistent easterly winds at certain times during the glacial periods of the Ice Age. Our area was then part of a vast steppe which stretched across central Europe and just reached eastern England.[2] The dust eventually settled around obstructions such as grass stems and accumulated to form a yellowish-brown soil known in the adjacent parts of France as *limon*. In the Channel Islands *loess* or *limon* survives mainly on the plateaux, but outliers may still be seen on some of the off-islets, for instance, Lihou off the west coast of Guernsey, and Green Island off the south-east of Jersey. Although the *loess* has usually been described as 'an ochreous clay' it is really a silt, the particles being finer than sand but coarser than clay. Nevertheless, it can form quite heavy soils, particularly in saucer-shaped depressions where drainage is impeded by the underlying head, and weathering has produced a deposit of finer clay particles.

Originally the *loess* contained some calcium carbonate, but this has long since been leached from the surface by rain, and the plateau soils tend to be naturally sour. In Jersey sand from some of the bays, containing a high proportion of calcium carbonate, was formerly spread on the fields along with the *vraic*; today lime is imported to correct the acidity and the *loess* becomes excellent agricultural soil. It is not as 'early' as the low-lying sands, taking longer to warm up and produce crops in the spring, but it retains water better and crops can continue to grow during a moderately dry summer. The water-holding property of *loess* is an important factor affecting the water supply of the islands. Its fine, even texture allows it to absorb a great deal of rain, which sinks quickly into the soil where it is retained, and is then fed slowly into the streams. Thus a high water table is maintained on the plateaux. In Jersey the water table is very high in the parishes of St. Mary, St. John, and St. Lawrence.

The steep slopes around the edges of the plateaux have a gritty, free-draining soil derived from granite or some allied rock and tending to be acid. On the cliffs and unworkable slopes the soil is thin, but in Jersey particularly, wherever it has been possible for a man to swing a spade the soil has been worked and enriched over the years by repeated applications of farmyard manure and *vraic*. In Jersey the slopes are called côtils, and those with a southerly aspect proved particularly valuable for early potatoes. By skilful manuring, some of the côtils have been made to produce potatoes without a break for almost a century. Today, with the virtual disappearance of hand digging, the côtils are less cultivated than they were.

Between the foot of the scarp and the low-lying coastal area there is a gentle slope where the soil is usually a fine, sandy loam, partly derived from raised beach material. This is an easily-worked soil that well repays manuring and irrigation. In Guernsey there is a broad belt of this sandy loam, much of it under glass, on either side of the Braye du Valle. In Jersey the sandy loam occurs mainly in the west and south, where it affords excellent soil for market gardening; the earliest land, for instance, at L'Etacq in the west and Gorey in the east, is used for tomatoes and the earliest potatoes. Most of the soil of Alderney is light and sandy; even the *loess* soil of the plateau is lighter than that of the other islands.

The low-lying coastal plains of Jersey and Guernsey are mostly based on sand, but here the nature of the soil depends very much on drainage. Where the run-off is good, as on the sandy plain at the foot of the Quennevais, or most of L'Ancresse Common, the soil tends to be dry. In other places, where run-off is impeded, the soil becomes swampy and peaty, with pools forming in the depressions. The most important of these, St. Ouen's Pond, is run with its surrounding reed-beds as a nature reserve. The water table comes to the surface also on Ouaisné Common at the east end of St. Brelade's Bay, and in a few hollows on L'Ancresse Common in Guernsey.

At both L'Ancresse and St. Ouen there is an interesting gradation in the acidity of the soil from west to east. At St. Ouen the soil near the bay is basic, the dunes containing plenty of lime in the form of fragmented shells. On the older dunes further inland, where the lime has been washed from the surface layers by the rain, the soil becomes acid.[3] At L'Ancresse there is a similar gradation, the soil being basic at the western end of the bay, but becoming acid towards Fort Le Marchant. On Herm Common the soil is particularly rich in shell fragments and lime-indicating plants such as rue-leaved saxifrage, salad burnet and burnet rose grow, and yet in the middle of the Common conditions of extreme acidity are indicated by a tiny *Sphagnum* bog.

Flora and Fauna

Despite their diminutive size, during the 10,000 years that have elapsed since the last glaciation the Channel Islands have accumulated an extremely rich flora, and an interesting, though more limited, fauna. The number of plant species, in particular, is high when compared with an equal area of either the British mainland or the neighbouring parts of France. The large number of species is partly explained by the wide variety of habitats that the islands contain, each with its own characteristic animals and plants. Further, their mild climate place the islands within the range of a number of plants and animals of southern Europe and the Mediterranean, some of which extend up the Atlantic coast of Europe as far as the Channel Islands, where they overlap with northern species, and this again adds to the diversity of the flora and fauna. The ormer and the green lizard are examples of southern species that reach their northern limit in the Channel Islands. But it is the plants, and particularly the trees, that contribute most to the landscape.

Trees and Woodland

Both Jersey and Guernsey were once well wooded. We have seen how the remains of a former forest lie preserved in the coastal peat beds; inland the forest probably covered most of the area of the islands except for sandy and rocky places where the soil was unsuitable. In the next chapter we shall see how the woodland was cleared in stages in prehistoric and medieval times. In Guernsey some indication of the former forest cover is given by the parish names Le Forêt and St. Pierre-du-Bois, but today the only considerable area of woodland is in Jersey. Even here, it represents a small proportion of the island: a survey of 1967 puts the area covered by mature trees at about 2¼ per cent. of the total land area, with a further 3 per cent. covered by scrub. Yet even this is more than existed at the beginning of the present century; many early photographs and postcards depict a landscape in places almost devoid of trees.

The original forest contained a mixture of trees of which the oak was almost certainly the commonest, and oaks, perhaps descended from those of the primeval woodland, still dominate many of Jersey's wooded côtils. The species is the pedunculate oak, characteristic of lowland Britain and central Europe. It is frequent as a hedgerow tree, and stunted specimens can be found in many places on the cliffs; but it is in Jersey's inland valleys and on the côtils that the oak comes into its own. It is particularly beautiful during the brief period in May when its fresh yellow-green leaves have just broken and the elms are not yet in leaf. Bright autumn colour is not a feature of the Channel Islands, and in some years gales hardly give the leaves a chance to develop their autumn tints before blowing them from the trees. Nevertheless, autumn colours are very mellow, and in a favourable year Jersey can be quite ravishing on a golden October day when the oaks and sweet chestnuts are aflame, and the elms are just beginning to colour.

On a small scale there are several stands of oak in the Talbots Valley, Guernsey, and nearby in the Fauxquets Valley a delightful hanging wood, predominantly of oak, skirts the lane above the Moulin de Haut.

A closely-related tree, though vastly different in appearance, is the holm oak. This is a tree of southern Europe which is native as far north as Brittany; it may possibly be native also in Jersey, for wind-pruned specimens grow in several inaccessible places on the cliffs. It was planted extensively in the last century in both Jersey and Guernsey, and large specimens are to be seen inland, often close to houses. Sometimes, as at La Hougue Boëte in St. John, Jersey, it forms an avenue. These planted trees have seeded themselves in many places; there are even some small but flourishing specimens on the dune plains at the foot of the Quennevais. With its dense, evergreen canopy and hard leaves which are slow to rot when they have fallen, the holm oak discourages other vegetation and imposes on its surroundings a distinctive atmosphere of its own.

Hazel, a regular feature of English oak woods, is surprisingly rare in the Channel Islands. In Jersey it grows sparingly in a few of the valleys carrying streams south into St. Aubin's Bay, while in the other islands it is almost unknown. This is particularly puzzling as hazel nuts and pollen have been found in abundance in the coastal peat beds, and the plant is still common in the neighbouring parts of Normandy.

Sweet chestnut, probably introduced several centuries ago, is a common tree in Jersey and occurs sparingly in the other islands. Some of the larger Guernsey houses have trees of enormous girth in their grounds; a venerable specimen survives outside the entrance to the Beau Séjour leisure centre. Sweet chestnut is common in woods in Jersey, for instance at Grève de Lecq, and is a feature of many of the côtils, where the trees were felled for fuel during the Occupation. The chestnut stools have now grown again to maturity, each with several trunks.[4] Other côtils are now dominated by sycamore, an introduced tree that has made itself thoroughly at home in all the islands. In the woods it tends to produce spindly saplings, but in the open it makes a splendid tree and is to be seen in hedges, waste places, and even growing out of walls and buildings. Because of its prolific ability to seed itself sycamore is often regarded as a weed, yet it is one of the few trees that thrive in the salt-laden winds to which the islands are subject, and it will even grow close to the exposed west coasts.

Ash, beech and holly were all constituents of the primeval forest, and may still be seen today. All the present-day beech trees appear to have been planted, but ash and holly grow wild in many hedgerows and valleys. The ash has a bad reputation with farmers, who consider it to be a hungry tree that tends to improverish the soil around it. In Guernsey there is a saying,

Bastard dans son lignage vaut mux qu'aën fresne sus s'n héritage—a bastard in one's ancestry is better than an ash on one's property.

Jersey has a similar saying, but there the unfortunate tree is likened to a lunatic in the family. In spite of its dubious reputation a mature ash is a beautiful tree, and there are some fine specimens by the roadsides of Jersey and Guernsey. The ash is not as prolific as the sycamore and usually grows singly, though in Sark there is a wood of ash saplings in the Dixcart Valley.

The commonest tree in all the islands today, and a vital element in the landscape, is the elm. Elm pollen lies preserved in the coastal peat beds, but this was probably wych elm, a woodland species that is rare in the islands today. The ubiquitous hedgerow elms are various forms of field elm; not the common English elm, but forms that closely resemble the elms to be found in Normandy. It has been suggested[5] that they were brought from Normandy along with the apple trees when the cider orchards were established in the islands. Their purpose was to shelter the apple trees, and they still play an important role in sheltering the cattle and crops in the fields, as well as protecting buildings in the more exposed places. In Jersey, particularly, the hedgerow elms are often kept cut back so that they bush out and filter the wind more effectively than would tall trees with clean trunks.

In Guernsey, virtually all the hedgerow elms fall into one of two well-defined types. The first is a tall, pyramidal tree with small leaves. The trunk stands stiffly erect, the branches ascend at a steep angle, and the twigs turn up so that their ends stand vertically. It belongs to the same species, *Ulmus minor,* as the Cornish elm, but the Guernsey form can always be distinguished by the upturned twigs. It has been used fairly widely in amenity planting in England, and is known to nurserymen variously as the 'Jersey' elm, the 'Guernsey' elm, or *Ulmus sarniensis.* The name 'Jersey' elm is a misnomer, for this form of elm is uncommon in Jersey, whereas in Guernsey it accounts for perhaps two-fifths of all the trees in the island. The other elm of Guernsey has large leaves and is a much more irregular tree with the trunk inclined and bending, even when growing in sheltered places. In older trees the trunk is covered with bosses. The branches leave the trunk almost at right angles, and the lower branches seem unable to support the weight of their leaves, and hang downwards. This elm has a hybrid origin, with the small-leaved elm and the wych elm somewhere in its ancestry.

Although their leaves are of different sizes, the two elms are most easily distinguished in winter, when the straight trunks of the 'Guernsey' elms stand against the skyline, and their ascending twigs contrast with the lattice-like arrangement of the floppy hybrid. Each type is so uniform that they must have been propagated by cuttings or suckers. Sometimes in a hedgerow the point can be made out where the farmer ran out of one handful of cuttings and started on some more from a tree of the other kind.

Jersey also has two main forms of elm, each very similar to the corresponding type in Guernsey. But the small-leaved elm of Jersey lacks the stiffly ascending branching system of its Guernsey relative. Some Guernsey elms have, however, been planted in Jersey in the past; some fine examples have recently been felled in the avenue outside St. Ouen's Manor, and some line the road on the hill near La Haule Manor. In both islands the small-leaved form used to be known as the 'male' elm, while the floppy 'female' was particularly prized for making the hubs of cart-wheels for, as anyone who has chopped the close-grained, knotty timber will know, it is not easily split.

Elms grow, though less abundantly, on the smaller islands, and both Herm and Jethou have little woods of extremely picturesque, gnarled elms on some of their rocky slopes, the ground carpeted in May, as the elm buds break, by bluebells.

Dutch elm disease has existed in the islands for some years in a mild form from which most of the affected trees recovered. But in 1974 the aggressive strain of the disease, which has wiped out so many elms in the United Kingdom, struck Jersey, and in 1977 it reached Guernsey and Sark. The States of both Jersey and Guernsey, recognising the importance of elm in the environment, at once instituted a campaign of felling infected trees. Sark, on the other hand, decided to let the disease run its course, thus making the campaign in the other islands less likely to succeed.

If the elms were to be wiped out, the effect on the landscape would be devastating. This is particularly the case in Guernsey, where about 80 per cent. of the trees are elms. Guernsey's hedgerow elms give the island a deceptively wooded appearance and if they should go, not only would the shelter be lost, but also the corridors of green that at present screen the various built-up areas from each other. In Jersey, which has relatively more oak and other trees than Guernsey, the wooded côtils would remain, but the elm is still the commonest tree, and on the plateau the effect would be profound. Other trees could be planted, but the elm is particularly well suited to Channel Island conditions. It is tolerant to salt, the leaves are not easily damaged by wind, and they are extremely late in appearing in the early summer, thus missing the worst of the spring gales. In the autumn the leaves are retained until well into November, and can take advantage of the occasional Indian summer.

An almost universal feature of the island scene is ivy. Like elm, it does not mind salt-laden winds, but revels in the damp, mild conditions. Besides climbing up trees it sprawls over hedgebanks, and in woods it often covers the ground. It hides the rock faces of old quarries, and on the cliffs it even flourishes within reach of the sea spray. Ivy is often denounced as a parasite (which it is not), but it provides food and shelter for birds, nectar for bees, and contributes to the landscape by softening hard outlines. The islands would seem gaunt without it.

As might be expected, many of the animals and plants normally associated with woodland are confined in the Channel Islands to Jersey. The red squirrel, introduced in the mid–19th century, is now firmly established; in fact, Jersey is one of its few remaining strongholds in the British Isles, for there are no grey squirrels. The jay, also introduced in the last century, is now fairly common, and most woods have a pair of these attractive but undesirable birds, which prey mainly on the eggs and young of other species.

Contributing more to the landscape is the wild daffodil or Lent lily. Daffodils have been cultivated in the islands for a century, and many of the old cultivated varieties have become completely naturalised in fields, hedges and woods. But in Jersey the true wild daffodil flourishes in many of the wooded valleys, such as St. Peter's Valley and Grève de Lecq; it also dances in early spring among the dead bracken on parts of the northern cliffs. The cultivated varieties spread only by the bulbs dividing and so grow in clumps, but the Lent lily, which has fertile seeds, is evenly spread over the ground. It is a smallish daffodil by garden standards, standing perhaps a foot high with a yellow trumpet and slightly paler petals. Another flower that gets on well with bracken is the bluebell, which contributes a blue sheen to many valley sides and stretches of cliff in all the islands in April and May. The coarser, paler bluebell that will be encountered, particularly in Alderney, is an escaped garden plant.

Sea Cliffs

The greatest scenic glory of the Channel Islands is the considerable amount of unspoilt cliff scenery that still exists in all the islands. Because of their inaccessibility, the steeper parts of the cliffs support the only vegetation in the islands that could be considered entirely natural and unaffected by man, though even here the effects of the burrowing and grazing activities of rabbits, which were introduced by man, can be seen.

The cliffs are at their best in May and early June, when they form a natural rock garden which, when seen against the blue sea far below, can be breathtaking. Banks of thrift and sea campion cover the slopes with splashes of pink and white, while sheep's-bit provides cornflower blue. Beside the cliff paths are drifts of red campion and ox-eye daisies. Gorse, which has some flowers all the year round, is now in full bloom, its golden flowers contrasting with the lemon yellow of broom. On some exposed cliffs, for instance near la Corbière and near Le Pinacle in Jersey, is a prostrate form of broom whose silvery-grey sprays creep over the rocks and cover them in early summer with yellow. It also grows at the Pleinmont end of the Guernsey cliffs and on the south-western cliffs of Alderney. Prostrate broom breeds true from seed, but although it is so well adapted to exposure it cannot stand frost, and only grows in the mildest corners of the British Isles.

Almost everywhere the thin soil between the rocky outcrops is studded with the tiny, succulent-leaved English stonecrop whose cushions are entirely hidden in May by white, star-like flowers, tinged with pink. Where the soil is deeper there are thickets of blackthorn or bramble, with the occasional stand of foxgloves, while in the more sheltered hollows are drifts of bluebells, to be covered later in the year by bracken, whose young shoots are just now growing up among them.

Although the cliffs vary in their geology, they are all composed of hard, ancient rocks that weather reluctantly to form a thin, acid soil. The differences in vegetation are due mainly to the aspect and degree of exposure of the various cliffs. In Jersey the red granite cliffs of the Noirmont and La Moye headlands face the sun and also the full force of south-westerly gales. In early spring they are ablaze with colour, but later they become parched and bare until the heather comes into bloom in late summer. This is also the time when autumn squill is at its best. This tiny relative of the bluebell is widespread on the cliffs and in short coastal turf in all the islands. The little pyramids of purple flowers appear from July to September, to be followed by a mat of curly, wiry leaves which sometimes almost cover the otherwise bare clifftops.

A speciality of the sun-baked headlands of western Jersey is annual rock-rose. The petals, which open and fall the same day, are pale yellow with a red spot at the base. As with so many cliff flowers, the best time to see it is in May and early June. Apart from a small colony on the Alderney cliffs, it grows in none of the other islands.

Jersey's north coast, which has the loftiest and longest stretch of cliff scenery in any of the islands, has quite a different character, becoming overgrown in summer with bracken and brambles, and in the damper hollows with water dropwort and hemp agrimony. Some flowers that otherwise are confined to woods grow on these shaded northern cliffs; there are Lent lilies, bluebells, and even in places wood sorrel.

In Guernsey the cliffs extend all along the south coast from Pleinmont to St. Martin's Point, then north as far as La Valette, just south of the town. The wildest parts are at the western end, towards Pleinmont Point, where the wind-swept vegetation includes prostrate broom and tight cushions of thrift, sea campion and English stonecrop. A particularly beautiful stretch of these cliffs is at Les Tielles, which can be reached from the Pleinmont Road just east of Torteval church. The lane is narrow and the car park, on the very brink of the cliff, is small, so a Sunday visit is not recommended. Access and parking are easier further west, near the television masts.

Further east, around the tourist beaches of Petit Bôt, Saints and Moulin Huet, the cliffs are more densely clothed with thickets of bramble, blackthorn and bracken. Kaffir fig, a fleshy-leaved mesembryanthemum with showy yellow or pink flowers, covers some of the slopes around the bays. A native of South Africa, it has been deliberately planted elsewhere on the coast as a ground cover to beautify coastal defence work and German fortifications. It is frost-tender and was nearly wiped out by the severe winter of 1962–3, but Kaffir fig and other, smaller-leaved mesembryanthemums have now spread on to the cliffs and even reached the most inaccessible off-islets, doubtless carried by gulls, who like to use it as a nest-building material.

The east-facing cliffs between St. Martin's Point and the town are sheltered from the prevailing wind and have a character very much their own. To the north and south of Fermain Bay wood sage, bracken, ash and oak grow right down to the high-water mark. The 'Pine Forest' is little more than a handful of pines among the bracken on the cliff-side, but the view between their branches across the Russel to Herm, Jethou and Sark is particularly fine. On some of Jersey's east-facing coasts, too—for instance Belcroute near St. Aubin and Anne Port near Gorey—the vegetation grows right down to the water's edge.

The south coast of Herm has cliffs very similar to those of Guernsey, and as in Guernsey there is a continuous cliff path; beginning at the Rosière landing steps the path climbs to the top of the cliff at the south-west corner of the island, affording a fine view across the Little Russel to Guernsey, with the neighbouring island of Jethou in the foreground. The path continues along the indentations of the south coast until the view is across the Great Russel to Sark, with the coast of Normandy on the horizon. Flying low over the water from rock to rock and calling in an agitated manner are oystercatchers, and there will be groups of shags sitting on the outlying rocks, perhaps holding out their wings to dry their saturated feathers. Bobbing on the water there may be guillemots and the occasional pair of puffins.

Sark is ringed by cliffs and her coastal scenery, whether viewed from the sea, from La Coupée or from the various headlands, is unsurpassed. Access to the cliffs is in many places difficult as they become heavily overgrown in summer and there is no continuous cliff path. One convenient path leaves Harbour Hill quite near the bottom and climbs the cliff southwards towards the landing place at Les Laches. Striking inland again one can join another path leading on to the Hog's Back, a bare-topped headland between the bays of Derrible and Dixcart. From Dixcart an attractive path continues along the cliff, emerging on the road near La Coupée. Sark's west coast is more difficult to see, though paths lead to various vantage points—from Beauregard, for instance, paths to Havre Gosselin and the Gouliot Headland afford magnificent views.

The cliffs of Alderney extend from Essex Castle, round the south coast and north again as far as Fort Clonque. The scenery around Telegraph Bay is particularly fine—again at its best in early summer with thrift, sea campion and prostrate broom in abundance. From the headland a little further to the west is a view of Les Etacs, an impressive sea stack surrounded in the breeding season by a cloud of wheeling gannets; white sea birds, as large as farmyard geese, with black tips to their long, slender wings. When fishing they plummet headlong with half-closed wings, closing them just before entering the water with a resounding splash. Often a whole party of birds will dive together, causing a salvo of splashes.

The gannets took up residence in Alderney during the Second World War. When the inhabitants returned from exile after the German occupation they found a colony on Ortac, an isolated stack between Alderney and the Casquets, and a smaller one on Les Etacs. Both colonies flourished, and by 1966 there were 2,000 pairs of the massive birds on Ortac and Les Etacs, covering practically every inch of rock. After breeding the gannets disperse until the following season. Parties are often seen off the other Channel Islands, and birds ringed as nestlings in Alderney have been recovered from places as far apart as the North Sea and the coast of West Africa.

A little further north, with the gannet colony still in view, is an expanse of gorsy heath, the Giffoine. On many clifftops there is a narrow belt of gorse or heather-covered heath between the cliff and the cultivated land, but in some places, as on the Giffoine, this broadens out to cover a considerable area. One of the largest of these clifftop heaths is Les Landes in the north-west corner of Jersey, where western gorse flourishes. This forms a much neater, smaller bush than common gorse, and its flowers are of a deeper gold. Western gorse flowers later in the summer than common gorse so that in August and September the ground is covered by the purple cushions of heather and the gold of western gorse. A very similar landscape may be seen at Cap Fréhel on the north coast of Brittany, now run as a nature reserve.

Western gorse grows sparingly in the other islands—in Alderney there is some by the zig-zag path opposite Fort Clonque, and on the Giffoine, but on most of the clifftop heaths it is the much larger common gorse that covers the ground. These gorsy places provide a habitat, all too rare in the British Isles today, for the stonechat. The diminutive cock bird, with his black head, white neck and rusty red breast is still a familiar sight in all the islands as he perches on the summit of a gorse bush, making a noise like two pebbles being chinked together. Some gorsy headlands in Jersey, Guernsey and Alderney are also the home of the Dartford warbler, a bird of southern Europe that just reaches as far north as Alderney and one spot on the south coast of England. It is a tiny bird, darker than other warblers, with a long, slender tail which is flicked erect from time to time.

Sprawling over some of the gorse bushes are the matted, wiry red stems of the parasite dodder, whose pompoms of pink flowers later in the summer smell strongly of honey.

Gorse or furze was formerly used as fuel, and as shelter for cattle. It was sown on the earth banks between fields and in patches of land where the soil was too thin for the plough. Every three or four years it was cut, taking care to leave a few inches of stem to sprout again. Its main use was to fuel the great bread oven that every old house possessed, either in the kitchen or in a separate building, the *boulangerie*. When about three faggots had been burnt in the oven the ashes were raked out and enough heat remained stored in the brickwork for the day's baking. In Jersey, at least, this versatile plant was also used as fodder for horses, and for lightening the soil around the roots of young apple trees.[6] Many farms have a field, now brought fully into cultivation but still known as La Geôniéthe or Jânnière (in Guernsey Jaonière) meaning a furze-brake, and Jaonnet, the bay between Petit Bôt and Icart in Guernsey, also takes its name from gorse.

The harvesting by rotation of the gorse meant that there was always some fresh young growth. Gorse is no longer cut as fuel, but from time to time fires break out on the cliffs and these have the same effect. Provided the fire is not too intense the old, leggy plants are soon replaced by new shoots from the old roots, and by a multitude of seedlings. But occasionally there is a fire of such violence that the roots and seeds lying in the soil are killed, and the cliffs remain bare and black for several years. In the great drought of 1976 fires broke out in a number of places. In Guernsey one raged around La Corbière on the south coast from which the cliffs have yet to recover.

Sand Dunes and Dune Grassland

Before man began to involve himself in coastal defence, the sandy bays were backed by mobile dunes, whose sand was not fixed by vegetation but was free to blow with the wind. Certain specialised plants could grow on these dunes and as they gradually stabilised them, other plants became established until the vegetation had become continuous and the dune was 'fixed'. As a little soil built up the vegetation continued to change until the dunes were covered by grassland. Left to itself, this would then develop into a scrub of gorse and bramble, but in many places the dunes have been kept at the grassland stage by grazing or mowing.

Mobile dunes have become something of a rarity in the Channel Islands. Some have succumbed to the insatiable demand for building sand and have been replaced by 'landscaped' grassland or car parks—the dunes that formerly existed across the road from *L'Erée* hotel in Guernsey have suffered this fate. Others, cut off from the beach and protected by a sea wall have become dune grassland. Miles of sea wall, beautifully constructed of stone, were build during the last century, and the work of severing the hinterland from the direct influence of the sea continued in the early years of the present century and was virtually completed (in concrete) during the German occupation. Alderney and Herm are the only islands still to have a significant proportion of their sandy shoreline unprotected by a wall. Herm Common still depends on a bulwark of mobile dunes that form a rim right round the northern part of the island. Where the dunes have been breached, as has happened in recent years near the Pierre aux Rats obelisk, erosion has eaten rapidly into the sandy plain of the Common. In Alderney the picturesque horseshoe of Saye Bay is contained by mobile dunes, and they survive also at Braye, where marram, fennel, sea holly and sea spurge grow right up to the door of the *Sea View* hotel. But Longy Bay is separated from the common behind by a wall of German concrete.

In Guernsey, L'Ancresse Common is protected from its bay by a German wall, and there is some form of coastal defence along most of the sandy west coast. A few mobile dunes survive at Grandes Rocques, Port Soif, and around Grand Havre. In Jersey the Germans severed the connection between the largest sandy area and the beach by completing the middle section of the sea wall in St. Ouen's Bay. A narrow belt of mobile dunes survives here and there behind the wall, particularly at the southern end of the bay, and on the summit of the Quennevais, where the former plant cover has been breached by rabbits and by trampling, there is now an increasing area of unprotected mobile dune. On the east coast the sea is still in direct contact with the sandy hinterland in a short stretch of Grouville Bay—elsewhere around lowland Jersey there is a continuous sea wall, though the St. Clement's coastal strip is still sometimes eroded during storms, and residents complain of losing their gardens.

The most obvious and characteristic plant of the mobile dunes is marram grass, which can grow in loose sand where nothing else is growing. Since it can only grow in mobile dunes it is not as common as it used to be, but it has been planted deliberately in some places to fix the sand. The tussocks of tall, sharp, blue-green leaves arise from a mat of creeping rhizomes which stabilise the sand and allow other plants to gain a foothold. Such plants are sea bindweed, sea holly, yellow horned poppy, and at Braye in particular, sea spurge. Often a row of tussocks of the small, grass-like sand sedge can be seen striking out in a straight line across a bare area of sand, indicating the position of a rhizome beneath the surface.

When all the sand has been covered by vegetation the dune is 'fixed'. Marram grass dies out at this stage and is replaced by a variety of other plants. Fixed dunes and dune grassland still occupy a fair proportion of all the islands except Sark; the position and origin of the more important of these areas were briefly described at the end of the last chapter. Although there are many thickets of gorse and bramble scrub, much of the area is covered by dune grassland. The springy, wiry grass is red fescue and there are several other grasses as well, but grasses are by no means the only plants of dune grassland, where the turf is closely cropped it is extremely rich in wild flowers. Many of them are so small that the only way to see them is to search the dunes on hands and knees; if one is prepared to run the risk of being mistaken for an escaped lunatic an astonishing number of different plants can be seen. Twenty species of flowering plant in a square yard of dune turf is not uncommon, besides mosses and lichens, with numerous ants, snails and beetles going quietly about their business among them.

The richness of the dune turf depends very much on grazing, which prevents the stronger-growing plants from crowding out the smaller species. Some of the dunes are grazed by cattle, but by far the closest grazing is by rabbits. These are so abundant on even the smallest off-islets today that it is difficult to believe that they are not native animals, yet they were introduced into north-west Europe as a source of fresh meat by the Normans. During the 13th and 14th centuries they became much prized as a delicacy and commanded a high price. The right to hunt them was jealously guarded by the lords of the manor, who kept them in warrens or *garennes,* and employed warreners to see that they did not escape, and to protect them from poachers.

In Jersey the first implied mention of rabbits is in 1253, when Richard Grey, *Gardien des Iles,* was ordered by Henry III to guard well the royal rabbit holes. It is difficult to imagine the present Lieutenant Governor receiving an order from Her Majesty to this effect, and it shows the importance that must have been attached to the rabbit as a source of meat and income in the Middle Ages.

In 1261 Prince Edward (later Edward I) granted the right of 'free warren' to the seigneur of Anneville in Guernsey, and in 1309 his heirs claimed in court that they had always enjoyed the right 'to chase conies with a dog and staff without other engine, from the month of September up to the month of February'.[7] La Garenne d'Anneville still exists, tucked away behind the bungalows and greenhouses of St. Sampson's. It is an area of land some 100 yards square, surrounded by a bank and ditch and containing a wilderness of bracken, gorse and bramble that has remained essentially the same for perhaps 700 years.

The rabbits soon escaped from the *garennes* and spread throughout the islands. In 1274 Edward I claimed the right to any rabbit anywhere in Jersey, which implies that they had been escaping from the king's warrens at Gorey Castle and La Moye.[8]

In England the rabbit became a major pest to agriculture during the 18th and 19th centuries, when the enclosure of the arable land by hedges provided it with breeding sites running conveniently through its feeding grounds.[9] It remained a pest until the outbreak of myxomatosis in 1954. In Jersey and Guernsey enclosure began early and was virtually complete by the end of the 18th century; the rabbit population increased accordingly, aided by the fact that they were no longer considered to be of value, until today they may be seen, particularly at their main feeding time in the early morning, on agricultural land, on cliffs and commons, and even on the beach.

In 1958 myxomatosis took hold in Jersey, and the importance of the rabbits' grazing on cliffs and dunes at once became apparent. Frances Le Sueur has described[10] the magnificent sight during the first summer as flowering plants hitherto nibbled by rabbits, attained for the first time their full stature. Soon, however, the more delicate plants were crowded out by the coarser ones such as cock's-foot grass; if this had continued, the cliffs and commons would be dull indeed.

The rabbits are back, and although there are still limited outbreaks of myxomatosis, the rich, short-cropped turf has returned to the dunes. The rabbits of Alderney were also affected by myxomatosis, but in Guernsey, although cases have been reported on many occasions, the disease has never spread over more than a limited area. Herm, more than any other island, has a rabbit problem, and all the farmland has to be surrounded by rabbit-proof wire. On Herm Common the grazing is so intense that in places the sand is covered only by lichens and minute specimens of buck's-horn plantain, early forget-me-not and rue-leaved saxifrage.

Judging by the uses to which man has put the sandy areas, the two ideas they universally suggest to him are building-sand and golf. The extraction of sand has had a disastrous effect on the environment, particularly where the authorities have insisted on pits being filled with hardcore, covered with soil and re-seeded with grass. The characteristic dune relief, with the contrast between the dry dunes and the damp hollows between, has been lost for ever. The effect of golf has been more beneficial, for this land-hungry game has kept open areas of dune grassland that would otherwise have been developed in some other way, and has preserved the encroachment of scrub on to the fairways.

By far the largest sandy expanse is the St. Ouen–Quennevais area of western Jersey, which includes an 18-hole golf course, several smaller golf courses, and numerous sand pits of different ages. The largest pits have been used for dumping household refuse, but in the abandoned pits that remain, several rare plants survive. Most of these are of interest only to the botanist, but one, Jersey thrift, is a striking element in the landscape. This southern species, which reaches the extreme northern limit of its range in St. Ouen's Bay, is a larger plant than the common thrift and has broader leaves with a characteristically tangled appearance. It flowers comparatively late in the year; while common thrift begins to flower in April and is at its best in May, Jersey thrift is not out until June and is still in full flower in August. It is not confined so closely to the coast as common thrift. Mrs. Le Sueur has vividly described[11] how a century ago a sheet of Jersey thrift stretched from Noirmont through St. Brelade's Bay, across the Quennevais and down into St. Ouen's Bay. Being at the extreme edge of its geographical range the plant is extra sensitive to changes in its environment and today it is abundant only on the western side of the Quennevais and in St. Ouen's Bay, and particularly on disturbed ground where competition from other plants is temporarily removed.

A flower that still grows all over the St. Ouen's dune system is burnet rose, whose creeping stems, covered with small prickles and bristles, will have drawn themselves to the attention of anyone who has attempted to sit on the dunes. The large, creamy-white flowers are at their best in June. Burnet rose flourishes particularly well where crushed shells give the soil a high lime content, as at Les Blanches Banques and Les Quennevais. In Guernsey it grows on L'Ancresse Common, and the massed flowers are particularly fragrant and beautiful on the closely-cropped turf of Herm Common. The plant spreads by suckers and its densely-matted roots help to bind the dunes. Among tussocks of grass the stems can grow fairly tall, but where grazing by rabbits is intense, as on Herm Common, they remain flat on the ground.

Another attractive plant of short dune turf is hare's-tail grass, a small annual grass whose white, oval head looks like a rabbit's tail. It is so abundant in parts of Jersey that it is difficult to imagine that it has not always been there, yet it is known to have been introduced to Jersey in the late 1870s. Starting from a small patch at St. Ouen it spread the whole length of the bay and beyond, and today it grows in sandy places in the south and east of the island as well; it has been widely used for Battle of Flowers exhibits. The seed planted at St. Ouen almost certainly came from Guernsey, where it has grown in the north and west at least since the 18th century. It may be a native plant in Guernsey, but it has been suggested[12] that it was accidentally introduced from southern France in the early Middle Ages when there was a flourishing trade between Gascony, then a British possession, and Guernsey. In those days Grand Havre was an important port of call between Bordeaux and England, and the soft, cottony heads of hare's-tail still dance in the wind on the dunes nearby.

Chapter Three

MAN IN A LANDSCAPE

*To glorify the past and to condemn the present has always been the
way of the scholar.*—Chung-Tsze, *c.* 400 B.C.

THE FIRST MAN to set a tentative foot in the Channel Islands did so well over
100,000 years ago, during the third of the four main glaciations of the Ice Age.
Palaeolithic man came to hunt such Arctic game as mammoth, woolly rhinoceros
and reindeer. During his hunting trips he took shelter in caves that had been cut
by the sea in a previous interglacial period. The caves were now many miles
inland, overlooking a tundra plain that stretched to the horizon. Although all the
Channel Islands were part of the continent the remains of Palaeolithic man have
only been found in Jersey; evidence of his occupation has been found in la Cotte
à la Chèvre, a small cave high on the cliffs to the east of Grosnez Point, and to a
much greater extent in La Cotte de St. Brelade, a gash in the headland that today
forms the south-eastern boundary of St. Brelade's Bay. La Cotte de St. Brelade
is one of the most important Palaeolithic sites in Europe. Serious excavation
began here in 1910 and from then until it was sealed in 1979 the cave was
excavated almost continuously, yielding a great deal of information about the
lives of successive Palaeolithic tribes who used the cave until the early part of
the final glaciation, some 50,000 years ago.

After 50,000 B.C. there is a long gap in the record; if the later Palaeolithic
men, who were responsible for the famous painted caves of southern France and
Spain, set foot in the area no trace of them has been found.

The parties of Mesolithic hunters who roamed Europe after the Ice Age may
have visited our area while the sea slowly rose between the islands, but the
evidence that they did so is doubtful. Small flint flakes of the type made by
Mesolithic man have been found in Jersey and Guernsey; on the other hand
similar flakes have been found in deposits that are undoubtedly much later. In
contrast, the evidence for a Neolithic occupation of all the Channel Islands is
very strong indeed; moreover, the people of the Neolithic, or New Stone Age,
were the first to have a significant influence on the landscape, and some of their
tombs and standing stones remain as landmarks today.

The Megalith Builders

The Neolithic settlers arrived when the sea-level was lower than it is at present;
their tools have been found in the forest bed under the sands of St. Ouen and
Vazon, and in excavations in St. Helier. While previous cultures had made tools

by chipping flint, Neolithic man ground his stones to the exact shape he wanted, producing the beautiful range of polished stone axes which may be seen in the island museums. With these axes he made clearings in the forest and planted his crops.

The Neolithic people who brought agriculture to the Channel Islands seem to have come by sea from the Mediterranean. Hitherto on the inaccessible fringe of Western Europe, at some time around 4,000 B.C. the islands suddenly found themselves part of a trade route which had built up between the Mediterranean basin, Spain, Portugal and Brittany, and which was now extending northwards towards Britain and Ireland. The arrival of agriculture allowed the islands to support a far larger population than could have been maintained by hunting and fishing. Among the evidence for this large Neolithic population is the number of stone axes that have been picked up over the years (the Guernsey museum has an enormous collection, though only a small selection is on display at Candie). But of greater importance in the landscape are the megalithic monuments; tombs and standing stones built, as the name suggests, of great boulders, which may still be seen in Jersey, Guernsey, Alderney and Herm.

Unfortunately for the archaeologist, the dwellings Neolithic man built for the living were considerably less substantial than those he built for the dead, and the only habitation sites so far discovered are in Jersey. Even here there are very few. A possible dwelling site is at the foot of Les Blanches Pierres sand dunes at the southern end of St. Ouen's Bay, but the only definite Neolithic settlement site to have been excavated is at the Pinnacle—a vast tooth of rock projecting from the west-facing cliff to the north of St. Ouen's Bay. The saddle between this rock and the upper part of the cliff has proved a rich source of material, ranging in date from the Neolithic to the 4th century A.D. The lowest, and therefore oldest, level produced a distinctive type of pottery that has also been found in the megalithic tombs, showing that these Neolithic settlers were the first megalith builders in the islands.[1]

The Neolithic love of monumental tombs and standing stones, combined with a superabundance of great boulders with which to build them, has left the Channel Islands with a concentration of megalithic monuments second only to the Carnac area of southern Brittany. As in Brittany, a wealth of folklore has accumulated around them. The tombs were thought to be fairies' caves, or the entrance to fairyland, and there are horrific stories of what happens to those who interfere with them. Despite this there are few left on agricultural land, those that formerly existed having been cleared to make way for the plough. Most of those that survive are in the coastal areas and commons, but even here many have been destroyed by quarrying or, particularly in Herm, broken up and used as quarries themselves. Even fewer would have survived had it not been for the Guernsey antiquarian, F. C. Lukis, who rescued and excavated a succession of burial chambers in Jersey, Guernsey and Herm between 1811 and his death in 1871. It was Lukis who realised that the megalithic chambers were tombs; in the early 19th century they were thought to be Druids' altars, and shallow, circular depressions in the stones known as cup-marks were pointed out as receptacles for the blood of the victims, in spite of the fact that most of the cup-marks are on the vertical faces of the uprights. A sign post to the Druids' altar survived until a year or two ago at Bordeaux in Guernsey. The burial chambers are now generally known in the islands as dolmens—the name applied to similar tombs in Brittany.

The larger dolmens, which were used as communal tombs and in which the remains of many burials have been found, are such an important feature of the Channel Islands landscape, both visually and because of the atmosphere of antiquity which they impart to their surroundings, that they will be described in some detail. The largest and most spectacular are the passage graves; cave-like tombs with a single, small entrance facing approximately east. It is easy to imagine how they came to be associated with fairies, particularly when the tomb is covered by a tumulus and the opening seems to lead into a hillside. In fact, it leads into a low, narrow passage which opens out into a fairly roomy burial chamber. The walls are of large boulders set on end and the roof is of even larger boulders laid across the uprights. Although these great stones are all that remains of many of the dolmens, the gaps between them were originally filled with dry-stone walling and the whole structure covered by a circular tumulus which was bounded by a low retaining wall. Besides the Channel Islands, this type of tomb is characteristic of southern Spain, Portugal, north-west France, Wales, Ireland, and Scotland.

Le Déhus passage grave, near Beaucette yacht marina in Guernsey, has been much restored, but it shows roughly what the external appearance of many of the dolmens would have been like. Internally it is one of the more elaborate tombs, having four side chambers opening from the passage, beside the main chamber at the western end. On the underside of the second capstone from the end of the main chamber are the crudely carved face and hands of a human figure. This is the only carving at present known in the Channel Islands tombs, but as it only becomes visible when a light is held from the side at a particular angle, it is possible that others await discovery.

By far the most impressive megalithic tomb in the Channel Islands is La Hougue Bie; indeed, it is one of the largest and best preserved passage graves in western Europe. The huge tumulus, standing in an oasis of trees on the plateau of south-east Jersey, on the northern border of Grouville parish, is today 40 feet high and surmounted by two medieval chapels. Although now covered by a single roof, these are of widely different dates. The western chapel, Notre Dame de la Clarté, dates from the early Middle Ages and may have been built to Christianise the hougue to which some pre-Christian veneration still clung. The Jerusalem chapel, to the east, is said to have been built in 1520 by Dean Mabon, on his return from a pilgrimage to the Holy Land. (It may, however, be older, for a will of 1496 seems to refer to it.) Some slightly dubious miracles performed by the dean attracted numerous pilgrims to this chapel.

After the Dissolution of the Monasteries, when even tiny chapels were confiscated and sold, the hougue had a succession of owners, one of whom, James d'Auvergne, built in the 18th century the romantic Gothic 'Prince's Tower' that crowns the hougue in many old prints. This was one of the show-places of Jersey—the view from the top was eulogised by many a guide-book—until it had to be demolished in 1924.

Later in the same year the passage grave was discovered. By then the hougue had been acquired by the Société Jersiaise. When, for reasons of safety, the crumbling 'Prince's Tower' had been demolished, a trench was driven into the tumulus at ground level. When it had penetrated 30 feet into the mound, a stone was encountered which proved to be the second capstone from the entrance of a magnificent passage grave some 70 feet long. The passage, itself 32 feet long and 4½ feet high, opens out into a chamber whose headroom averages about 6½ feet. There are three side-chambers, giving the tomb a cruciform plan. A few of the great stones had collapsed and had to be re-erected during the 1924 excavation, but the dry-stone infilling between the boulders was still in excellent condition, and the tomb was completely dry. It had been plundered at some time, either during or before the early Middle Ages; such objects as remained for the excavators are now in the Jersey Museum.

Two miles south of the Hougue Bie, on a spur of high land to the west of St. Clement's church, is the passage grave of Mont Ubé. This tomb, some 40 feet long, was discovered in 1848 by workmen looking for building stone. F. C. Lukis, who hurried over from Guernsey as soon as he heard of the discovery, found the covering tumulus already removed and the capstones destroyed. He was, however, in time to save the walls of the tomb, which is unusual in having small internal compartments built against the walls of the chamber. It is now owned by the Société Jersiaise and may be visited by following a wooded track indicated by a sign by the road just to the east of Samarès Manor. Some 560 yards to the south, at Le Haguais, is a single standing stone known as La Dame Blanche or La Blanche Pierre. It is the largest menhir known in Jersey, standing about eight feet above the present ground level, and it is the only one in the east of the island. It is quite possible that other, unrecognised menhirs may exist as gate-posts or built into walls and hedges, but the only other standing stones known at present are clustered around St. Ouen's Bay.

Another dolmen belonging to the Société Jersiaise is La Pouquelaye de Faldouet, an enigmatic monument on the plateau just inland from Anne Port, where a spur of elevated land extends towards Gorey Castle. It is basically a large passage grave with a horseshoe-shaped eastern chamber roofed by a capstone that must weigh some 24 tons. Between the passage and the chamber is a circular courtyard which has apparently never been roofed, surrounded by small, box-like cists. D. E. Johnston considers that the western chamber was originally a simple passage grave and that the courtyard and cists were added later.[2] Although the dolmen has been badly mutilated it is full of atmosphere, having that air of mysterious antiquity that clings to megalithic remains in the remote parts of Brittany.

The circular courtyard and cists of Faldouet are reminiscent of a tomb which formerly existed on Mont de la Ville, the site now occupied by the Fort Regent sports centre. If the reader wishes to view this part of the Jersey landscape he will have to travel to Henley-on-Thames, for in 1788 it was presented by the

Vingtaine de la Ville to the Governor of Jersey, Marshal Conway, as a small token of gratitude from the island he had so greatly benefited. The Marshal caused the 45 stones to be shipped up the Thames in a barge and re-erected at his home, Park Place, just upstream from Henley, where they joined a Roman amphitheatre, a grove of cypresses, a grotto, and a bridge which incorporated some of the few remaining stones of Reading Abbey.

Jersey's remaining passage grave, a much more typical one, is the Dolmen des Monts Grantez, which crouches among the fields near the brink of the escarpment overlooking the northern part of St. Ouen's Bay. This is a fine specimen, with a single side-chamber. Most of the capstones are still in position, but the main chamber is open to the sky. At the foot of the escarpment, in the sandy plain behind St. Ouen's Bay, are several menhirs including Les Trois Rocques, grouped almost in a line in a field to the south-east of St. Ouen's Pond, and the White Menhir, built into a modern field wall 200 yards further south. Further south again, on the Quennevais, are some small menhirs and the remains of a small chamber that yielded so many bones when it was excavated in 1922 that it has since been known as the Ossuary.

Occupying a magnificent cliff-top site on a promontory to the east of Rozel Bay is the Dolmen du Couperon. This is not a passage grave, for the chamber, about 27 feet long and three feet wide, is parallel-sided and there is no passage. The covering tumulus has long since disappeared, but the outer ring of stones suggests that it was oblong, and not round as in the case of the passage graves. Le Couperon is one of the few Channel Island examples of a gallery grave—a type of communal tomb that is fairly common in the adjacent parts of France, where they are known as *allées couvertes*.

Le Couperon has a particularly rugged appearance, for the boulders are of the local Rozel conglomerate. The stone at present blocking the western end of the chamber has had a semi-circular opening cut out of it; unfortunately, the dolmen has been excavated and restored so many times that the original position of this stone is no longer known.[3] Judging by some very similar *allées couvertes* in the Paris basin, it probably formed part of an internal partition dividing the chamber in two, with a similar stone to complete a 'port-hole' which would have been just large enough to permit the passage of a body. The remains of a second gallery grave, side by side with a smaller tomb that was probably intended for a single burial, may be seen in the municipal park at Ville-ès-Nouaux, near First Tower.

Guernsey has three large passage graves, all near the coast. The Déhus has already been mentioned; the others are La Varde and Le Creux-ès-Faies. La Varde is a sandy hillock on L'Ancresse Common, just to the west of the road to Pembroke Bay. Its summit, some 70 feet above sea level, is shared by a passage grave and a German bunker. The passage grave has the largest chamber of any of the Channel Island tombs, with a single side-chamber. It was discovered in 1811, when some troops were digging a redoubt and came upon an 'artificial cavern'. The young Lukis was present when the troops began shovelling out human bones and pottery, but it was not until 1837 that he excavated the tomb systematically and found evidence of many burials.[4]

From the entrance of La Varde dolmen there is a fine view eastward across the Russel to the northern hillocks of Herm, where there are more megalithic monuments. There are several smaller tombs on L'Ancresse Common; across the road to the south of La Varde, among the gorse and brambles between two golf fairways, is La Platte Mare, a small burial chamber notable for a fine row of 'cup-marks' on the end of the northern prop-stone, and across the road to the east of La Varde, near a small pond, is another chamber, La Mare ès Mauves. Other, more ruined, remains may be noticed by the walker who is intrepid enough to brave the volleys of golf balls that fly over this beautiful part of Guernsey.

The third Guernsey passage grave is built into a hillock on L'Erée peninsula, skirted by the lane that leads from the coast road to the car park overlooking Lihou Island. It is known as Le Creux-ès-Faies and, as the name implies, it was known to Guernseymen of old, who thought it to be a fairies' cave. The tomb is 28 feet long and, as in the case of La Varde, it now shares its hill with a German bunker.

A little over half a mile to the north-east the coast road rounds a spur of elevated land, Le Catioroc, and in full view of the coast road as one approaches from the west, is Le Trépied dolmen. The burial chamber, which has no passage, is 18 feet long and roofed by three massive capstones. Like Le Creux-ès-Faies, Le Trépied is associated in Guernsey folklore with fairies, but it is more famous as the meeting place of a coven of witches, and is repeatedly mentioned in the records of a spate of witch trials that took place at the beginning of the 17th century. According to confessions extracted from some of the victims, the devil would sit on the centre capstone in the shape of a black goat, while the witches danced around him.[5]

Le Catioroc still has a strong atmosphere of mystery and antiquity, though marred by a cutting through the hillside, now used as a silage pit, which the Germans caused to be made for a railway that ran round the west coast during the occupation.

Guernsey has no surviving gallery graves, though a ruined structure in Delancey Park may be the remains of one. The stones are among the gorse bushes near the tennis courts at the north-eastern entrance to the park. Many smaller megalithic graves are recorded and some may still be seen, though it cannot be claimed that they contribute much to the landscape. A number of menhirs, however, do contribute greatly to the character of the Guernsey scene. The traveller who arrives by air will pass a small menhir, Le Perron du Roi, immediately after leaving the airport. It stands four feet high and at present forms the end of the wall at the corner between the main Forest Road and the road down to Petit Bôt, opposite the Forest Stores. Its original position was the other side of the road, where in the Middle Ages it served as a boundary mark for the royal fief. *Perron* means boulder, but it can also mean a mounting block, and as such it was used during the *Chevauchée de St. Michel,* a colourful medieval ceremony in which a great deal of fun was had by everybody under the pretext of inspecting the island's roads. Three cup-marks, the most obvious of which is just above ground level and full of tar, show the stone's prehistoric origin; the lettering was added comparatively recently, perhaps in the 18th century.

Turning from the airport in the opposite direction and heading towards I'Erée, the road passes the largest menhir in the Channel Islands, La Longue Rocque des Paysans. This rugged column of grey granite stands 11ft. 6ins. above the ground and is over 10 feet in circumference. It is 200 yards or so to the south of Les Paysans farmhouses, in the middle of a field on the plateau, overlooking Rocquaine Bay. It stands on private property, but Guernseymen have an opportunity of renewing acquaintance with it once a year, when its field becomes the car park for the West Show.

Besides these unhewn standing stones, Guernsey has two statue-menhirs, carved to represent female figures. Both are associated with churches; doubtless the churches were sited so as to Christianise places which had a tradition of pagan veneration. The older of the two stands just outside the west door of the Castel church. She was found buried a foot beneath the floor of the north chancel when the church was being restored in 1878, and erected in her present splendid setting under the trees, the view behind her commanding most of the north of the island. Although there is no detail to the face the stone conveys an excellent impression of a veiled figure. Around her head is what appears to be a crown or chaplet, and she wears a long necklace. Ridges on each side of the head suggest a veil. One breast has been mutilated; perhaps the figure was defaced and buried to prevent a veneration that persisted in spite of the building of the church. The nearest parallels to the Castel scuplture are mother-goddess figures which have been found in certain gallery graves in the Paris basin.[6] The site has further associations; the flat stones at the foot of the figure mark the site of a feudal court, and there is a tradition that the church was built on the site of a castle—hence the name of the parish. Certainly the position, at the centre of the island and on the brink of the plateau, would be a good one to defend.

The second female figure, *La Grandmère du Chimquière* (cemetery) at present serves as a gate-post at the entrance to St. Martin's churchyard. Unlike the Castel statue the face is carved in some detail, though the rest of the figure is merely suggested by ridges and grooves. She seems to be wearing a tightly-fitting head-dress, with tresses of hair hanging over her shoulders. Below the bust a pair of stylised, curving arms are just visible. The carving undoubtedly took place in two stages. The shoulders, breasts and arms seem to belong to the megalithic period, while the face has been touched up at a much later date, perhaps in the early Iron Age. La Grandmère formerly stood within the churchyard, somewhere between her present position and the church door. Even in the last century she was regarded with some awe, and was broken in two and removed by an over-zealous churchwarden to prevent such superstition. The people of St. Martin's were so outraged by this vandalism that she was cemented together and erected in her present not very satisfactory position, where she is in some danger from passing traffic. Small gifts of coins and flowers are still occasionally found on her head after weddings, and the writer is glad to number her among those present in the photographs taken after his own wedding.

A unique structure which is older than all these megalithic remains was excavated at Les Fouaillages, L'Ancresse Common, between 1979 and 1981.

The results of the excavation have yet to be published, but it appears to consist of a pair of small burial chambers in a triangular walled enclosure. It has been dated by pottery to 4,500 B.C., and must have been built by some of the first farmers in Western Europe.

The northern end of the island of Herm is rich in megalithic remains. Kendrick[7] lists 17 structures and it is extremely likely that more await discovery beneath the sand of the Common. Those that are at present visible have clearly been used as a source of stone by quarrymen, and tantalisingly little is known of their original form.

Walking north from the harbour, just before the path opens out on to the Common it passes a hill which has been partly quarried away. On the very summit of this hill (confusingly named Le Monceau, a name shared by the two hills on the Common) are the remains of a grave enclosed by a circle of stones. When Lukis visited the site on one of his customary rescue operations he found the quarrymen in the act of destroying it while two human skulls were being trodden to pieces under their feet. All that is visible today is a horseshoe-shaped arrangement on the brink of the quarry.

On reaching the Common the path strikes north-east across the closely-cropped turf to 'Robert's Cross' where several tracks meet in the plain between Le Petit and Le Grand Monceau. Looking now north-west towards Le Petit Monceau, Herm's largest dolmen lies partially buried at one's feet. It is a parallel-sided chamber about 16 feet in length, with most of its capstones still in place. There is a second burial chamber 27 feet to the north-west; this is at present buried in the midst of a large bramble-patch. Continuing up the spur towards the summit of Le Petit Monceau the remains of three small tombs can be made out by the side of the path. Another lies by the path near the bottom on the other side of the hill.

On Le Grand Monceau, the hill in the south-east corner of the Common, there are four recognisable ruins. The easternmost may possibly be the remains of a passage grave.

The stone obelisk on the dunes on the north coast of the Common is La Pierre aux Rats. It is said to have been built to replace a tall menhir that was destroyed by quarrymen, but which was needed by fishermen as a sea-mark. According to another version, it replaces a large dolmen with five capstones. Finally, since the last war a small tomb has been exposed by the erosion of sand at the extreme north-western tip of Herm. It lies at the top of the beach at Oyster Point, and appears to be empty.

The Percée Passage, between Herm and Jethou, takes its name from La Pierre Percée, a stone with a neat round hole drilled through it. If the tide is too low to use Herm harbour and the traveller is about to land at Rosière Steps, he will pass close to this rock on his port side. It is now usually known as the Gate Rock and there is a popular fancy that it served as a gate-post when fields extended between the two islands. A more plausible explanation is that it was used for mooring barges which were waiting to load stone from the quarries of Herm and Jethou.

Sark was certainly inhabited in Neolithic times, for numerous polished stone axes and other tools have been picked up and 10 dolmens are said once to have existed there.[8] Of these, only two small chambers have been seen in recent years, both in Little Sark.[9] The larger of the two lies near the clifftop overlooking Brenière Bay. Though smothered in gorse it can still be seen from the sea, or by looking east from the path leading down to Venus Pool. The other tomb is even less accessible, at the southern end of Vermandaie Bay.

Alderney was formerly rich in megalithic remains, but most of them have been irreparably damaged by the various spates of fortification that have rent the island during the last 200 years, culminating in the German occupation. The north-west corner of the island was the richest in megaliths: Les Porciaux, on a plateau above Longy Bay, were a particularly important group of tombs until they were incorporated into a German gun emplacement. The best surviving tomb is the miniature Tourgis Dolmen, which stands in a clearing in the gorse by the side of the unfenced road above Fort Tourgis, at the other end of the island. It was recently excavated by the Alderney Society. Although no trace of the occupant was found, it is easy to imagine why he chose to be buried here, with a splendid view over Clonque Bay and the Swinge.

Only the larger tombs and standing stones still visible in the islands have been mentioned. The previous existence of many more megalithic monuments is indicated by certain place-names. Thus in Guernsey Colonel T. W. M. de Guerin[10] found evidence for 68 tombs, of which 15 were still standing, and 39 menhirs, of which only six were still standing when he published his paper in 1921. The former existence of menhirs in both Jersey and Guernsey is indicated by names such as La Longue Rocque, La Longue Pierre, and La Blanche Pierre. La Rocque and its diminutive La Rocquette also indicate megalithic remains, usually menhirs, in Jersey, Guernsey and Alderney. St. Stephen's vicarage in Guernsey stands on the site of a field named Le Courtil de la Grande Longue Rocque, which suggests that more than one menhir stood in the area; across the road *Les Rocquettes* hotel tells the same story. Thus, while medieval churches were often built on megalithic sites by design, St. Stephen's is a Victorian church built on one by accident.

The names that most commonly indicate dolmens in Guernsey are La Pouquelaie, Le Trépied and Le Déhus, Déhusset or Tuzet. La Pouquelaie is also frequently found in Jersey. La Hougue, which may also mean a natural hillock or rocky outcrop, is commonly applied to dolmens, especially in Jersey, as in the case of the largest of them all, La Hougue Bie.

The Bronze and Early Iron Ages

The megalithic culture in the Channel Islands was extremely long-lived. Objects found in the tombs show that they continued to be used through the Bronze Age and even into the early Iron Age. Although the islands were certainly inhabited during the Bronze Age, there is no evidence at present that this period has left any appreciable mark on the landscape. The early Iron Age, however, has left its mark in the form of several earthworks in Jersey, one in Guernsey, and a possible one in Alderney.

The most impressive Iron Age monument is the promontory fort of Le Câtel de Rozel in Jersey. The tongue of land in Trinity Parish between Bouley Bay and Rozel Bay was cut off by a rampart extending north-west and south-east, from the clifftop at the eastern side of Bouley Bay to the steep-sided valley leading down to Rozel. All that remains is a 200-yard length near the clifftop, but this is well preserved and is still about 20 feet high, and some 30 feet wide at the base. On the promontory side of the rampart the ground is level; on the south-west side the land is lower and slopes away for some distance. This indicates that the position was a defensive one—it has been suggested that the promontory was a refuge for hard-pressed Gauls from the Continent.[11]

Inland in the same parish is the earthwork of Les Câteaux, a few hundred yards south-west of Les Augrès Manor (better known as the Zoo). Traces can be seen of an inner and an outer rampart, which may be Iron Age or later. And on the clifftop immediately to the east of Grève de Lecq is the tiny promontory fort of Le Câtel de Lecq, where a natural eminence has been improved by earthworks. Of occupation sites the Pinnacle, already occupied in the Neolithic, was still in use in the Iron Age, and a newly-discovered Iron Age occupation site is at present being excavated at Broad Street in the centre of St. Helier. At present the earliest Iron Age occupation site known in the islands is the pot factory already mentioned (p. 23) at Les Houguettes, at the extreme eastern end of the Alderney golf course.

At Jerbourg in the south-east corner of Guernsey is a peninsula some three-quarters of a mile in length and half a mile in width, joined to the rest of the island by a neck of land only 500 yards across, from Petit Port in the west to Pied du Mur, the little bay south of Bec du Nez on the east coast. The peninsula was converted into a promontory fort during the Iron Age by building a series of ramparts and ditches across the isthmus. Fortunately, the earthworks were mapped by La Société Guernesiaise during a too-brief excursion in July 1923, for since then they have been obscured by two German bunkers, two car parks, a public lavatory (two, if you count the sexes separately), an electricity sub-station, and a beer garden. There seem to have been three ramparts. On the west side they ran together from the clifftop overlooking Petit Port, where they can still be seen, towards the Doyle Column. To the east of this, two ramparts can still be made out running down through the bracken to Pied du Mur, while the third diverges and meets the coast further south at Divette.

No trace of the banks can be seen on the summit, for in the 14th century a fortification known as Jerbourg Castle was built, which itself has disappeared to be replaced by the Doyle Column. With the earthworks across the isthmus, the Jerbourg peninsula would have been an ideal defensive position, with a fair-sized area of plateau land surrounded on nearly all sides by 200-foot cliffs.

The first Iron Age settlement site to be found in Guernsey came to light during the drought of 1976, when crop-marks in a field in St. Saviour's were noticed in an aerial photograph. The site, a village of circular huts, has been excavated and has yielded evidence of a considerable traffic between Gaul, Guernsey and England during the first century B.C. and the opening years of the Christian era.[12]

The Roman Period

Imperial Rome seems to have made remarkably little lasting impression on the Channel Islands. With the Roman conquest of Gaul and of Britain, new trade-routes were established between Gaul and south-eastern Britain which left the Channel Islands out of the mainstream of events. Apart from a most exciting shipwreck just discovered in the St. Peter Port roadstead, Guernsey can boast no Roman remains whatsoever. In Jersey, the foundations of a building that can be seen on the col at the foot of the Pinnacle are certainly of Roman date. The building was probably a small temple with an inner shrine and an outer verandah. Some Romano-British pottery from the site suggests that the shrine was still in use at the beginning of the 4th century A.D. In Alderney the Nunnery may possibly be of Roman date.

The Nunnery is the rectangular, fort-like building with rounded corners beside the slipway leading down to Longy Bay. It is so close to the beach that parts of it have fallen into the sea. It has never been a nunnery—the name was probably coined by the inmates when it was converted to barracks in the 18th century. It is private property and the courtyard is today occupied by flats. Several interesting features, however, can be seen from the outside. The Nunnery was evidently built as a fort; the curtain-walls are massive and have round bastions at the corners. They are built of horizontal courses of irregular blocks of stone set in a mortar containing shell fragments and pieces of brick and tile. Some of the courses are of stones set on the slant to give a herring-bone pattern, with flat slabs between the courses. The architecture, the brick and tile fragments, and the herring-bone pattern all suggest that the Nunnery is of Roman date—perhaps one of a string of forts built along the Channel coast in the 4th century A.D.[13] At that time Longy would have been the main harbour of Alderney.

This, apart from isolated finds of pottery and coins and the capital of a Roman pillar that will be described later, appears to be the sum total of Roman remains in the Channel Islands.

The Dark Ages

In common with many parts of the British Isles, practically nothing is known of events in the islands during the long centuries that followed the collapse of Imperial Rome; the little that is known is based on extremely scanty material evidence. Some of the churches probably owe their foundation, though not their present buildings, to the period before the Viking invasions, and a very few habitation sites have been dated to this time.

L'Ile Agois is an isolated stack of rock at Crabbé, in Jersey's parish of St. Mary. It is separated from the main island by a narrow gorge with cliffs 250 feet high, and yet on it are the remains of several dwellings. Most are circular, earth-embanked 'pit dwellings', but near the top are the remains of three built of stone, and on the summit are the foundations of two rectangular buildings. A Dark Age date is indicated by one piece of pottery, and by the fact that a hoard of Roman coins was found below the wall of one of the huts.

L'Ile Agois is a good example of the full use man has made of Jersey, even of the most unpromising off-islands. Besides being a habitation, the islet has been used for grazing sheep; the seaward slopes, carpeted in spring with primroses and bluebells, still bear traces of sheep-runs. This is one of the most picturesque parts of Jersey's north coast. The headland immediately to the east, Le Col de la Rocque, belongs to the National Trust for Jersey and a visit is well worth while, particularly in early spring, when the wild daffodils are in bloom. It can be reached from the lanes to the north of St. Mary's church, by bumping down a cart-track for about a quarter of a mile. There are two cliff paths, one for pedestrians and one for horses, and the views to the neighbouring headlands in both directions are magnificent.

It has been suggested that a small community of hermit monks may have lived on l'Ile Agois. The only evidence for this are the cell-like huts and the rectangular foundations which may have been oratories, but certainly the Celtic saints were attracted to remote islets, and certainly the names of several of them are associated with the Channel Islands. Christian refugees would have discovered the islands in the 6th century when, having been forced out of Wales by the advancing Anglo-Saxons, they sought refuge in Armorica in such numbers that it became known as Brittany, the land of the Britons. One of the founders of the Breton church was St. Sampson, who became Bishop of Dol in about 552. He must have visited Jersey, for his name appears in field-names at St. Brelade, a chapel was dedicated to him at La Rocque, and his name is associated with l'Avarison, the islet on which Seymour Tower now stands—the square fortificattion a mile and a quarter out to sea from La Rocque Point. But St. Sampson is mainly associated with Guernsey, where a parish church is dedicated to him. According to tradition it was he who brought Christianity to the island, building his church on the beach at the spot where he first landed. The only real evidence for this is the dedication of the church, but certainly the inlet that is now St. Sampson's harbour would have been the best haven at that time, and St. Sampson's church was once nearly on the beach; the land between it and the harbour has been built up comparatively recently.

St. Sampson was succeeded as Bishop of Dol by his nephew, St. Magloire or Mannelier, who in 565 founded a monastery in Sark, in the little wooded valley running down from La Seigneurie to Port du Moulin. The community is said to have consisted of 62 monks, who undertook the education of the children of noble families from the French mainland—the earliest seat of learning in the Channel Islands. The monastery was sacked by marauding Danes in the 9th century, but seems to have continued in some form into the Middle Ages. The monks built a water-mill to grind their corn; traces of one of the mill-ponds survive near the bottom of the valley, and the dam is commemorated in the name of the adjacent property, L'Ecluse. The mill also gave its name to Port du Moulin.

The 'window' in the rock was blasted by a thoughtful 19th-century Seigneur to provide a look-out for tourists. All that remains of the monastery itself is the name of the valley and the property at its head, La Moinerie.

St. Magloire's missionaries visited both Guernsey and Jersey. Mrs. Stevens has pointed out[14] that the obvious place to land in Jersey from Sark would have been Grève de Lecq, or perhaps Bonne Nuit, and indeed there are a number of place-names in the area that indicate the sites of monasteries and chapels. The full title of St. Mary's parish is St. Mary of the Burnt Monastery. Although there is a mass of legend concerning the Celtic saints, it is perhaps these indicative place-names that provide the best evidence for their visits. Visible material remains are extremely rare. One valuable exception may be seen standing on the floor of the south transept of St. Laurence's church. It is the upper part and capital of a Roman pillar of the Doric order, fashioned from granite in the 3rd or 4th century. It was found buried beneath the floor of the nave in 1891. One side of the pillar is flattened, as it if were intended to stand as a pilaster against a wall, perhaps of a Roman villa. The top of the pillar is carved with an early Christian inscription. The lettering suggests Celtic influence from the British Isles rather than the Continent. Widely different translations are possible, depending on whether you think the inscription is in Latin or a Celtic language, but there is agreement that it is the epitaph of a priest who died about the year 600. At a later date, perhaps in the 8th or 9th century, the flat back of the pillar was embellished with a Celtic plaited design. Although there is no guarantee that the pillar was made in Jersey, it does provide evidence of a flourishing Celtic church in the island before the Viking conquest.[15]

The tombstone of another early missionary, bearing the fish emblem, is built into the west wall of St. Mary's church. In Guernsey, a tombstone standing at the west end of the Vale church bears a cross, an alpha and omega and an inscription which suggest British Celtic work of the 7th or 8th century. It was discovered in the churchyard in 1933. As recently as 1977 a piece of granite bearing a Celtic cross was found built into the wall of a barn at Maison d'Aval, St. Peter's, Guernsey.

Jersey's St. Helier, who established himself in conditions of extreme discomfort on a rock 300 yards south of the islet on which Elizabeth Castle now stands, did not come from Wales, but from the Low Countries. In the 12th century a tiny chapel was built on the supposed site of his cell, and in 1872, when the rock was incorporated into the breakwater, half of it was blasted away. The chapel, still known as the Hermitage, survives.

Although the former existence of oratories and chapels is indicated by place-names, names that are themselves Celtic in origin are extremely rare in the Channel islands, if they occur at all. Names that can be traced to the Vikings, whose forays reached this corner of Europe in the 9th century, are far more numerous. As is to be expected of a seafaring people, many of the Scandinavian words are connected with the sea. To begin with, the names of the islands themselves are Norse, the suffix -ey denoting a large island (Jersey, Guernsey, Alderney, Sark, formerly Serquey, and Chausey) and the suffix -hou indicating a small island (Lihou, Jethou, Burhou, Brecqhou, Ecrehou). Then the descriptive names of rocks, which are repeated many times in charts of local waters, are also Norse: étac (stack in English) means a large rock; grune, a rocky shoal, usually just visible at low water; raz, a tide-race; and boue, a rock formation below the water which causes a tidal eddy or 'overfall' as the tide races over it.

Several names of coastal features, although apparently French, are, in fact, Scandinavian in origin: crocq indicates a low point of land; nez a more prominent one, as in Mannez (Alderney), Bec de Nez (Guernsey), and Ronez (Jersey). Mielle means a sand-dune and banque a low cliff (not a bank in the English sense). Hougue, a cairn or barrow, and varde, a beacon or lookout point are also Scandinavian words, and usually refer to features that are visible from the sea.

At first the Norsemen came on brief plundering expeditions, returning home for the winter, but eventually they settled down and farmed the land. One area they settled at the beginning of the 10th century became Normandy—the land of the Northmen. Perhaps they settled and farmed the islands as well, for another group of Scandinavian names common in the islands is connected with farming: bel, a farmyard; cotte, a hut or sty; and haugard, a rickyard.[16]

As in the case of the Celtic saints, although there is circumstantial evidence for the presence of Vikings in the islands, evidence in the landscape is scanty in the extreme. But the inclusion of the islands in the Duchy of Normandy and the establishment of the feudal system resulted in changes which still colour the scene, and which are responsible for much of the special character of the islands.

Chapter Four

NORMAN ISLES

Some of our great historians have written on the assumption that feudal and evil are synonymous.—G. F. B. de Gruchy, Seigneur de Noirmont, d. 1940.

IN THE YEAR 911, by the Treaty of St. Clair-Sur-Epte, Charles the Simple ceded Normandy to the Viking chieftain Rollo, who thus became the first Duke of Normandy. The Channel Islands were probably added to the Duchy in 933, when further territory was granted to Rollo's son, William Longsword. However, it was probably not until the beginning of the 11th century that the islands came under the full control of the Dukes of Normandy, who had by that time adopted the French system of granting fiefs of land in return for feudal service. The duke kept some land to provide himself with revenue, and parcelled out the rest to his followers. They, in turn, sub-divided their fiefs among their own henchmen. The holder, or seigneur of a fief did not own the freehold of the property; he merely owned certain rights over it, in return for some service which varied with the fief. One of the features of the Channel Islands which make them of special interest is that even today they are divided into fiefs, each held by a seigneur. The difference is that the seigneurs' rights have been drastically curtailed, while their obligations to their tenants have been abolished completely.

The earliest recorded feudal grant in the Channel Islands dates from about 1020, when Duke Richard II divided the island of Guernsey into two, granting the western half to the Vicomte du Bessin and the eastern half to the Vicomte du Contentin. The western fief consisted of St. Pierre-du-Bois, St. Saviour's, the Castel, and that part of the Vale parish, the vingtaine de l'Epine, that formed part of the main island of Guernsey. (The rest of the parish, le Clos du Valle, was at that time a separate island and was presumably unproductive waste land, for it was not included in either fief.) The eastern fief consisted of the parishes of St. Sampson's, St. Peter Port, St. Martin's, Forest, St. Andrew's, and, surprisingly, Torteval.

The boundary between the Fiefs du Bessin and du Cotentin was probably not made by the Normans, but followed some existing administrative division.[1] This ancient boundary, perhaps the oldest in the island, can still be traced along lanes and field hedges, except where it crosses the airport. It corresponds with the parish boundaries, and when plotted on a map it forms a remarkably clean line dividing the island diagonally from south-west to north-east. Only the parish of Torteval, which was included in the eastern fief, although detached from it, breaks the line.

In the troubled years of the 11th century the two great fiefs changed hands rather frequently, as the loyalty of successive holders was called in question. Displayed in Candie Museum is a charter of about 1060 by the then Vicomte du Cotentin, confirming that Duke William (soon to become the Conqueror) had granted the six churches of the eastern fief to the Abbey of Marmoutiers, near Tours. On several occasions the fief was seized back by successive dukes; small parcels were subsequently granted to various abbeys and private families, but the manorial rights over much of the area, Fief le Roi, still belong to the Crown.

At some time, nobody seems to be able to discover exactly when or in what circumstances, half of the western fief came into the possession of the abbey of Mont St. Michel. This territory, which is still known as Fief St. Michel, includes the four churches of St. Saviour, St. Pierre-du-Bois, Ste. Marie-du-Castro (the Castel), and St. Michel-du-Valle. It also contains the wasteland that was not included in the original fief, including part of the northern island, le Clos du Valle. The other half of the western fief, Fief le Comte, was sub-divided and granted to various knights with holdings on the mainland of Normandy.

The islands of Alderney and Sark did not form part of the original share-out but were retained by the Dukes of Normandy. For a short time they were given to the abbey of Mont St. Michel, but were then transferred to successive bishops of Coutances, while Mont St. Michel was given another rather barren area, the fief of Noirmont in Jersey, as compensation. In the case of Alderney there was no feudal tenure; the holder does not seem to have had any duties to perform in return for his territory. Sark, like parts of Guernsey, was eventually held by several seigneurs holding other property on the Norman mainland.

In Jersey, too, successive dukes granted fiefs of different sizes to their followers in return for a guarantee of service and manpower in times of trouble, while retaining some part of the island for their own use, in order to provide themselves with a source of income. The larger fiefs were granted to important Norman families: St. Ouen to the de Carterets, for instance. The seigneurs of the great fiefs such as St. Ouen and Samarès had power of life and death over their tenants, and even minor seigneurs held feudal courts at which dues were collected, stray cattle sorted out and fines imposed. In Jersey the Queen's feudal court, l'Assize d'Heritage, is still held twice a year, and some of the minor courts continued to be held until recently. In Guernsey the Queen's court, Chief Pleas, is held three times a year, and a few of the minor courts are still held annually.

Feudal Courts and Colombiers

In Jersey the minor courts did not meet at any particular place, but in one of the houses on the fief, or perhaps at the scene of some controversy. Guernseymen were hardier, or perhaps more suspicious of each other, and met in the open air at a spot where seats were provided for the seigneur and his officers. Some of these feudal courts survive, and are a characteristic feature of the Guernsey landscape.

The largest and most powerful of Guernsey's feudal courts was that of St. Michel. This sometimes met in the Vale church and sometimes in the Castel churchyard, at a spot marked by some flat stones which may still be seen outside the west door of the church. When the statue-menhir was found beneath the floor of the church in the last century, she was erected in a place of honour behind these stones. In the lanes not far away, at the corner of Le Frie Plaidy and Les Pelleys, is the court of Fief de la Court; the place is marked by three comparatively modern stone seats built into the wall.

The court of Fief des Eperons is near the entrance to the farm of that name in St. Andrew's, down the lane leading south from 'The Last Post'. The name of the fief derives from the feudal due its seigneur owes to the sovereign; a pair of gilt spurs or their equivalent in money. The Duke of Normandy seems to have been rather heavy on his spurs. Several other Guernsey fiefs owed him an annual pair, and in Jersey the seigneur of the Fief des Blancs Esperons owed a pair of white spurs.

The court of Fief de Beuval is at Les Sages, St. Peter's. The road running down the valley from St. Peter's church widens at a cluster of houses, all bearing, in the true Channel Island tradition, the same name. The stone seats are in the front garden of the pink-painted farmhouse, against a high bank topped by elms. Someone with a poetic turn of mind has added a stone mushroom for good measure.

The main road leading up the hill from the reservoir towards St. Saviour's church passes the old parish school (now Le Mont Varouf School). The court of Fief des Gohiers is about 100 yards down the lane that leads off to the left, just above the school. The rude stone seats can still be seen in the broad grass verge of the lane, embellished by hydrangeas. Returning to the main road, continuing up the hill for a quarter of a mile, and turning right just before St. Saviour's church, the road dips down into the valley of Sous l'Eglise. From the bend at the bottom an upspoilt stone-paved footpath climbs the hillside towards the churchyard. It ends in a flight of steps up to the churchyard; beside these steps are the stone seats of Fief Jean Gaillard. The de Gaillards were a Gascon family who became influential in the Channel Islands of the 14th century.

The court of Fief d'Anneville is still held outside the front door of the manor house, in the lanes a quarter of a mile to the north of the Camp du Roi crossroads. After serving for many years as a stable, the house has recently been given the full restoration treatment. The fief takes its name from a family, who, in common with many others, lost their island property with the separation from Normandy in the time of King John. Near the manor is the *garenne* or rabbit warren, which has already been described (p. 37).

The court of St. Michel in Guernsey had the responsibility for organising the most colourful and elaborate medieval ceremony in the Channel Islands— *La Chevauchée de St. Michel*. This was supposed to be held every three years, and was ostensibly an inspection of the main roads of the island, to make sure that they had not become overgrown. Even in Norman times the custom must have been ancient, for it included dancing round such megalithic monuments as

Le Perron du Roi (p. 45), and there were features which some students of folklore have pointed to as the remains of a fertility cult. A full account of the *Chevauchée* will be found in Raoul Lemprière's book on the customs of the Channel Islands.[2] The custom was last enacted in 1837, with a revival in 1966 to mark the 900th anniversary of the Battle of Hastings. *La Chevauchée* is commemorated by *La Table des Pions* at Pleinmont. Just beyond the car park at Les Pezeries, at the extreme end of the road beyond Portelet Bay, is a grassy mound surrounded by a circular trench. It was here that the footmen or *pions* who attended the mounted dignitaries on the cavalcade, had their lunch, sitting in a circle with their feet in the trench.

Not all the feudal courts were held in the open, even in hardy Guernsey. Immediately opposite the third milestone from town, on the road between Saumarez Park and King's Mills, is a small, chapel-like building which is the court house of the major fief Le Comte. The court of Fief Le Comte was formerly held in the chapel of St. George which stood beside a sacred well in the demesne. For a time the chapel also served as a parish schoolroom, and a right of way through the estate was established which the parishioners refused to give up, even after a new school had been built elsewhere. One of the 18th-century owners of the estate was so annoyed by the constant trespass that he demolished the chapel, and since then the court has been held in the little court house by the gate.

Guernsey's other court house is the square building with the overhanging first floor, beside the imposing main gates of Sausmarez Manor, St. Martin's. The upper storey was probably added in the early 18th century, but the lower part is much older; it is probably the earliest building of brick with lime mortar in the island.

If Jersey lacks the sites of its feudal courts, it can boast of no fewer than 11 colombiers, or dovecotes, to Guernsey's one. In the Middle Ages, when most of the farm animals, apart from breeding stock, were slaughtered in the autumn, pigeons were an important source of fresh meat during the winter. Only the seigneur of the fief was allowed to have a colombier, which could house up to about a thousand pairs of birds. They cost the seigneur nothing to keep as they fed themselves on the peasants' crops; indeed, they were one of the causes of the French Revolution. The typical Norman colombier is a circular tower, the inside wall being lined by pigeon holes in which the birds nested. Each pair of birds had the privacy of a niche which was usually on the left side of the hole, so that a right-handed man could easily collect the squabs and eggs. The advantage of the circular plan was that every niche could be reached by a man on a ladder, which rested on arms projecting from the central upright pole, which could rotate. Most of Jersey's colombiers are of this circular pattern, but if the rotating gear ever existed there is no trace of it now.

The colombier was normally near the manor house (but not too near, because of the noise of the birds), and most are still on private property. The National Trust for Jersey, however, owns a fine example behind Longueville Manor. It can be reached from La Rue St. Thomas, to the east of the hotel grounds. A colombier at Longueville is mentioned in a document of 1299, though this may have been on a different site. The present building was erected in 1692, it was restored in 1873 and again, by the National Trust, in 1970. The cobbled floor came to light during the last restoration. Inside the circular wall are 700 nesting holes. Three quarters of a mile to the south is the colombier of Samarès Manor, which has survived in good condition. The colombiers of Trinity and St. Ouen's Manors are reconstructions; in the case of St. Ouen, even the site of the original one is forgotten.

The largest colombier is at Diélament, Trinity, with accommodation for over a thousand pairs of birds. It was rebuilt in 1573 on its original foundations and is still in good order, although the original manor itself has gone; only the rather grandoise gateway survives, opening blankly into a field. The Rozel colombier was unusually close to the manor house, but again the original manor house has gone and only the colombier survives.

At La Hague, St. Peter, the colombier was rebuilt in 1629 and is still in a good state of preservation, with a conical roof. The property known as Le Colombier, near St. Laurence's church, has a dovecote bearing the date 1669. This property was the manor of the fief Jourdain Payn.

The remaining round dovecote is at Les Colombiers, St. Mary, at the head of the Grève de Lecq valley. This property is unique in having possessed more than one colombier; indeed, it probably had three. Until recently all were in ruins, but one has been well restored, even to the conical roof with a sort of dormer window for the birds to enter by.

Finally, Jersey has two square dovecotes: one is at La Haule Manor, St. Aubin, and the other at Hamptonne, St. Laurence. The Hamptonne dovecote was built in 1445 and rebuilt in 1674.

Guernsey's only surviving colombier, a circular one, stands behind the farm-house of that name, in the lanes to the north-east of Torteval church. It stands on the Fief Janin Bernard, and was in existence by 1330. Being on the plateau it can be seen from many parts of Torteval and St. Peter's. By the beginning of this century it was in a ruinous condition, the ivy-covered walls reduced to 14 feet in height, but during the 1950s it was restored at the expense of a trust administered by La Société Guernesiaise, which also financed the restoration of the court house at Sausmarez Manor. Le Colombier stands on private land, and permission is required to view it.

There was formerly a colombier on Lihou Island. The circular foundation can be seen near the ruined priory, on the inland side of the path. In Sark, the ornate colombier in the Seigneurie gardens dates from 1730, when the property became the residence of the seigneurs.

Although only lords of the manor were allowed to build colombiers, other gentlemen of standing were permitted to own a few birds, which were housed in holes in the wall called *volières à pigeons*. These are not uncommon in Jersey and Guernsey, usually in the walls of farm buildings, but sometimes in the gable of the house itself. At La Tourelle, a farm in St. Martin, Jersey, four rows of *volières* are built into the top part of the projecting tower that houses the staircase. The tower, *la tourelle,* is an exceptionally fine one and gives its name to the property. The splendid farmstead of The Elms, half a mile south-east of St. Mary's church, has a double row of pigeon-holes above one of the two great archways leading into the farmyard. They are on the inside, facing the yard.

In Guernsey there is a barn gable bristling with pigeon-holes at La Maison de Haut, St. Peter's. Another example, easily seen from the main road, is the wall of a farm building in King's Mills, opposite Orange Lodge.

Bouvées, Vergées and Perches

One of the Norman legacies retained by the islands is their system of land measurement. At a time when the English acre is giving way to the hectare, the Channel Islands cling obstinately to their vergées and perches. The vergée, being smaller than the English acre, is a convenient unit for measuring the diminutive, but valuable, fields of the islands, and is still used when buying and selling property, leasing land, and calculating the application of fertiliser.

In both Jersey and Guernsey a vergée consists of 40 perches, but since the Jersey and Guernsey perches differ slightly in area, their vergées also differ. In Jersey a perch is an area of land 22ft. by 22ft., or 484 square feet. The vergée is an area of 2,151 square yards, i.e., four-ninths of an English acre, so there are approximately 2¼ vergées to the English acre.

In Guernsey the perch is slightly smaller, 21ft. by 21ft., or 441 square feet. Thus the vergée of 40 perches is an area of 1,960 square yards, and there are approximately 2½ Guernsey vergées to the English acre.

Though the vergée and the perch are still alive and well, larger units of land measurements which were used in the Middle Ages have long fallen into disuse. They do, however, survive here and there as place-names. In Jersey four vergées were equal to an old Jersey acre, six Jersey acres made one bouvée, and 10 bouvées made one carucate.[3] Guernsey had the same units, but authorities differ on how they were related to each other. The early, major grants of land were in carucates, which were sublet by bouvées. The word bouvée is obviously related to bovate of the Danelaw, though the areas involved are very different. It was originally supposed to be the area that could be ploughed by a team of oxen in a year, but by the time the word reached the Channel Islands it had lost this meaning, and was simply a conveniently-sized feudal holding. Similarly the vergée is reminiscent of the old English virgate, but a virgate consisted of several acres, while a vergée is a fraction of one acre. Charles Stevens derives the word from the Latin *virga,* a slender branch—hence a measuring rod.

The task of mapping the boundaries of the feudal holdings has proved surpris-ingly difficult and a great deal of detective work remains to be done. In a few cases the exact boundaries have been worked out. In many more cases the approximate location of a fief is known, but the boundaries have been lost, while some fiefs that are known to have existed have not been located at all. A map of the fiefs so far located in Jersey, together with a list of the unlocated ones, will be found in Volume II of Joan Stevens' magnificent work on old Jersey houses.[4]

In Guernsey the work of defining the feudal boundaries is helped by the *Livres de Perchage*. These are lists of all the tenants of a particular fief, giving details of their holdings and the area (*perchage*) of each. The court of every fief had the responsibility of compiling a *Livre de Perchage* once in each generation, with a maximum interval of 20 years. In some fiefs the practice has been kept up to the present day.

The 25-inch Ordnance Survey map of Guernsey had, until the new edition came out recently, the areas of the fields marked in vérgees and perches, and it is hardly surprising that these areas, obtained by modern surveying methods, are not exactly the same as those given in the *Livres de Perchage*. Nevertheless, by using a combination of the names of the field and its neighbours, the area of the field and inspired guesswork, it is usually possible to locate an entry in a *Livre*. Then, by working back from book to book, a history of the property can be obtained.

Patterns of Settlement

The Norman Conquest of Britain in 1066 had little significance in the Channel Islands, which had already been part of the Duchy of Normandy for over 100 years. Of far more importance was the separation from Normandy that began in 1204, when King John lost control of Continental Normandy, and was completed in 1259, when the islands were formally recognised as British. The islands, which until then had lain at the centre of a unified empire, suddenly became of strategic importance, and the first great wave of fortifications began, including Gorey Castle and Castle Cornet. The Channel Islands, as the only friendly territory on a hostile coast, became important ports of call between England her territories in southern France, and the development of St. Peter Port began.

The landscape of the medieval islands would have been one of open fields and nucleated settlements—groups of farm buildings and houses clustered together for mutual protection, each settlement with its common fields nearby. The fields were unfenced, and each was divided into strips cultivated by the different families. Between the settlements was oak forest where the soil was good, or on the poorer soils heathland or *landes*. In Alderney this arrangement survives intact, making the island of particular interest as one of the very few open field systems still to be seen in the British Isles. The farm buildings were clustered together in St. Anne and the cultivated land was on the plateau to the south and west of the town. The area is still known as La Blaye, a word doubtless related to the French *blé*, meaning a cereal crop. Part of it is now occupied by the airport, but most of it is still cultivated and it remains unfenced except for the occasional electric wire around a patch of grazing land. Narrow lanes or *Venelles* led between the farmsteads of the town and radiated out on to the Blaye. Beyond the Blaye was common grazing land, or *Terres*. Some of this was low-lying and marshy (Le Marais), some sandy (Les Mielles), some grew gorse which was used as fuel (Les

Genêts, Les Jaonnières) and some grew bracken, which was useful as bedding (Les Fougères). Le Prè (now the road between St. Anne's church and Valley Gardens) was valuable pasture land.

The open-field system was widespread in Europe and there is no reason to suppose that it was not practiced in all the islands; however, in Jersey, Guernsey and Sark it has been superseded and almost obliterated by the enclosed fields and widely scattered farmsteads that make up the rural landscape of those islands today.

The landscapes of Alderney and Sark make a particularly interesting comparison. Both are small islands slightly over three miles long and slightly over a mile across at the widest point, and both consist of a plateau surrounded by cliffs. The chief physical differences are that Sark has a narrow waist where Great and Little Sark are connected by the Coupée, so that Sark's total area is less than that of Alderney, and Sark is almost entirely plateau, while Alderney has a considerable area of low-lying dunes. But because of their histories, the man-made landscapes of the two islands offer a complete contrast. Alderney, which was inhabited continuously throughout the Middle Ages and where the feudal system did not operate, retains its open fields and its nucleated settlement to this day. Sark, on the other hand, was colonised from Jersey in the 16th century, after a period of perhaps 200 years during which it had had no settled population. The landscape is one of scattered farmsteads, each surrounded by its own fields, enclosed by high earth banks.

If there were ever open fields in Sark all trace of them has disappeared except for two small pieces of evidence; one place-name, Les Camps, and the fact that when the Jersey colonists arrived in Sark they were surprised to find a complete absence of hedges. Les Camps are the fields in the northern part of the rectangle enclosed by roads opposite the Seigneurie gates, and A. H. Ewen has suggested that the nucleated settlement would have been close to the site of St. Magloire's monastery.[5]

In the rural areas of both Jersey and Guernsey the open-field landscape has been almost entirely obliterated by dispersed farmsteads with enclosed fields. In both islands, however, vestiges of the strip system of cultivation survive. In Guernsey, clear evidence of the medieval open fields survive in documents, and in place-names containing *camp*, the local equivalent of *Champ*. Also, although villages in the English sense are not characteristic of the island, there are certain clusters of old buildings that are clearly nucleated settlements of the same type as St. Anne. Clustered round St. Martin's church is a group of farmhouses, La Bellieuse, whose arable land lay to the south and east around the 'Old Mill'; the district is still known as Les Camps and Les Camps du Moulin. In the Forest parish there was a settlement by the church at Le Bourg; Les Camps were just to the east. In St. Andrew's again there was a settlement round the church, with Les Camps just to the north. Beyond the fields, forming a kind of no-man's land between one parish and the next, was the wilderness or *landes*. The word survives as a place-name in numerous parts of the island, often on the boundaries between parishes.

In the Castel parish there is a well-defined nucleated settlement at King's Mills, formerly Les Grands Moulins. This is not centred on the church, which is strangely sited at the extreme edge of the parish, but on three water-mills that made use of the Talbot Valley stream. The first, Le Moulin de Haut, is idyllically sited at the foot of the Fauxquets Valley, up the lane that leaves the Talbots Road at a green island. Le Moulin du Milieu is by the Rue à l'Eau and Le Moulin de Bas was in the centre of King's Mills, its site now occupied by a water pumping station of almost unbelievably municipal design. As recently as 1945 there were 12 working farms in King's Mills, their land extending up the hillside behind, and on to the water meadows of La Grande Mare. In the Middle Ages the open fields of the district were at Les Beaucamps, where there is now a secondary school; as usual, all traces of the fields have gone, except for the *camps* in the place-name. Vestiges of strip-cultivation do, however, survive at Pleinmont, and they give a fair idea of what the open-field landscape was like. La Rue du Banquet, above the National Trust property of Le Vau de Monel, is unfenced for part of its length, and to its north is a large open field sloping down to give a splendid view across Rocquaine Bay to Lihou Island. The field is still divided into strips, separated by low balks of earth, and as would have been the case in medieval times, the strips belong to a variety of owners. Further examples of strip cultivation may be seen near the television mast at Pleinmont.

In Jersey the last considerable area of unenclosed cultivated land, in that part of the Quennevais which lies in the parish of St. Peter, is now covered by the airport. Some strip cultivation survives, however, particularly in the western parishes. Near St. Ouen's Mill there are several strips with earth balks between them. It is significant that a previous name of St. Ouen's Mill was Le Moulin de la Campagne, while the partially unfenced road which passes it and leads south to Mont Rossignol is La Rue de la Campagne. In Jersey, as in France, the word *campagne* can mean country as opposed to town, but it also implies open, unfenced terrain. Besides St. Ouen, the word occurs in St. Martin and Grouville.

G. F. B. de Gruchy[6] did not consider that there were ever nucleated settlements of the St. Anne type in Jersey, and indeed he was not very impressed by the evidence for them in Guernsey either. Certainly by the late Middle Ages the Jersey farmer liked to live at a decent distance from his neighbours, relying for protection on the fort-like layout of his farm buildings. Jersey has no villages in the English sense; no village green, with clusters of cottages nestling round a church. Settlements have grown up around the harbours and at the foot of Gorey Castle, but these are commercial rather than agricultural in origin. What Jersey does have is a number of small groups of houses, named Ville followed by a family name (La Ville ès Nouaux, La Ville ès Gaudins, La Ville ès Philippes). These probably arose simply by younger sons building upon their share of the land near the family home. The word ville is still in common use in Jersey—it may simply mean 'the town' (St. Helier), but it can also mean a country house, a farm, or a hamlet.

Much then remains to be discovered about the early settlement patterns in both Jersey and Guernsey. Much more is known about the settlement of Sark, since it was a planned operation, undertaken for strategic reasons.

The Elizabethan Settlement of Sark

Although Sark had been inhabited at various times during the Dark Ages and the early Middle Ages, by the first half of the 16th century it was deserted except for bands of pirates; Rabelais described it as an island of crooks, thieves, brigands, murderers and assassins. Then in 1549 it was occupied by the French, and although they were evicted in 1553 the vacuum left by the uninhabited island at the centre of the archipelago was a cause of concern both to the British government and to the authorities in Jersey and Guernsey. Particularly concerned was Helier de Carteret, seigneur of St. Ouen, from whose fief in the north-west of Jersey the cliffs of Sark were a mere 10 miles distant. Helier's solution was to propose to the British government that he should be granted the island of Sark as an extension of his Jersey fief; in return he would provide a permanent, loyal population and guarantee the defence of the island. Permission was granted, and in the summer of 1565 Helier crossed to Sark, cleared some land and made a trial sowing of wheat. The result was sufficiently encouraging for him to return the following year with a party of his tenants from St. Ouen.

Under the terms of the Letters Patent which Helier received in 1565 from Queen Elizabeth, he was obliged to see that Sark was permanently settled by at least 40 men would be capable of bearing arms in the island's defence. Accordingly he divided the island into 40 tenements or holdings. Some he granted to his own tenants of St. Ouen, some to volunteers from other parts of Jersey, and a small group of tenements in the west were even granted to Guernseymen. Each tenant built himself a house on his own holding in the manner already well established in Jersey, and in complete contrast to the nucleated settlement of Alderney.

The whole island was rabbit-infested and overgrown with brambles, bracken and gorse. There do not appear to have been any trees, for the settlers had to bring timber with them, for use both as building material and fuel. Indeed, everything they needed had to be brought from Jersey; horses, cattle, tools, seeds, young trees, food, drink, and fodder. Helier apportioned the land so that each tenement had some fertile plateau land for cultivation, and some slopes and cliffland for grazing. The area of fertile land varied from 10 to 40 vergées, according to the importance of the tenement. The fields were enclosed by massive hedges, following the practice already established in Jersey. These Elizabethan hedges are still one of the major elements in the Sark landscape.

Helier reserved for himself some 300 vergées of plateau land in the middle of Great Sark, where he and his wife established themselves close to the ruins of St. Magloire's priory. The property is still known as Le Manoir. Their first dwelling is said to have been the ruined chapel of the priory. This was probably one of the row of cottages which face the Greffe and school across the road.

Later, they built the fine, two-storey house, in the pattern of a Jersey farmhouse, which faces south down the Dixcart Valley and across the sea to their old home at St. Ouen.

A water supply was obviously of prime importance in the siting of the tenements; Helier's was a spring that still rises at the head of the valley, a few yards in front of his house. Another important consideration was the defence of the various landing places. One possible landing beach was le Port du Moulin, at the foot of the valley where there had previously been a water-mill and dam. No fewer than six tenements were located here, taking advantage of the shelter of the valley, the water from the mill-stream and perhaps using the monastic buildings as a source of stone. The tenements were La Moinerie, La Moinerie de Haut, La Perronerie (now La Seigneurie), L'Ecluse, La Rondellerie, and La Rade. A further group of four tenements—Le Fort, Le Grant Fort, La Tour and La Genetière—were established in the north-east corner of Great Sark to guard the landing places of L'Eperquerie and La Banquette. They doubtless made use of stone from a fort that had been built by the French in this area.[7]

Half a mile to the south was the tenement of Le Carrefour (the crossroads). Immediately to the east of this another cluster of houses commanded the zig-zag path that leads up from Grève de la Ville, and took advantage of the stream that descends the cliff at this point. The tenements are La Ville Roussel, La Ville Roussel de Bas, Clos de Manage, Clos de la Ville, and La Ville Farm. A quarter of a mile to the south-east, La Valette de Haut and La Valette de Bas sheltered in a small valley close to the headland where the lighthouse now stands.

At the head of the valley now known as Harbour Hill stood three tenements, again taking advantage of the stream that runs down the valley; La Collenette, La Fripponerie, and the tenement now known as Aval du Creux. (Creux refers to the tunnel which was driven through the cliff soon after Helier's death to gain access to the bay that became Creux Harbour.) A little further to the south La Forge commanded Derrible Bay, while Le Petit Dixcart overlooked the lower part of the Dixcart Valley and the Hog's Back. Further up the Dixcart Valley, and blocking what was probably the most likely invasion route, were Le Clos de Dixcart, La Pomme de Chien, and La Jaspellerie. Their water supply was the stream that rises in front of Le Manoir. A few yards up a side valley to the west was Le Grand Dixcart, and on the plateau, overlooking Dixcart Bay from the west, was Le Clos Bourel.

Grande Grève, the bay on the Guernsey side of la Coupée, was left undefended. Although it has a fine, sandy beach it was perhaps not considered an invasion risk because of the precipitous ascent to the Coupée. The next bay to the north, Le Port ès Saies, although it is impossible to reach from inland today, was guarded by Le Dos d'Ane, a tenement which takes its name (the donkey's back) from the dip in the road as it passes the tenement on its way to the Coupée.

Havre Gosselin is a deep-water anchorage surrounded by towering cliffs which lies just to the south of the Gouliot Passage between Sark and Brecqhou. It takes its name from Nicholas Gosselin, who with his father, the Bailiff of Guernsey, had smoothed the way with the authorities in that island for Helier's takeover of Sark. Gosselin was granted as a sub-fief a large area in the west of Sark, over-looking Brecqhou with Guernsey, Jethou and Herm in the distance. Since in the terms of his lease he had to provide four men for the defence of the island, Gosselin divided his fief into four tenements. The largest, Le Grand Beauregard, which commanded his anchorage of Havre Gosselin, he kept for himself. (The obelisk at the summit of the track from the landing commemorates Jeremiah Pilcher, who with four companions attempted to cross to Guernsey in an open boat one stormy night in 1868. His body was eventually recovered from the Isle of Wight.) Near Gosselin's own tenement was Petit Beauregard, while further to the north Le Vieux Port and Le Port à la Jument defended the bay known as Port à la Jument.

The remaining tenement of Great Sark, Le Vaurocque, was on the plateau at the junction where the road to Beauregard meets the main road to Little Sark.

Little Sark was divided into five tenements: La Sablonnerie, La Pipeterie, La Duvallerie, La Moserie, and La Donnellerie. The problem of water supply seems to have been the deciding factor in the siting of the farmsteads, for they are all clustered round a spring.

When Helier de Carteret died in 1581 he left a thriving, self-supporting community and 40 tenants, each armed with a musket and each with a strong incentive to defend his home and his island. The farmsteads they built, the fields they cleared and cultivated, and the hedgebanks they threw up are to be seen wherever one looks in Sark. Superimposed on the Elizabethan landscape are features such as corrugated iron bungalows and electricity cables which will be dealt with in the appropriate chapters. Most of these modern features are associated with the island's status as a haven from the two main evils of the 20th century—the motor car and income tax.

Chapter Five

THE AGRICULTURAL LANDSCAPE

The inhabitants of Guernsey are nothing so industrious in tilling their ground as those of Jersey.—William Camden, 1586.

THE LOWER PALAEOLITHIC people who lived in La Cotte de St. Brelade and elsewhere on the peninsula that is now Jersey were hunters who probably had little influence on the landscape, and there is no evidence that they reached the other islands. For thousands of years after their departure the Channel Island area would seem to have been deserted except for the occasional hunting expedition which may have penetrated to these remote promontories of western Europe. But at some time in the fourth or perhaps even the fifth millenium B.C. a sea-route was established between the Mediterranean and the Atlantic coast of Europe, and the islands were colonised by a people who brought with them an advanced Neolithic culture. This included the ability to cultivate the land, grow crops, and rear farm animals.

Although today the only obvious Neolithic remains are the megalithic tombs and standing stones, the arrival of the first farmers must have had a profound effect upon the primeval landscape. Clearings were made in the forest by burning and by felling with polished stone axes, the rich forest soil was loosed by primitive ploughs which were little more than large hoes, and the first crops were sown. In the cereal seed which the Neolithic farmers brought with them from the Mediterranean basin were the seeds of arable weeds, many of which are still to be seen in our fields and gardens.

It is possible that some of the small mammals, such as the house mouse, also arrived in the islands at this time, having been carried in grain and fodder aboard the Neolithic ships.

Evidence that the megalith builders were also farmers is provided by the peat beds which occur around the coasts of the islands. Samples of peat from Vazon Bay, for instance, have been examined at Cambridge and found to contain abundant pollen from a variety of agricultural weeds, including docks, nettles, daisies, buttercups, corn spurrey and three species of plantain.[1] Besides pollen grains, the peat contains some recognisable non-microscopic plant remains; these are mainly of water and marsh plants, and apart from one nettle seed no weeds are represented. But the abundance of weed pollen does indicate that cultivation was going on nearby. The sea level at this time was lower in relation to the land than it is today, and Jersey was probably having one of its periods as a promontory of the European mainland. All the same, the plant remains in the peat show that conditions in what is now Vazon Bay would have been too swampy for cultivation, rather as parts of La Grande Mare are to this day. The cultivated clearings must have been further inland, at a site yet to be discovered.

A. H. Ewen has pointed out that the presence of megalithic monuments well inland in Guernsey show that much of the island was opened up in the megalithic period.[2] He further points to certain areas positively bristling with place-names such as La Longue Rocque and Le Trépied, which indicate the former existence of many more such monuments. Ewen suggests that these clusters indicate the sites of Neolithic settlements. They are all on the drier, higher ground, and the cultivated land would not have been far away. The standing stones may even have marked the boundaries of the arable fields.

On the heights overlooking Vazon Bay are two such areas. To the east, the area around the Castel Primary School includes the sites of two medieval chapels, St. George and St. Germain, probably built on pre-Christian sites, and fields with names such as La Blanche Rocque and La Longue Pierre, indicating megalithic remains. Overlooking the southern end of Vazon there was a dolmen at Le Mont Saint and there are numerous indicative place-names in the vicinity of St. Saviour's church, which was itself built on a megalithic site. Similar groups of megaliths can be traced in all the Guernsey parishes except Torteval, which with its cliffy coastline and densely wooded hinterland was probably not penetrated until the end of the megalithic period.

The same argument may be applied to Jersey. Although many of the smaller inland remains have been cleared to make way for the plough or used as handy sources of building stone, tombs such as La Hougue Bie demonstrate that the megalith builders penetrated the forested hinterland of the island, and surely a labour force of the size necessary to raise La Hougue Bie could not have been supported without agriculture.

In Alderney, Ewen considers that the Neolithic arable fields were within a triangle bounded by Les Autels, Les Rochers and La Longue Pierre, to the south and south-east of the present town. His only evidence for this view seems to be the place-names, which all have megalithic associations.[3] Sark, too, was inhabited during at least part of the megalithic period.

The Neolithic fields were probably very small clearings in the wilderness or forest, designed to satisfy the settlers' own needs, without producing a marketable surplus. Unlike the long medieval strips they were probably square or irregular, excavations in England suggest that they were ploughed in two directions, giving the simple man-drawn plough a better chance of breaking up the soil.

The Open Fields

While we know that some form of agriculture was practised in the islands during the megalithic period, we know absolutely nothing of how it developed in the Bronze Age, the Iron Age, or the centuries that followed the collapse of the Roman Empire. All we can say with some degree of certainty is that by the end of the 'dark ages' (dark to us, that is) the settlements we now call parishes had been established, each with its area of agricultural land in the forms of open or common fields.

Attention has already been drawn to Alderney as a living example of the open-field system. The only comparable area in the British Isles is in Nottinghamshire where the parish of Laxton has retained its open fields to the present day. The farmsteads are all concentrated in the village of Laxton, and although the land immediately around the village has been enclosed, beyond these small enclosures are three large open fields, crossed by unfenced roads and grass tracks. The tracks divide each field into several parcels of land called furlongs, and each furlong consists of a number of long, narrow strips. This is typical of a system of agriculture that was already widespread in Europe by the early Middle Ages.

We know from documentary evidence that in the days of the first Queen Elizabeth when Helier De Carteret was establishing his tenements over the length and breadth of Sark, the entire population of Alderney, numbering some 700 souls, was concentrated in the town of St. Anne.[4] The cultivated land was all in the area known as the Blaye, which had no hedges or walls of any description, but was divided into strips, each belonging to an individual member of the community.

Although the population of Alderney is no longer confined to St. Anne, but has spread freely over the former waste land to the north and east, the open-field system of the Blaye survives, and is organised on the same principles as Laxton. The Blaye is divided into rectangular blocks known as *riages,* each of about 36 vergées. These in turn are divided into parallel strips. In some *riages* the strips run north and south; in others, east and west. Across one end of each *riage* is a strip called a *vaindif,* on which the ox-team turned when the plough reached the end of the furrow.

The strips today vary in size from a few perches to several vergées, having been sub-divided and amalgamated many times as they have changed hands down the centuries.

One advantage of the open-field system was that no land was wasted by broad banks and hedges. A more important advantage was that the land could be distributed fairly between all the members of the community. The strips belonging to one man did not lie together but were scattered among the various *raiges* so that each family had a fair share of both good and bad land.

Although the strips were individually held, it was not left to the holders themselves to decide which crops to grow, or when to begin sowing or harvesting. Each *riage* was managed as a single unit, and either sown with a crop or left fallow. This encouraged efficiency and co-operation, at least in theory. An ox-team, for instance, might plough a whole *riage*, one strip after another, without anyone having to wait too long before he could get on with his sowing. Also, since each man held strips in various parts of the Blaye, he could grow enough of each crop for his own use. The cropping pattern was decided by an elected committee of 12 men known as the Douzaine, who also inspected the *riages,* settled boundary disputes, and imposed fines for failure to erect the temporary fences which were set up around the Blaye in the growing season, to protect the crops from wandering cattle. The animals might be allowed to graze the *riages* that were left fallow—another advantage of managing the strips together.

If an over-enthusiastic strip-holder were to plough an extra furrow and encroach upon his neighbour's strip, the Douzaine would be called and would settle the dispute by making the owner dig a hole in which they would set a large standing stone. Before the hole was filled in each douzenier would drop in a pebble known as a *temoin*—a witness stone. Unfortunately, the boundary stones were removed during the German occupation, causing some confusion when the population returned in 1945.[5] It is interesting that the open fields of Laxton are also inspected by a court of 12 men, with power to levy fines.

Although several advantages have been advanced in support of the strip system, they were probably outweighed by the disadvantages. The scattered strips were extremely wasteful of time, the unploughed balks which divided the strips would have bred weeds in profusion, and a single neglected strip could provide enough seeds of weeds such as ragwort to foul all the others. This is only too evident on the Blaye today. Altogether it is not surprising that as soon as the enclosure movement reached the other islands, it was adopted with such enthusiasm.

The picture which Alderney and Laxton allow us to form of the system that was once widespread in the Channel Islands is of more than academic interest. We tend to think of our familiar enclosed landscape as having been there for ever. Yet the present tendency of farmers to grub up hedges and bulldoze banks to make room for modern machinery is producing a landscape which resembles more and more the old open fields. The difference is that beyond the medieval open fields was wilderness and forest; beyond the new open fields lies a stark landscape of housing estates and hurrying traffic.

Banon and Mession

The medieval landscape of the islands, then, was one of open fields surrounded by forest and heath; in Guernsey, at least, there were nucleated settlements of the St. Anne type corresponding in most cases with the parishes, each settlement with its own fields. In Jersey there were certainly open fields, but there is no evidence at present of nucleated settlements.

Beside the open fields, each settlement also had its common pastureland, where the inhabitants had the right to graze their animals. During the growing season, between seed-time and harvest, temporary fences were erected around the common fields and the cattle were restricted either to the commons or to any small enclosures which their owners might have near their farmsteads. The period when the ban was in force was known as *mession*. The word recalls the French *moisson* (harvest), but in the islands *mession* meant the growing period, not the harvest itself. If an animal was found straying during the *mession,* it was impounded, and a fine had to be paid before it could be reclaimed. The fine was doubled at harvest time.

After the harvest the fences were removed and the animals were allowed on to the stubble. The right of the inhabitants to allow their animals to graze the cultivated fields was known as *banon*. It applied to all the land except for the enclosed paddocks, and lasted from harvest to March or April. The exact dates of *banon* and *mession* were fixed by law from time to time. Because of their destructive habits, in Norman law the right of *banon* was not extended to goats or pigs, nor in Jersey at least to stallions or geese.[6] In Guernsey pigs were allowed loose only with a ring in the nose.

The main crop of the open fields was corn, and although this was overtaken in importance after the enclosures by cider, roots and other crops, cereals were still being grown in some quantity within living memory. A very small acreage is still grown. The ricks were circular, and often built on a raised platform supported by mushroom-shaped stones which prevented rats from entering the rick. These 'stone mushrooms' are known locally as *pilotins,* and many are still to be seen embellishing drives and gardens. Some are made of local granite; others, of cement or sandstone, were imported from England where they are called staddle-stones. The rickyard or *haugard* was near the farm building and a few examples of covered *haugards* survive. One, with a roof supported by circular columns of masonry, is at La Pouquelah, just across the lane from the Folk Museum entrance to Saumarez Park in Guernsey. And across the main road in the property known as Les Mourains is another, complete with rat-proof *pilotins.*

Besides the stone mushrooms, many farmyards still contain some of the stone weights that were used for measuring farm produce. These were made from large pebbles selected on the beach and the weight was adjusted either by chipping pieces off or by making a hole and adding lead. They were equipped with a ring for lifting, secured by a staple packed by lead into a hole in the top of the weight. In Guernsey the weights are usually entire pebbles, lying on one side, with the weight carved in Roman numerals on the upper face. In Jersey the pebble was usually cracked in half to make a flat base, with a ring at the end of the pebble and the weight marked in Arabic numerals. A few Jersey weights use a very early 'tally' notation in which a stroke represents one unit, and one cancelled by a transverse stroke means ten.[7]

A fine collection of these weights may be seen in the courtyard of the Société Jersiaise Museum in Pier Road, St. Helier. They were so numerous that many are still to be seen in gardens and even in houses, where the smaller ones make convenient door-stops. The numerals incised on the weights are in pounds, but the islands used the *Poids du Marc* measure in Rouen, which was slightly heavier than the English pound. The ancient weights and measures (with the notable exception of vergées and perches) were abolished in Guernsey in 1916 and in Jersey in 1917, though most of them had fallen into disuse long before then.

The Hedgerow Revolution

The enclosure of agricultural land began early in both Jersey and Guernsey. There is documentary evidence in both islands that some enclosure was going on in the 14th century.[8, 9] Sometimes the seigneur would make an enclosure (we would call it a paddock) near the manor; sometimes he would give permission to one of his tenants to do the same. The existence of early enclosures is indicated in Jersey by the name *Clos* and in Guernsey by *Courtil*. (In Jersey *côtil* has a different meaning, a cultivated slope, while *courtil* has the sense of a garden.)

The next land to be enclosed was presumably the open fields themselves. It has already been pointed out that the position of these is often indicated by the place-name *Les Camps*. The name in the plural indicates a whole field of strips, particularly when it is found that several adjacent modern fields bear the same name. The title often includes a personal name, indicating some former owner or even the individual who enclosed the field. The houses in the Green Lanes, St. Peter Port, for instance, stand on the site of Les Camps Collette Nicolle. *Le Camp* in the singular indicates a single strip—Le Camp du Roi was the king's strip.

The enclosure of the open fields proceeded rapidly in Elizabeth's reign; Camden, writing in 1586, saw very little open-field farming in Guernsey. When the fields had been enclosed the hedges crept round the common pastures, finally eating into areas that had been *landes* or heath. Unlike the United Kingdom there were no Enclosure Acts in the Channel Islands; owners and tenants seem just quietly to have got on with building their walls and hedges. In Jersey those with common grazing rights seem willingly to have seen the commons disappear in return for the benefits they derived from enclosing their own holdings.[10] In Guernsey things did not proceed so happily, and during the 17th century there were constant cases of peasants breaking down the enclosures on the former commons to allow their animals to wander freely. In 1614 the Royal Court ordained that

> . . . the enclosures being the cause of frequent disputes between neighbours, and the disturbance of the public peace, it is absolutely forbidden, on pain of corporal punishment, to break down walls or hedges.

The problem of wandering animals breaking through the hedges, whether sabotaged or not, continued all through the 17th century, and numerous laws were passed which provided for stray animals to be impounded and fines to be levied when they were claimed. Judging by the number of times the same laws were reinacted, the former commoners were taking little notice of them. In 1710 cattle and sheep were ordered to be hobbled during the *mession,* and finally in 1717 *banon* was abolished in Guernsey. Animals were no longer allowed loose, even in winter, except on the few remaining commons.

By the end of the 18th century the enclosure of Guernsey was virtually complete. We are now on firm ground because in 1787 the first official survey of the island was made. It is generally known as the 'Duke of Richmond's Map' since it was commissioned for defence purposes by the third Duke of Richmond, Master General of the Ordnance. The actual survey was carried out by a party of five men under William Gardner. It is a beautifully executed and detailed survey of the island, in two sheets to a scale of six inches to the mile. Every building, lane, hedgerow, stream and orchard appears to be shown, and when it is compared with the modern Ordnance Survey maps its accuracy is apparent. Relief is indicated by hatching and, most important to our purpose, land use is indicated by a variety of symbols. The only serious drawback to the Richmond map is the scarcity of place-names. Those names that do appear are spelt in an interesting way, as though the surveyors had the greatest difficulty in understanding the natives.

In 1795 Gardner executed a similar survey of Jersey, this time in four sheets. Statistical studies of the land use shown in these two splendid maps have been made by Dury.[11, 12]

The Richmond map of Guernsey shows that by 1787 nine-tenths of the island was already enclosed, even though the reclamation of the Braye du Valle was still to come. The parish of St. Andrew, with no coastline, was entirely enclosed; the other parishes had an unenclosed strip of varying width along the coast. The northern island, Le Clos du Valle, had a broad belt of unenclosed common on its northern and western side, most of which is still unenclosed today. On the west coast the promontories such as Hommet and Pleinmont were unenclosed then as now, and a belt of open land ran along the southern cliffs. It was particularly broad in the Forest parish, from La Corbière to Petit Bôt. This strip, grazed by sheep belonging to the Forest parishioners, was not enclosed until 1834.[13] The maps defining each parishioner's holding may be seen in the Greffe. They show enclosures extending to the very brink of the cliff. Now that sheep are no longer grazed on the cliffs these plots have been allowed to revert to gorse and bracken, but the walls can still be seen plunging down the cliff when the vegetation has been stripped by a fire.

One of the most interesting features of the Richmond map of Guernsey is the area around the Old Mill, St. Martin's, which was still unenclosed. The map shows a windmill standing at the intersection of a number of unfenced roads which crossed the open fields of the parish. The legend reads 'Moulin de Saumerez on Les Camps'. The area is still known as Les Camps, but today it is heavily built over, and the base of the mill stands sadly beside a housing estate.

In Jersey, as in Guernsey, the enclosure movement seems to have begun in earnest in Elizabeth's reign, but here the evidence is conflicting. Jean Poingdestre, in his *Discourse on the Island of Jersey,* published in 1682, said that 100 years previously the island had lain almost open, with few enclosures. Yet Philip Falle, in his account of Jersey in 1734, mentioned the hedgebanks and said that they dated back some 150 years, which would bring us to 1584. And as we have seen, when Helier de Carteret colonised Sark in 1565 he took enclosure for granted. In any event by 1682 the hedges were up in Jersey, for Poingdestre not only mentions them but explains in detail how they were made. They were built of earth with a ditch on each side and were so high that a man with a three-foot staff could not reach the top. When they were within a foot of the summit a row of hawthorn seedlings were laid crossways on top, four or five inches apart, so that their heads just projected on both sides. Then they were covered with a further foot of soil from the ditch. The result was a hedge thick enough to stop the most determined beast. These hedges have lost some of their height in the course of natural erosion, but their remains are still to be seen, particularly in the northern parishes.

Poingdestre also tells us why the hedges were built; they were to shelter the apple trees of the booming cider industry. He disapproved of this. In the days of the open fields Jersey had grown enough corn to feed her own population and still have a surplus to export. Now, in 1682, far from exporting it she had to import at least half her needs.

The swing to cider was caused partly by a drift of labour from the land to the fishing industry, and partly by the fact that producing cider was much more profitable than growing corn. More and more land was enclosed and turned into orchard, and a huge export trade was built up. Already in 1682 Poingdestre claimed that every house in the island had at least one cider orchard, and by the middle of the 18th century so much land had been enclosed, largely but not entirely for orchards, that *banon* was officially abolished in Jersey in 1771.

The Richmond map of 1795 shows Jersey in a less advanced stage of enclosure than Guernsey. The parish of St. Saviour, which has virtually no coastline, was entirely enclosed, but other parishes, particularly in the west, were still largely open. Dury calculates that St. Brelade was only 26.5 per cent. enclosed. The map shows in an impressive manner the density of cider orchards, especially in the eastern parishes. Nearly 40 per cent. of St. Saviour was covered by orchards. The Guernsey map shows that, although a larger proportion of the island was enclosed the density of orchards was far less. In only two parishes, St. Peter Port and St. Andrews, did orchards cover more than 10 per cent. of the area. Clearly the cider industry in Guernsey, though considerable, was less important than in Jersey. The question then arises, why was Guernsey so completely enclosed at an earlier stage than Jersey? The reason usually given for the Guernsey enclosures is that they correspond with the introduction of root crops, particularly parsnips, which necessitated winter ploughing. This could not have been done in the open fields during the *banon*. But this argument would apply with equal force to Jersey and there is much scope for further work on the subject. Part of the problem when comparing the histories of the two islands is that they have been studied by different people, observing from different viewpoints. The island differences may therefore be more apparent than real.

My apology for dwelling at length on these events long past is that the legacy they left us of tree-lined hedges is still the most important element in the rural landscape of the two largest islands.

So far in our discussion of enclosure we have relied on documentary evidence and place-names. Another method of dating the hedges is now available, based on botanical evidence from the hedge itself. After sampling many hedges from different parts of England Dr. Max Hooper of Monks Wood Experimental Station has found that there is a correlation between the number of species of trees and shrubs in a hedge and the age of the hedge. Further, he finds that a 30-yard length of hedge will on the average contain close to one species of tree or shrub for every 100 years of the hedge's life.[14] This simple rule may seem too good to be true, but it has been tested many times in the United Kingdom, and as a rough rule of thumb it has proved remarkably reliable. Presumably, the original enclosing banks were planted with one species—in our case usually elm or hawthorn—and approximately one new species has managed to establish itself in the hedge, per 30 yards, per century.

It does not follow that Hooper's Hedgerow Hypothesis will necessarily apply in the Channel Islands, but a few counts I have made on my own property in Guernsey suggest that it may well do so. A hedge bordering one of Doyle's military roads, which was cut diagonally through a field in 1810 and was presumably planted soon afterwards, has an average of two species in each 30-yard length, while the hedges on either side of a cart track that was already there when the Richmond map was made in 1787 have 4 and 4.5 species respectively.

Clearly there is abundant scope for further work on this subject as well. It would be an interesting project to make a survey of all the hedges in, say, a parish, and to test the hypothesis against hedges of known age. It is not sufficient to take a single 30-yard length; several lengths of each hedge must be sampled, and they must be picked at random, not selected because they contain a particular tree which it would be nice to include. One side of each hedge is examined and all tree and shrub species are recorded, whether they are in the form of trees or low, bushy growth.

Hedges differ considerably from place to place, and not all of them have trees. In Jersey the tall thorn hedges described by Poingdestre are quite different from the walls of St. Ouen, and in Guernsey the broad banks of grass and wild violet on the windswept escarpment overlooking the west coast are very different from the elm hedges of the sheltered valleys. A further project might be to see whether there is any connection between the number of herbaceous species (bluebell, 'stinking onion', hart's-tongue, etc.) and the age of a hedge.

Work in England would lead one to expect that the oldest hedges are those that form the parish boundaries, but this again needs to be tested in the Channel Islands. If the Ewen model is correct, of ancient nucleated settlements with their fields, each separated from the next by wilderness or *landes*, then the parish boundary hedges would be no older than the other hedges enclosing the *landes*.

Cider, Roots and Vraic

The cider industry, one of the two main causes of the enclosures, flourished throughout the 17th and 18th centuries and reached a peak in the middle of the 19th century. Then it declined rapidly, although cider for home consumption continued to be made until quite recently. The decline coincided with the introduction of new export crops, particularly potatoes, which will be dealt with in the next chapter. A few representatives of the old Norman varieties of cider trees survive in the corners of fields and gardens, but the industry's main contribution to the modern landscape is the network of tree-capped hedges intended to shelter the orchards, and which now shelter other crops and cattle, as well as hiding one subtopian disaster from the next.

The building in which the cider was made (*le prienseu* in Jersey, *le prinseux* in Guernsey), is still to be seen in many a farmyard. In it, the apples were first reduced to pulp in a circular stone crusher, *le tour,* then the pulp was shovelled into a massive oak press which extracted the juice. *Le tour* typically consisted of nine heavy granite sections hollowed out to produce a circular trough in which the apples were crushed by a stone wheel. The wheel was pierced by an axle which was attached to a rotating upright piece of wood in the centre of the circle. The axle projected beyond the wheel, and was harnessed to a horse which plodded round and round *le tour.* In Guernsey instead of a stone wheel, there were usually two wooden ones, one behind the other. The well-impregnated timber was said to add an essential flavour to the cider. The wooden wheels have long since rotted away, but stone ones may be seen here and there, especially in Jersey. They may be mistaken for millstones, but the grooves are on the perimeter, not on the flat face.

Occasionally a complete *tour* may be seen adorning a front garden or public place, and individual sections are to be found in many a farmyard and field where, with ends blocked up, they serve as drinking troughs.

The other main cause of the enclosures was almost certainly the popularity of root crops. Roots have been grown in Jersey and Guernsey for many centuries, and the parsnip is particularly associated with the islands. It was already being grown in Guernsey in the 13th century and until recently it was the main winter fodder crop, being used to fatten cattle and pigs as well as going into the pot for human use. Poingdestre in 1682 wrote that in Jersey parsnips were particularly esteemed as a vegetable, boiled and mashed with butter. (He also mentions turnips, and this was some 70 years before 'Turnip' Townshend popularised the turnip as an agricultural crop in England.)

Parsnips have extremely deep roots and require a deeply-dug soil. At first this was achieved with a spade—it was said that an experienced man could dig four Guernsey perches a day. Later a heavy wooden plough was introduced, *La grande charrue* (*querrue* in Guernsey) which could slice a furrow up to 18 inches deep. The big plough is said to have been introduced into Guernsey towards the end of the 18th century, though de Gruchy considers it to have been a characteristic feature of Jersey agriculture for at least four centuries.

La grande charrue was an expensive piece of equipment and required so many beasts to pull it that several farmers would own one jointly, and plough each other's fields in turn. A yoke or two of oxen were usually harnessed nearest to the plough, with three or four pairs of horses in front. When the horses reached the headland and started to turn, the slow but powerful pull of the oxen was necessary to finish the furrow.

Examples of *la grande charrue* and many other traditional agricultural implements may be seen at the museums at La Hougue Bie in Jersey and Saumarez Park in Guernsey.

With adequate manuring a yield of 15 tons of parsnips to the acre was quite common, and in some years 20 tons were achieved. But then a fat steer would eat up to a hundredweight of parsnips a day.

Mangolds, cattle beet and even parsnips and carrots are still grown as fodder by dairy farmers of the old school, but the seed is slow to germinate and easily choked by weeds, and the labour involved in hoeing, singling and pulling them is making a field of roots an increasingly rare sight.

Channel Islanders have long realised the value of manure, and besides using all their farmyard manure they made liberal use of seaweed or *vraic*. With their rocky coastline and wide tidal range the islands afforded (and still do afford) a plentiful supply of this excellent fertiliser, free for the taking. Sometimes it was spread directly on the fields, and sometimes it was piled into stacks and dried for use as fuel, or burned and the powdery ash used as a fertiliser. With the high cost of artificial fertilisers it is surprising that more use is not made of *vraic* today, though the occasional lorry may still be seen loading up on the beaches in the winter, and very occasionally the smoke from a burning heap drifts over L'Erée in Guernsey or La Pulente in Jersey. However, the magnificent granite slipways that were built to give access to the beaches by horse and cart are still a useful and attractive part of the landscape. They were built of heavy stone setts set on edge, each with a projecting angle designed to give a grip to a horse's hooves as it hauled a boxcart loaded high with dripping seaweed up from the beach. Many such slips still exist around the shores of Jersey and Guernsey, having withstood to a remarkable degree the onslaught of the waves over the years. Nearly every bay has at least one, and in some cases even tiny coves and creeks are served by slipways, which could only have been of use for gathering *vraic*. An example is the gracefully curving slip leading to a rocky cove at Pezeries, on the Pleinmont peninsula of Guernsey.

Pigs, Sheep and Cattle

Pigs, once so numerous that they had to be excluded from the *banon* and were only allowed on common land if they were equipped with rings in their noses, are now a rare sight in the islands. There is no bacon factory, and only a comparatively few farmers rear pigs for pork. But until a few years ago every farm had a few sows and many cottagers fattened a pig for Christmas. The sties in which they lived are still to be seen in many farmyards, often in pairs, or in Jersey, three in a row. Each sty has a house, usually roofed with pantiles, and an open area surrounded by a low wall, pierced by a chute down which the farmer's wife would throw her kitchen refuse and buttermilk. The chute leads into a granite feeding trough. An interesting variant of the usual pig-sty is found in the north-west of Jersey. The covered area has a domed roof of granite slabs, covered in rough cement. This type seems to be confined to the three adjacent parishes of St. Ouen, St. Mary, and St. John.[15]

A fig tree was often planted against the wall of the sty. Thus the pig benefited from the waste from the kitchen and dairy, the fig tree benefited from the waste from the pig, and the family benefited from the fruit of the tree. Some of these trees may still be seen in cottage gardens, even though the sty may long since have been demolished.

The 19th century scenery of the Channel Islands has been depicted in many delightful prints, notably those published in Jersey by P. Falle, and in Guernsey by M. Moss. Although some of them display a certain artistic licence, together they form an excellent record of the landscape in the last century. One of the most striking features of those prints that portray coastal scenes is that the cliffs appear to be devoid of bushy vegetation, and not overgrown by brambles, gorse and blackthorn as they are now. The explanation is that they were grazed by sheep. Today the Channel Islands are associated mainly with cattle, while sheep are an uncommon sight, but from the Middle Ages until the 18th century sheep were far more numerous than cows. At first they were kept on the common land, and allowed on the open fields during the *banon*. When most of the commons had been enclosed and *banon* abolished they were confined to their owners' sheep runs, which included cliff land that has since been abandoned and allowed to grow over. Sometimes walls are exposed by a cliff fire, although they are now so low that it is difficult to imagine how they could contain an active sheep. Even the precipitous Ile Agois by Crabbé Bay on the north coast of Jersey has the remains of sheep-runs, suggesting that the islet became separated from the rest of Jersey after the Middle Ages.

The sheep provided wool for a knitting industry that was already in existence in the 15th century, and built up to such proportions that the bulk of the wool had to be imported. Stockings, jerseys and guernseys were exported both to England and the Continent. Men and women knitted; fishermen would knit in their boats as they waited for the tide, and agriculture suffered, for in 1606 the States of Jersey had to pass a law which forbade knitting at harvest and *vraicing* times. The industry declined during the Civil War and again when England and France were at war in the early 19th century. A few sheep continued to be kept on the cliffs and commons, but today the only ones that will be seen are a small flock in Sark and the occasional pet sheep in Jersey and Guernsey.

The former existence of sheep pens, where the animals were collected for shearing, is indicated by the place-names La Bergerie and Le Bigard. The only surviving pen is a small, triangular enclosure bounded by rough dry-stone walls, in front of the cottage Le Ménage ès Feuvres in La Rue des Landes, in the extreme north-west corner of Jersey. It has recently been presented to the Société Jersiaise.

While sheep were declining in importance in the 18th and 19th centuries, cattle were coming into prominence, and today they are the only farm animals that will be seen in any numbers. The drinking of milk is a comparatively new phenomenon—cattle were originally draught animals and producers of beef. (The use of steers and even cows for ploughing and pulling carts continued until early this century, and was revived through necessity during the Occupation.) During the 18th century the emphasis shifted from beef to butter, and Channel Island cattle began to earn a reputation for their rich milk, which was ideal for butter-making. Thousands of animals were sent to England from Jersey, Guernsey and Alderney. As there was free movement of animals between the islands and France it is doubtful whether there was any appreciable difference between the island breeds at this time: they were generally lumped together as 'Alderneys'. These small deer-like animals were much in demand to grace gentlemen's parks and to provide cream for the dairy. Although some of them were capable of a high yield, quantity of milk was the last consideration. It took five Alderneys to supply the rectory at Steventon where Jane Austen was born and brought up. Alderneys were also bought by ships' captains to provide fresh milk on long voyages.

As the island herds began to improve, laws were passed forbidding the importation of cattle into the islands, first from the Continent and finally from the United Kingdom, and even between Jersey and Guernsey. At first these were quarantine measures to protect the island herds from the cattle plagues that were raging on the Continent, but they also had the effect of maintaining the purity of the island breeds. Apart from beef animals for immediate slaughter, it has been illegal to import cattle into Jersey since 1789 and into the Guernsey bailiwick since 1819. Skilled selective breeding since then has produced the two distinct breeds which are now famous throughout the world.

The Jersey is a neat, lightly-boned animal with large, soulful eyes and a 'dished' face, concave between the eyes. The colour varies between shades of fawn, brown and grey; the neck and head are often a darker brown, with light grey 'spectacles' around the eyes, and a light muzzle around the dark nose. The shape of the head is similar to the brindle and white *Normande* breed of the adjacent parts of France, to which the Jersey is closely related, but the *Normande* is much larger, having been crossed with the British Shorthorn in the 1830s in order to produce a dual-purpose dairy and beef breed.

For its size the Jersey produces a high yield, and the milk is extremely rich, having a butterfat content of well over 5 per cent.

Dairy farming is less important in Jersey than it was earlier in the century, but the beautiful cows, often wearing coats, are still mercifully a characteristic part of the island scene.

The Guernsey is a larger animal than the Jersey and the colour is a more uniform fawn and white, though the shade of fawn varies from dark red to a pale sandy colour. The face is longer and straighter than the Jersey and the nose is flesh-coloured. The milk is rich in cream of a characteristic yellow colour, especially when the cows are grazing grass during the summer.

The Guernsey breed resembles very closely the *Froment du Léon* breed which was once common in the northern coastal parts of Brittany. Unfortunately the *Froment* is nearly extinct. The only survivors are a few elderly cows living in the neighbourhood of St. Brieuc, and we will probably never know how they are related to the cattle of Guernsey.

All the cows of Guernsey, Alderney, Sark and Herm are Guernseys. The Alderney cow is said to have been smaller than the Guernsey, but it is doubtful whether Alderney ever had a true breed of its own and certainly the present herd is descended from animals that were shipped from Guernsey after the Occupation.

The light cream beef animals that may be seen here and there in Guernsey are a Charolais-Guernsey cross. Recently the regulations have been relaxed to allow local cows to be inseminated with imported Charolais semen. The reason is that a pure Channel Island calf has very little value as meat and is uneconomic to rear except as a replacement for the dairy herd. It is therefore more profitable to inseminate the less good cows, whose calves would not be kept for breeding, with beef semen. The hybrid calves grow rapidly and command a good price. Cross-bred bull calves have to be castrated and heifers slaughtered before they are two years old, so there is no danger to the purity of the Guernsey breed.

Both the Channel Island breeds are efficient converters of food. Many English black-and-white herds include one or two Jerseys or Guernseys to improve the butterfat level and provide milk for the farmhouse. It will often be noticed that these animals are still grazing, clearing up the less palatable grasses, long after the others have settled down to chew the cud. For this reason and for their small size, they are ideal for the small fields of the Channel Islands.

Although the cows of both the Channel Island breeds are docile and friendly, the bulls have a reputation for ferocity and it is not advisable to approach them too closely.

Until quite recently all the island cattle were tethered and some herds are still managed in this way. Each cow is attached by a chain around her horns to a stake driven into the ground, which has to be moved three or four times a day, using a mallet made from apple wood, or failing this an elm log. In the summer she is milked in the field, where she spends her night. In winter she is milked and spends the night in the stable, but unless the weather is severe she is led out to the field during the day. It used to be a common sight to see herds being moved along the road, each man surrounded by a bunch of half a dozen cows, and the driver may still be held up in the lanes of Jersey and Guernsey by this soothing spectacle.

A milking cow needs to drink many gallons of water each day, and providing it for tethered cattle is a laborious process. A characteristic sight in the fields of all the islands is the improvised water carrier made from a tank and some lorry or cart wheels. In former times some fields were provided with wells, and the stone well-heads which covered them can still be seen, though the wells themselves have usually been filled with rubbish. The well-heads have an opening in the side, with a door to prevent accidents, and are usually covered by a single slab of granite. Inside the well-head was a wooden capstan, now usually gone, to raise the bucket of water, and a niche in the wall for the bucket when not in use. Some well-heads have a flat stone projecting on the outside near the sill of the door, on which to rest the bucket when full of water. Beside the well was a granite drinking trough; this, being a valuable item today, has usually disappeared. In Guernsey there are a few examples of party wells, set in a hedge with two doors to serve the fields on either side.

The tethering system made good use of the limited area of land. The cows were tethered in a line and worked their way across the field, so that as soon as they had passed, the grass could begin to grow again. The disadvantages were that moving the stakes and watering the animals involved much labour; in dry weather the ground became hard and it was difficult to hammer in the stakes, and in wet weather the cows could pull their stakes out of the ground. In most herds tethering has now been abandoned in favour of the electric fence and the cows, which no longer need horns for the attachment of a chain, are 'disbudded' as calves so that their horns never grow. At first strip-grazing was used, the electric wire being moved each day a few yards further into the field. This was in effect very like tethering, and like tethering it involved some labour. The much more labour-saving paddock system is now coming increasingly into favour. The grazing land is divided into permanent paddocks and the cows are simply turned into a fresh paddock each day.

The main disadvantage of the paddock system is the fragmented nature of many of the farms, which would entail moving the cows along narrow and busy roads to reach outlying fields. Many of the larger dairy farmers have overcome this problem by zero-grazing. The cows are kept in one of the large, concrete and asbestos sheds that are appearing next to the old farm buildings, and the grass is brought to them, having been cut in the field by a forage harvester, which blows it up a spout into a trailer. Examples of every system from tethering to zero-grazing are to be seen both in Jersey and Guernsey.

Forage Crops

The best food for cattle is grass, and in the mild, damp climate of the islands this crop has a long growing season. It does, however, tend to dry up in the late summer, when in most years there is a drought. This is one reason why permanent pasture is sometimes ploughed and re-seeded with a ryegrass ley. The young, vigorous grass plants keep growing after the older pastures have dried up. They also come into growth much earlier in the spring. The dark green colour of these grass leys is the result of heavy manuring with an artificial fertiliser containing nitrogen. Slightly over half the area of grassland is grazed throughout the year, either directly by the cows or indirectly by the forage harvester. The rest of the area is either harvested in May, again by the forage harvester, to be made into silage for winter feed, or mown in June and July as the weather allows for hay. Those fields that have yielded silage will provide grazing later in the summer. In the case of the hay fields, given a reasonably wet summer some grazing is usually possible on the aftermath.

The giant Jersey cabbages, with stems 10 feet or even 15 feet high, were once grown as cattle fodder in that island, but are seldom seen today except as a curiosity in gardens. Marrow-stemmed kale, a cabbagy plant with stout, succulent stems which the cows devour with noisy enjoyment, has been widely grown, particularly in Guernsey, which has its own variety. It had declined in recent years but is becoming popular again as the price of imported feed increases. Perhaps the biggest change in Guernsey's agricultural landscape in the last decade has been the widespread adoption of maize as a fodder crop. It has the great advantage that it keeps growing in the late summer drought, when the grass has dried up. When the first visitors arrive the maize seedlings are just germinating. Later holidaymakers see the young plants growing strongly, and by the time the last visitor has left the canes are standing some 10 feet high and the fields have a tropical appearance. Some maize is cut at this stage and fed to the cows, but most of the crop is harvested in October and November by a powerful machine which chops it into small fragments, and it is then made into silage for feed when the cattle are indoors during the winter.

Potatoes, broccoli and flowers are also grown on an agricultural scale, particularly in Jersey. Indeed, Jersey's early potatoes occupy more land than any other crop, and the area devoted to broccoli is only slightly less than that devoted to pasture. But since most readers would perhaps classify these crops as 'market gardening', they are included in the next chapter.

Chapter Six

THE HORTICULTURAL LANDSCAPE

Perhaps there is no spot of ground in Europe of the same size, where there are more greenhouses, or hothouses, than in Guernsey.
—John Jacob, 1830.

NOWHERE ARE THE DIFFERENCES between the islands more marked than in the field of horticulture. Alderney and Sark, with their difficult communications with the outside world, export an insignificant amount of produce, and, in fact, do not even grow enough fruit and vegetables for their own consumption. By contrast, in the two larger islands the export of horticultural produce is a major source of income. Yet Jersey and Guernsey have developed their horticultural industries in completely different directions. Jersey's horticulture, though intensive, is an outdoor industry which adds charm and character to the landscape. Guernsey's 1,000 acres of glass certainly add character to that island, but few people would claim that they enhance its beauty.

Potatoes, Cauliflower and Outdoor Tomatoes

Potatoes have been grown commercially in Jersey since the end of the 18th century, and during the first half of the 19th century they gradually assumed importance as an export crop. Sir John Le Couteur described the method of cultivation in one of his contemporary letters.[1] Old grassland was broken up during the summer and left to rot, then farmyard manure was spread on the broken turf at the rate of 20 tons to the acre. (*Vraic* was not considered suitable for potatoes.) Two ploughs were used. First a big plough drawn by four or six horses would open a deep furrow, then a light single-horse skim plough would turn the turf and manure into the furrow, to be buried by the big plough when it opened the next furrow. Le Couteur claimed that in this way an acre would yield from 20 to 28 tons of potatoes.

Obviously at this time the aim was to achieve a high yield rather than an early crop. It was about the time of the Irish potato famine that Jersey farmers seem to have realised that they could grow their crop earlier than had been customary. The potato disease reached the island in 1845 and caused considerable damage, though the crop never failed completely. Whether by conscious design or not, the Jersey crop was early enough to miss the build-up of the disease which tended to occur later in the year. Planting early had the added advantage that the produce reached the London market before other new potatoes were available;

Le Couteur rightly foresaw that the day would come when, in order for the industry to survive, Jersey potatoes would have to reach the market a week or more ahead of foreign competitors. By the selection of better varieties and the liberal use of imported guano as well as local farmyard manure, the yield of the early crop was gradually improved, but a sudden surge in potato growing which occurred at the end of the last century was due almost entirely to the chance discovery of one remarkable variety.

It was in 1880, during the festivities which followed the co-operative effort of ploughing the fields with *la grande charrue,* that Hugh de la Haye of Bushy Farm, St. Helier, produced two enormous potatoes, which somebody had given him as a curiosity. One of them had no fewer than 16 eyes. During the evening the two tubers were cut into as many pieces as possible so that each piece had one eye, and the following day they were planted in one of de la Haye's fields, Le Côtil de Bellozanne. The following spring there was a fine crop of early potatoes. The progeny of one tuber in particular yielded so well that de la Haye selected from it and built up a stock which he distributed among his fellow farmers. He gave his new variety the name 'Royal Jersey Fluke'. Within a few years, re-named the 'Jersey Royal', it was to become the basis of a flourishing early potato industry that brought renewed prosperity to the island.

Of more importance even than the yield is the exceptional earliness of the Jersey Royal. Its shoots appear so early in the year that if they were grown in most parts of the United Kingdom they would be killed by frost. But in the light soil of Jersey's south-facing côtils the variety produces an early enough crop to command high prices on the British market.

The Jersey Royal was such an immediate success that within three or four years it was almost the only variety being grown on a large scale in Jersey. At the height of the industry, in the 1930s, about a third of the total area of Jersey was planted in potatoes. After the war this area was reduced, partly because of an outbreak of potato root eelworm; but in 1970 there were still 16,782 vergées of early and maincrop potatoes, or slightly over one quarter of the area of the island. With minor fluctuations, this proportion has been maintained to the present day. In 1978, 15,468 vergées were devoted to Royals, 206 vergées to other early varieties, and 937 vergées to maincrop potatoes.[2] This is a remarkable achievement since Jersey has had to face increasing competition in the British markets from other parts of Europe, particularly since the United Kingdom entered the E.E.C. Despite this, the Jersey potato crop still occupies more land than any other industry in the Channel Islands.

Much of Jersey's 'earlier' land is so steep that it can only be cultivated by hand. Until recently this has not been a problem, local labour being augmented seasonally from Brittany. The factor which limited the growth of the industry was not labour but the amount of available land, and this encouraged the intensive cultivation that is such a feature of the island. In the last decade it has become increasingly difficult to find anyone prepared to dig by hand; nevertheless visitors are still surprised to see the amount of work being done in the fields by hand and by horses. The steep côtils with their immaculately ridged soil, the potato plants sprouting dark green from the summits of the ridges, are an immensely satisfying sight in the early months of the year.

Potato culture was once important in Guernsey, though never on the same scale as in Jersey. In the 19th century 'potato spirit' was produced for export by several local distilleries. When this trade collapsed the potatoes themselves were exported. For a time Guernsey potatoes sold at a premium in London, but since the 1920s they have been unable to compete with Jersey and the Canaries. Today a small but steady acreage is grown, mainly for local consumption. Several new varieties are being tried at present, in the hope of finding the most suitable for local conditions.

The contraction of Jersey's potato industry after the war was more than offset by a rapid increase in the production of broccoli or winter cauliflower. During the summer and autumn the British market is supplied by home-grown cauliflower. The first frosts cut down the supply, and from January onwards Britain relies heavily on imported broccoli.[3] Jersey tends to concentrate its production in the early part of the year, so that the demands on labour do not compete with the early potatoes. Broccoli growing is labour-intensive in the sense that the curds are picked and packed into wooden crates by hand, but the flatter fields, which can be ploughed by tractor, are mostly used; thus the plots of broccoli tend to be larger than those of early potatoes or outdoor tomatoes.

Despite strong competition from the Continent and especially from Brittany, the area devoted to broccoli increased enormously between 1950, when only 276 vergées were grown, and 1970, when the area reached 8,122 vergées. The area now seems to have stabilised at around 6,000 vergées. Some 120,000 crates of cauliflower were exported to the United Kingdom in 1979.

Jersey grows many other vegetables on a commercial scale, of which courgettes are showing the most rapid expansion at the time of writing. These and other vegetables are often grown under polythene shelters.

Another element in Jersey's landscape that makes it unique is the outdoor tomato crop. The rows of plants, supported by bamboo canes or by wooden crosses and wires, cause the sunnier slopes of the valleys to resemble more than anything the vineyards of some parts of the Continent. Although Guernsey's tomatoes are entirely under glass, Jersey's sunny, south-facing slopes and her slightly more Continental climate enable the major part of her tomato crop to be grown in the open. About half the outdoor crop is concentrated in the south-east corner of Jersey, in the parishes of Grouville and St. Clement.

The industry seems to have started at the beginning of the present century and to have become a major source of Jersey's income between the wars. At first most of the tomatoes were grown as a second crop following early potatoes, but the prices fetched by early tomatoes increased to the point where it became worth sacrificing potato land for an early crop of tomatoes. Tomatoes are prey to a great variety of diseases including, since they are closely related to potatoes, the potato root eelworm. This and the vagaries of the weather have caused the value of the crop to fluctuate rather widely from year to year, and the tendency now is to reduce the area of outdoor tomatoes and grow more under glass. By 1978 the outdoor crop had decreased to 701 vergées, while the area of tomatoes under glass had increased to 200 vergées.

Daffodils and Narcissi

One of the delights of the Channel Islands is the succession of naturalised narcissi which flower in fields, banks and hedges from January to May. These are not the wild daffodils or Lent lilies of Jersey's cliffs and woodland, but survivors of old cultivated varieties, most of which have not been grown commercially for many years. The bulb and flower industry, in which all the islands have taken part, seems to have begun in 1864 when Charles Smith, founder of the Caledonia Nursery which still exists on the outskirts of St. Peter Port, sent a consignment of narcissi and double daffodils to London.[4] This was before daffodils had become popular in England, and before the Scilly Island bulb trade had begun. Smith's example was followed by other Guernsey growers, who scoured the gardens of the island for cultivated varieties which they bought, dug up and propagated. By the end of the century an interest in daffodils had been kindled in England, and there was a small but flourishing export trade in bulbs and flowers from both Guernsey and Jersey.

Early in the present century bulb eelworm was accidentally imported with some bulbs, and threatened to wipe out the industry until a cure was found by treating the bulbs with hot water. Eelworm is still a nuisance and serious bulb growers, mainly in Jersey, move their stock from field to field to avoid a build-up of the pest in the soil. The legacy of eelworm can still be seen in some former bulb fields, now grassed over. Each spring the turf is pierced by daffodil leaves, still in the rows in which the bulbs were planted, but patches of the field are devoid of leaves, where the bulbs have been killed by eelworm.

There was a strong recovery in the 1920s and '30s, when many tons of bulbs and blooms were sent from both islands. In the Occupation all the available land was used for producing food and most of the bulb stocks were lost. After the war new varieties were introduced which commanded much higher prices, and in the 1950s the industry became important again. In the last decade falling prices and increased freight charges have savaged the industry, and bulb growing in Guernsey is now at a very low ebb. In Jersey, however, either because the blooms reach the market earlier, or because more emphasis is placed on growing bulbs as opposed to blooms, the growing of narcissi still flourishes—1,225 vergées were devoted to it in 1978.

Early visitors are sometimes disappointed to find that, unlike the bulb fields of Holland, the island fields are not normally seen in bloom. This is because the flowers are picked when they are just beginning to crook, and long before they open. In this way they reach the market as they are just opening, and should have a fairly long life ahead of them. When a field of 'daffs' is seen in full bloom—and it is a stunningly beautiful sight—it is because it has 'missed the market' and the blooms are no longer worth picking.

Many of the narcissi that have established themselves in field hedges were dumped there as 'rogues' when another, newer variety was being grown in the field. When the object was to grow the bulbs for sale they were allowed to flower, and any with the wrong kind of flower were lifted and dumped in the hedge. These 'rogues' provide us with a record of the varieties that were grown in the past. Unlike wild daffodils, which spread by seed, the cultivated narcissi reproduce only vegetatively, by the division of the bulbs. Thus the present naturalised specimens are identical with those that were cultivated years ago.

Some 50 or 60 of the old varieties still grow in hedges and fields. Two of the commonest of the ordinary yellow 'daffs' are Golden Spur and Princeps. Both date back to the 19th century. Princeps, whose rather long and delicate petals are of a paler yellow than its trumpet, closely resembles the native wild daffodil but it always grows in clumps, while the wild daffodil, spreading by seed, tends to be evenly scattered over the ground. Double daffodils have not been sent to market for many years, but still bloom in odd corners; their descriptive names include Eggs and Bacon, Fried Eggs, Butter and Eggs, and Poached Egg. The sweet-smelling multi-flowered narcissi include the yellow Soleil-d'or and the cream Primo, which are still exported.

Despite the difficulty of getting their produce to market the smaller islands shared in the daffodil trade. Even Jethou has a few vergées of bulbs on its flat summit, and it is possible that they were also cultivated, together with potatoes, on the terraces cut in the cliff on the south side of that island. These terraces are overgrown with bracken now, but they can still be seen from a boat or from the outlying stack, Grande Fauconnière. Their age and original purpose are not known.

Many flowers are grown commercially beside daffodils and narcissi. In Jersey many of them are grown in the open, especially anemones, while carnations, iris, chrysanthemums and freesias are grown under glass. The area of glass in Jersey is increasing, and reached 285 vergées (126 acres) in 1978. It tends to be concentrated in the east of the island, about 30 per cent. of the area being in the parish of St. Saviour. There are 79 vergées of glass devoted to flowers.

In Guernsey the main flowers grown under glass are carnations, freesias and roses. Freesias are often grown in 'whale-hide' pots which stand in a shaded spot outside the greenhouse in the summer. For some years they have been Guernsey's main glasshouse flower crop, but rose growing is expanding rapidly and has nearly overtaken freesia production.

The Glasshouses of Guernsey

The traveller who approaches Guernsey by air can hardly fail to be struck by the sea of glistening glass which appears to cover most of the north of the island and a good deal of the south as well. Guernsey's glass is no new thing. In 1830 John Jacob wrote, in an elongated sentence typical of his time,

> This island may be deemed the garden both of common flowers and exotics; many
> of the latter have no need to shelter from the frost and snow, which are scarcely even

1. The Chouet peninsula, Guernsey from Les Amarreurs.

2. (*above left*) The south coast of Guernsey from the air, looking east. Herm and Sark are in the distance.

3. (*above right*) The Talbot Valley, Guernsey. This section of the valley is the property of the National Trust of Guernsey.

4. (*left*) Gully and natural bridge near Grosnez Castle in the north-west corner of Jersey.

5. (*above*) Le Rât Cottage, St. Laurence, Jersey, the property of the National Trust for Jersey. The small windows suggest a date before 1700.

6. (*below*) The cliffs at Pleinmont, Guernsey, looking east towards the German control tower.

7. (*above*) Le Pinacle, St. Ouen, Jersey. Foundations dating from Roman times may be seen on the right.

8. (*left*) St. Peter's Valley, Jersey, from the air; St. Aubin's Bay in the distance. In the right foreground is the National Trust property, Le Don Gaudin, with Quetivel Mill and the white Midvale Hotel beyond.

9. (*below*) German control tower at Les Landes on the north-west cliffs of Jersey.

10. (*above left*) The Island of Jethou from a lagoon in Herm.

11. (*above*) Monku Quarry and Fisherman's Cottage, Herm, with Guernsey in the distance across the Little Russel.

12. (*left*) Les Etacs, Alderney in September. The stacks off the south-west cliffs of Alderney are the breeding place of a huge colony of gannets.

13. (*below*) View of the south coast of Sark.

sufficiently powerful here to destroy the plants; yet perhaps there is no spot of ground in Europe of the same size, where there are more greenhouses, or hothouses, than in Guernsey, there being scarcely a gentleman's house without one or more, and many of the tradesmen have their graperies.[5]

As Jacob implies, these early greenhouses were adjuncts of private gardens. For many years the better-off citizens of Guernsey had been enclosing their gardens with high walls and growing a great variety of fruit, the more tender trees such as lemons and peaches being trained against south-facing walls. They were doubtless protected in winter by some form of covering, and it was but a short step from this to covering them by a permanent lean-to greenhouse.

The first greenhouse in the island is said to have been built in 1792 by Peter Mourant of Candie House. The Candie estate has been the property of the States since 1886. The house is now the Priaulx Library. The Museum and Art Gallery are on the site of Peter Mourant's ornamental garden, and Lower Candie Gardens, where he grew his vegetables and fruit, are now public gardens. Two of his prototype greenhouses are still to be seen against the south wall of the lower gardens, one near the bottom and one at the top of the gardens. Their most striking feature is the heavy construction, with massive timbers and narrow panes. The carpenters, perhaps used to building ships, were not taking any risks with these unfamiliar structures. By comparison with modern glass the light in these houses must be very poor, but they were built to last and are still used by the Parks and Gardens Department for raising plants.

Among the fruit formerly grown in the open against south-facing walls were grapes, and these prospered so well under glass that before long they were being grown on a commercial scale. In 1830, the year Jacob wrote his piece about greenhouses, 3,474 pounds of grapes were exported.[6] The first mention of a commercial hothouse is in 1847, when W. A. Crousaz erected a range of houses heated by hot water. During the next 40 years numerous vineries were built— so many indeed that a holding of glass, whether it contains tomatoes, freesias or roses, is still called a vinery. By 1887 1,000 tons of grapes were being exported each year.

At first only lean-to houses were built. Sometimes they were backed by a wall of wooden boards, but in many cases stone walls were built specially for the purpose. These tall granite walls, beautifully constructed with string coursing, are particularly numerous in the town parish, where many lanes and alleys are bounded by them on both sides. If one is inquisitive enough to pry behind such a wall the lean-to house and sometimes even the vines may still be seen. Often, however, a more profitable use has been found for the land and the wall is hiding an office block or a housing estate. In either case the walls are still a vital element in Guernsey's landscape.

In some vineries the lean-to houses formed three sides of a rectangle. An example may be seen in the Talbot Valley; the high granite wall is on the south side of the road, three-quarters of a mile above King's Mills.

At some stage it occurred to someone to dispense with the wall and build a span house, and this proved so much more efficient that before long spans were appearing all over the island. Some masonry was still involved, for these early greenhouses had no glass fronts, the span roof being supported on low stone walls (The *front* of a greenhouse is not the gable, but the glass 'wall' at right-angles to it.) Although the vines were trained up inside the glass they were rooted in the soil outside. Each vine entered the house through a hole in the front wall just above ground level. These holes, about the size of a small brick, are still a good indication of the original purpose of a greenhouse. It is possible that with some study the distance between the holes might be found to indicate the age of a house, for at first the vines were overcrowded and later it was found that the quality of the fruit was far better if they were well spaced out.

In lean-to houses peaches were very often grown against the back wall, with a catch-crop such as lettuce or asparagus between the peaches and the vines. It was in this position, in about the year 1874, that the first commercial crops of tomatoes were grown.[7] The first maincrop tomatoes were grown, in a span house, in 1884. Since the requirements of tomatoes and vines are completely different, these tomatoes, grown on their own, were much more successful than those under vines. By this time Guernsey grapes were commanding lower and lower prices on the London market, and growers turned to tomatoes with enthusiasm.

From the 1880s until the First World War vast areas of glass were erected. Many greenhouses were built by shipwrights who had been left without work by the change from wooden to iron ships. They were built to last, and are only being demolished today because they are no longer profitable. The heavy construction excludes too much light, and it is too expensive to heat a number of separate spans.

After the 1914–18 War the development continued, and by now a distinctive 'Guernsey greenhouse' had evolved. It consisted of a shallow-pitched span roof supported on low glass fronts, with a glass gable at each end. The standard panes were 12 inches wide and were 'round-and-hollow', the bottom of each pane being rounded with its lowest point in the middle, so that the rain water dripped from the centre of the pane, away from the wooden sash bars on each side. After every five panes, instead of a sash bar there was a principal rafter, the sash bars being supported by purlins which were mortised into the principals. Many of these houses are still in service—in 1978 there were 335 acres of 12-inch glass.

Tomatoes proved so profitable that glass continued to proliferate until in 1939 tomato exports amounted to 35,000 tons. This was brought to an abrupt halt by the Occupation, when many acres of glass had to be abandoned through lack of labour. The remaining glass was used for growing a variety of vegetables to eke out the meagre rations, though some tomatoes were exported to France.

Since the war the tendency has been for panes to become broader and sash bars narrower, and for single blocks of glass to be built instead of separate spans. The greenhouses being built at present have 24-inch panes supported by a light metal framework, high glass fronts and multiple spans so that several acres can be covered by a single glasshouse. The construction has perhaps evolved too far in the direction of flimsiness, for at least one large modern unit was destroyed in a storm in December 1979.

The method of growing the plants has also changed over the years. In the traditional houses the 'Guernsey arch' was used; wires were stretched the length of the house just above head level, and the plants were trained up strings which were tied to the wires. When they reached the wires the stems were arched overhead, across the path and down the other side. The 'Guernsey arch' will still be seen in many greenhouses, but in the new high-fronted houses the wires are much higher and the grower stands on an electrically-operated trolley to trim the shoots and pick the fruit. When they reach the height of the wires the plants are let down so that the lower, leafless part of the stem runs along the ground, and then the fruiting part of the stem is tied up further on.

At first the plants were rooted in clay pots; the kilns where these were made can still be seen at Oatlands, across the field from the Brae Side crossroad. Later the plants were grown in the soil of the greenhouse, which had to be sterilised between crops by steam from huge itinerant boilers which resembled primitive railway engines. A few survivors of the breed are still at work. If there is insufficient room within the vinery they simply park in the road, and traffic has to find its way round them as best it can.

For a time it was fashionable to grow the plants in 'whale-hide' pots, but the present method is to grow them in peat modules—pillow-like polythene bags containing Irish or Finnish peat. These are laid on their sides, holes are cut in the polythene, and the baby plants in fibre pots are placed on top, so that their roots can grow through into the peat. The modules have to be changed every year, and the disposal of the old ones is becoming a serious problem. The countryside is increasingly littered with the polythene, and even the peat is suspect because of the chemicals it contains.

Until the 1950s the greenhouses were heated by coal-fired boilers and hot water pipes. Because the boiler had to be at the lowest point in the circuit it was buried in a pit, into which the grower had to descend to attend to its needs. Stoking, riddling and clinkering the boilers was a time-consuming job which had to be done fairly frequently, often late at night. 'Ah well, I must attend to my boilers' was a frequently heard ending to a conversation. A typical growing property at this time consisted of a cottage or a bungalow, a couple of spans of glass, a boiler-pit and brick chimney, a pile of huge lumps of coal and a packing shed consisting largely of greenhouse glass. Many such properties are still to be seen, especially in the north of the island, but the pile of coal is no more, having been replaced by an oil tank standing in a concrete catchment pit. Now that the hot water is circulated by an electric pump there is no need for the boiler to be in a pit, so the oil-fired boiler is above ground in a corrugated asbestos boiler house, and the brick chimney has been replaced by an iron or asbestos pipe held up by wires. Some modern vineries are heated by hot air.

Someone in search of a project may like to make a survey of the remaining brick chimneys to find out whether their tops all lean in the same direction, and if so, why.

Greenhouse crops, and particularly tomatoes, consume huge quantities of water, and the various methods that have been used to supply it are still represented in the landscape. At first water was pumped from wells by hand for the vines. Then cisterns were built to collect rain water from the glasshouse roof, but the water still had to be pumped from the cistern by hand. Next, wind-pumps began to appear, which pumped water from wells or cisterns into tanks raised on tall legs so that the tomatoes could be watered by gravity. The forest of wind-pumps with metal sails turning and clanking in the ample wind became a feature of the skyline until growers either turned to the main water supply or fitted electric pumps. A few wind-pumps remain, their twisted sails adding a touch of desolation to the already depressing sight of run-down glass. The modern blocks of glass are supplied with water from round concrete towers, often fed from deep boreholes.

Since the war an increasing amount of glass has been devoted to flowers, especially to freesias and roses, but tomatoes are still the main greenhouse crop, occupying 63 per cent. of the glass in 1978.

The distribution of glass is interesting, not only from an academic point of view but because it presents a problem for those who plan the future development of the island. There is a concentration in the north, particularly on the reclaimed land of the Braye du Valle, but apart from this the glass is scattered in small groups almost uniformly throughout the island, inextricably entangled with the distribution of dwellings. This is because the Guernsey growing industry is essentially one of small family concerns, the family living and working on the same property. At first most of the greenhouses were built in back gardens to be worked as a spare-time occupation, though many prospered enough to grow eventually into whole-time family units. It was not until the industry was firmly established that investment capital moved in and the large vineries were built. Today the average vinery has an area of glass equivalent to a traditional span 811 feet long.

When the back gardens were full of glass and new land had to be bought, very different criteria operated in choosing a site from those which apply today. The last consideration was natural beauty or the amenity value of the land. The Island Development Committee had yet to be thought of and land must have seemed unlimited. The main considerations were the price of the land and its suitability for growing crops under glass. In the early days the first of these seems to have been the factor that weighed most heavily. The first generation of greenhouses tended to be on land which was not good for agriculture, either because this could be bought more cheaply or because the landowner placed his own glass where it would least interfere with his farming. This is why there is so much glass on the low-lying and sandy areas of the north and west.

P. J. Girard has studied the glass of the Vazon area and finds here that by far the greatest concentration of old glass is on land which is far from ideal for the purpose.[8] He considers the reason to be that this early glass was built by working men with little capital, who could only afford to buy land in the low-lying, swampy area immediately to the east of Vazon Bay. The level was first raised by dumping sand, which was cheaply available from the dunes at Albecq, which were themselves being levelled for glass. Above the 50-foot contour there is good agricultural land and far less glass, farmers having been reluctant to sell their best land while dairy farming was still profitable. A large proportion of the glass that does exist in this area is modern, including some very successful vineries in a belt extending northwards from Les Beaucamps to Cobo.

The profit margin from glasshouse crops has fallen enormously in recent years, partly because of the price of oil and partly because of subsidised competition from Holland. This makes investment in the far more efficient modern glass vital if the industry is to survive. Until the expansion of the industry came to a halt in the late 1970s, vineries were still being extended by building new spans beside the old. Since dwellings and glass were already inextricably mixed, this added to the muddle by bringing the glass even closer to the next group of dwellings. The mixture was made worse by the fact that the only land released for substantial groups of new dwellings was that containing obsolete glass, which was usually surrounded by other glass.[9] At present more and more unprofitable vineries are being abandoned, and there is pressure to develop the derelict land for industry or housing. Where the derelict vinery has become surrounded by industrial or residential development, this pressure is difficult to resist, but in rural areas it is vital to regard greenhouse land as agricultural rather than industrial, and to return it, if it is not required for new glass, to farmland.

Guernsey still has a thousand acres of glass, equivalent to the total roof area of a town of a quarter of a million souls. The industry plays such an important part in the economy, both as a money earner and by providing the framework for the Guernsey way of life, that the States have given it substantial aid in order to tide it over the present difficult years. Jersey's glasshouse industry, although proportionally less important than Guernsey's, is also a substantial one and consideration is being given in that island as well to providing the industry with financial support.

Although nobody could describe the glasshouse landscape as beautiful it has enormous character, and unlike some other aspects of the man-made landscape it is genuine and unselfconscious.

Chapter Seven

THE ARCHITECTURAL LANDSCAPE: (1) VERNACULAR ARCHITECTURE

It is not only the architectural facade of the building that matters;
it is that combined with a feeling for proportion, texture, colour,
materials, and harmony with the landscape.—Joan Stevens, 1977.

IN ISLANDS as densely populated as Jersey and Guernsey, buildings are bound to be a significant, even a dominant, feature of the landscape. For better or worse, islanders and visitors alike see architecture wherever they turn their eyes.

The traveller who is discerning enough to approach the islands by sea could scarcely wish for a happier introduction to the archipelago than the view of St. Peter Port as the boat steams down the Little Russel and turns between the pier-heads. Behind the massed masts in the Old Harbour, now a marina for visiting yachts, the buildings of the town crowd steeply up the hill, innumerable Georgian sash windows overlooking the harbour. On the narrow strip of level ground at the foot of the hill, a row of tall, gabled warehouses faces the quay. Today they are used as banks, offices and restaurants, and many of them have been rebuilt within the last 20 years, but they retain their crowded, vertical emphasis and their steeply-pitched pantile roofs. Behind them an intricate roofscape of red pantiles climbs the hill, and turns inland to follow the two valleys to the north and south of the town. On the skyline are the Regency terraces of the New Town, the blunt pink granite steeple of St. Barnabas, the tall, slender spire of St. Joseph, the Ionic cupola of St. James the Less, the towers and battlements of Elizabeth College, and the magnificent folly of Victoria Tower.

The airborn traveller has a less happy introduction to Guernsey. Assuming that he arrives at all, the three miles' drive from the airport to town takes him past some of the worst 20th-century ribbon development anywhere in the Channel Islands. Only when he reaches the outskirts of the town, and piecemeal development gives way to orderly and restful Regency and Victorian terraces, will he begin to realise that he is in an island of quite exceptional architectural interest. A few jettied houses dating from the 16th century or earlier survive in the medieval part of the town, centred on the Town Church, and there are several large 18th-century town houses, most of them comparatively unspoilt. The town expanded explosively in the early 19th century, and there are numerous Regency terraces as well as grander villas. Modern buildings have mainly been in the 'neo-Georgian' style which, if not very distinguished, at

92

least blends in quite well with the surrounding houses. There is only one building that could be described as a tower block: an 11-storey block of flats tucked away in the Charroterie valley. It is carefully sited and does not intrude upon the skyline, but there are no plans to repeat the experiment elsewhere in Guernsey.

The town of St. Helier is less impressive. Built mainly on flat, low-lying land, it lacks the narrow *venelles* and precipitous flights of steps with sudden views of of the harbour that give such charm to St. Peter Port. Early buildings are scarcer, several rows of mid–18th-century houses have been demolished in the last few years and very few good examples of this period survive. The town is rich in buildings of the 19th century, for as in St. Peter Port this was a time of rapid expansion. When the Regency and Victorian development had overrun the level land by the harbour it began to climb the slopes behind. Almorah Crescent, which overlooks the town from the north, is, with its continuous wrought-iron hooded balcony, the most impressive Regency terrace in any of the islands.

If the town of St. Helier lacks the character of St. Peter Port it nonetheless has a fine approach by sea. Two hours after leaving Guernsey the boat passes the broad sweep of St. Aubin's Bay and turns north around the breakwater which runs out from Elizabeth Castle on its high-tide island. From the middle of the breakwater rises a rock surmounted by the Hermitage, where St. Helier is said to have lived.

As one enters the harbour the town of St. Helier lies ahead to the north, but to the east, forming a backdrop to the harbour, are the pink granite ramparts of Fort Regent, with the space-age dome and roofs of the leisure centre peeping over the parapet.

Until the end of the 17th century the architecture of the Channel Islands, both in the towns and countryside, was extremely distinctive, and it is this vernacular architecture which is the subject of the present chapter. Building erected after 1700, when islanders began to look for inspiration beyond their own shores, will be described in the next chapter.

The Medieval Churches

The oldest buildings still standing in Jersey and Guernsey are almost certainly the medieval parish churches. Every one of the 12 parishes of Jersey retains its ancient church. In Guernsey, nine of the 10 medieval churches survive. The tenth, Notre Dame (later known, incorrectly, as St. Philippe) de Torteval had been allowed to fall into such a state of disrepair during the 18th century that it was demolished and replaced by the present church in 1816. In Alderney, too, the old church was demolished in the last century; all that remains of it is the clock-tower, standing in the old cemetery over the wall from the museum. For all its medieval appearance, with its squat conical spire and spirelets, the tower was only added to the church in 1767.

Although a great deal has been written about the ages of the medieval parish churches, the only certain fact is that they are all extremely ancient. The fact that the churches of St. Sampson, St Helier, and St. Brelade are dedicated to obscure saints who lived in the 6th century, and St. Ouen to a saint of the 7th century, strongly suggests that there were churches in these parishes in the Dark Ages, long before the arrival of the Normans. We have seen (p. 55) that some of the Guernsey churches are mentioned in a document of 1060; other charters of the same century mention the other Channel Island churches, and they figure in numerous subsequent documents. What the documents do not tell us is whether they refer to the churches we see standing today, or to earlier ones.

With their double naves and chancels, vaulted roofs and central steeples of idiosyncratic design the churches of Jersey, together with most of those of Guernsey, form a highly distinctive group which has no exact parallel elsewhere. The delightful church of St. Mary may be taken as typical of the group. It stands amid the fields on the northern plateau of Jersey, between the heads of the Gréve de Lecq and the St. Peter's Valleys. Although it serves the least populated parish in the island the church is surprisingly large—it has been suggested that this reflects the success of sheep farming in the Middle Ages.[1] It is beautifully maintained, but unspoilt.

The present church consists of two parallel naves and chancels. The roofs are not of timber but are vaulted, like those of all Jersey's parish churches, in solid masonry. Between the north nave and chancel is a square tower surmounted by a cement-covered octagonal spire, with four spirelets filling the corners where the spire meets the tower. There are several steeples of this kind in the islands, but St. Mary's is unusual in having raised ribs on the angles of the spire.

St. Mary's church was mentioned in a document of 1042 as St. Mary of the Burnt Monastery, from which historians have not been slow to deduce its possible origin. The earliest part of the church is the northern of the two chancels, built of rough stones, some of which appear to have been collected on the beach. In 1978 the outlines of two very early Norman windows were discovered, which may date this corner of the church to the 11th century. Some 200 years later a nave was built out to the west, with perhaps small transepts to make a cruciform church. At the crossing was a square tower, probably with a gabled roof similar to the one at St. Brelade.

The next stage was the building of a chapel which is now the south chancel. Set into the apex of the gable is a stone bearing the date 1342 in Roman figures. This is by far the earliest dated stone known in Jersey. The walls of this section are mainly of grey granite from the Chausey Islands. The wall between the two chancels was replaced by arches supported on round pillars. At least one of these pillars was removed during the 19th century. The risky process of removing a pillar has also been undertaken at Trinity (where the work was paid for by selling a pew in the space provided), at St. John, and at St. Andrew's, Guernsey. The reason seems to have been to allow the congregation a better view of the preacher in the pulpit. The elongated arches look a little awkward, but so far none has collapsed.

The octagonal spire was added to the medieval tower in 1834 and the final section of the church, the south nave, was begun in 1838—an unusually late date for a major part of a parish church. Again, the wall between the two naves was replaced by arches and pillars.

Beside the altar in the south chancel is a piscina—a niche in the wall in which, in pre-Reformation days, the priest washed the vessels after celebrating Mass. There would have been several altars in different parts of the church, each with a piscina, but at the Reformation, which was particularly vigorous in the Channel Islands, all the piscinas that could be found in churches and chapels were either blocked up or ripped out. Many found their way into private houses, where they are known as bénitiers. All the Guernsey medieval churches except St. Saviour's have retained at least one piscina: the Town Church has no fewer than six, and there is a particularly fine example in the north chancel of the Vale. In Jersey St. Clement's, St. Laurence's, and Grouville each have one, and a piscina from the Town Church is now in the Victorian church of St. Simon in St. Helier. But St. Mary's, with its carved trefoil head and rope-moulding, is perhaps the finest.

A holy water stoup, in which worshippers would dip their fingers on entering the church, has recently been uncovered in St. Mary's church beside a former door, now a window, in the south chancel. At the same time an aumbry was discovered to the left of the altar. In Guernsey there is a stoup at St. Martin's.

In Ste. Marie du Castel, Guernsey, the south-eastern of the four great piers which support the steeple is pierced by a rectangular hole, or squint. There would have been an altar to the west of the pillar, and the least improbable explanation so far advanced for the squint is that it afforded a chantry priest at this altar a view of the parish priest at the high altar, during the celebration of the Mass. In St. Laurence's, Jersey, there is a squint in exactly the same position, directed towards the altar in the Hamptonne chapel.

The walls of the medieval churches and chapels would have been covered with paintings of Biblical scenes and moral fables. At the Reformation these were whitewashed over, but some have since been uncovered, and many more certainly await discovery. The walls and vaulting of the 'Fishermen's Chapel' at St. Brelade are covered with paintings of the 14th and 15th centuries, depicting the Annunciation, the Massacre of the Innocents, the Entry into Jerusalem, the Scourging, the Crucifixion, the Resurrection, and the Last Judgement. The very similar chapel of St. Apolline near Perelle in Guernsey, which was built in the 1390s, has some paintings under the vaulting which may represent the Nativity. They are badly decayed—not surprisingly, as the chapel was used for some years as a stable. It has lately been restored for interdenominational use.

The Castel church has some 13th-century paintings under the vaulting in the north chancel. In the centre is a figure with a chalice, a flagon, and an axe, possibly St. Thomas Becket. To the east is the Last Supper. The Apostle on the extreme right was only uncovered when the frescoes were restored in 1962. The scene on the left illustrates a fable in which three courtiers on horseback encounter three walking skeletons. One of the courtiers has not noticed them, but the others, and even one of the horses, look suitably astonished. The same story is illustrated in the south transept of St. Clement's church, Jersey, but here only two dogs, two horse's legs and some French verse survive. In the north transept are St. Barbara, standing by her tower, and St. Margaret, with a wing of her dragon, and in the nave is a spirited rendering of St. Michael slaying the dragon. A painting is known to exist under the whitewash of St. Mary's church, and there were formerly some at Grouville.

Some of the parish churches began as chantry chapels. The church of St. Helier (the Town Church) grew from a chapel built perhaps in the 11th century near the beach, and dedicated to the saint who had lived, and according to legend, had been martyred, on his offshore islet. At St. Brelade were two chapels within a few yards of each other. One, whose dedication is not known, fell into disuse at the Reformation and for centuries was used for storing the Militia's guns; it was restored at the beginning of the present century as the 'Fishermen's Chapel'. The other, dedicated to St. Brelade, became the parish church. At St. Saviour in the same island there were no fewer than four dedications within the church, which some historians have taken to indicate four chantry chapels on or near the site of the present church. In these three parishes, as in St. Mary's, the original chapel became the chancel of the parish church, which was extended westwards to form a nave for the growing population. This was the case in most parishes, though in St. Clement and Grouville the original part became the nave, and a new chancel was built to the east. In St. Pierre du Bois and St. Saviour's, Guernsey, the oldest parts have also been considered to be the naves.[2] In most churches the oldest surviving parts appear to date from the 11th and 12th centuries.

All the churches were enlarged at various times during the Middle Ages, and by the time of the Reformation they had substantially reached their present form. In nearly every case the completed church consists, like St. Mary's, of two chancels and two naves lying parallel, each with a separate, vaulted roof of solid masonry. Externally the roofs are steeply pitched and have been tiled or slated in comparatively recent times in an attempt to render them waterproof. The vaulted roofs are often described as groined, but with the exception of the Hamptonne chapel, St. Laurence, and the south chancel of the Vale, they are completely plain and only groined in the sense that they are not 'Norman' barrel vaults but are shaped like a Gothic arch with a ridge line along the top. (The Town Church, Guernsey, has ribbed vaulting with bosses, but, except under the crossing, the ribs look like the work of John Wilson who presided over the early 19th-century restoration.)

Vaulted roofs of the same type were built in Ireland between the 6th and 12th centuries, and it has been suggested that they were brought to the Channel Islands by the Celtic missionaries and lingered here long after they had been superseded in Ireland.[3] An exception is St. Pierre du Bois, Guernsey, which has a central nave with side aisles and a wooden roof. This church is also notable for its sloping floor, the east end being 4ft. 8in. higher than the west. The south aisle of St. Sampson's and the western extension of St. Helier's also have timber roofs. St. Martin de Grouville has vaulted roofs but lacks the usual twin naves and chancels; a single nave and chancel are flanked by a pair of transept-like extensions.

The original medieval windows were small and either square-headed or with a shallowly arched head. Some have survived in this state, for instance the east window of the 'Fishermen's Chapel', St. Brelade, the south windows of St. Andrew's, Guernsey, and two square-headed windows in the south wall of the Castel church. The smaller of these is said to be a 'low-side window', a feature common in English churches of the 13th and 14th centuries, now thought to have been for ventilation. There is a very tall and narrow lancet window in the north wall of St. Martin de Grouville.

After the Reformation, when the nature of the services changed and more light was required, the square-headed windows were enlarged, often by removing the lintel and making an arch above it. Some of the chamfered and ornamented lintels that have been built into old houses doubtless came from the churches—the ogee lintel over the doorway of one of the old houses on the left of the road from St. Martin's church to Icart, Guernsey, is a possible example. To fill these pointed windows, devoid of tracery, in many Guernsey churches sash windows were fitted in the 18th or early 19th century. A lone survivor may still be seen over the west porch of the Castel church.

Many more windows were enlarged and Gothicised during the wave of restorations which swept through the parish churches in the last century, when it was considered that the only shape for a church window was pointed Gothic. The stone tracery in these 'Gothic' windows is often very obviously modern compared with the ancient stonework surrounding the windows. Examples of modern tracery are to be seen in almost every church. They are particularly obvious in the Town Church, St. Peter Port, where the wooden sash windows were replaced by tracery in 1839.

Some genuine medieval tracery does survive in the islands, and is particularly interesting to English visitors as it tends to follow the Flamboyant style which is uncommon in Britain. This style, so named because the sinuous curves of the tracery suggest a flickering flame, evolved in France in the 14th century from the Decorated Gothic introduced from England during the Hundred Years War. There was a great flowering of Flamboyant architecture in France in the 15th century, while in England the late Gothic architects were following the Perpendicular style. In the Channel Islands the local granite is so intractable that in most cases no particular Gothic style can be detected, least of all the delicate Perpendicular, but style does appear in the window tracery, and it is not surprising that it follows the Flamboyant style of France rather than the English Perpendicular.

Perhaps the best example of a Flamboyant window is the east window of the Hamptonne chapel in St. Laurence's church, Jersey. This was built by a wealthy rector, Louis Hamptonne, in 1524, and (apart from some Romanesque arcading in the Vale church, Guernsey) is the only consciously architectural piece of building in any of the medieval churches. On the outside the chapel is embellished by an ogee moulding over the window, crockets on the gable, a crocketed pinnacle and some robust gargoyles. Within, the vaulted roof is groined and ribbed, with a pair of bosses carved with a rose and the Hamptonne arms. In Guernsey,

St. Martin's church is notable for its Flamboyant porch. When the Flamboyant style is applied to the head of an opening the result is an ogee arch, alternately concave and convex. The moulding over the outer doorway is an excellent example.

St. Helier's church has its original tracery, some of it Flamboyant, and St. Saviour's church in the same island has a variety of windows of great interest. The two beautiful east windows make a particularly interesting comparison. The southern of these is a three-light window with reticulate tracery. This is a variety of Decorated Gothic with net-like tracery and cusped openings, which is sometimes found in English churches of the 14th century. The northern window of the pair has four lights and Flamboyant tracery. Seen together, the pair illustrate how the Flamboyant style evolved from the Decorated.

Many other Flamboyant windows, ancient and modern, may be seen in both islands. In Guernsey the east window of the north aisle of St. Michel du Valle still has its original Flamboyant tracery. The modern tracery of the Town Church is supposed to have been copied from this, and from famous examples at Beauvais and Caen, but although the same *mouchette* or dagger-like motif is used, the tracery is crude and heavy. While the east window of the Hamptonne chapel seems positively to flicker as you look at it, the windows of St. Peter Port are lifeless—the one weak feature in a magnificent church.

St. Peter Port church is basically cross-shaped, with a pair of transepts forming the arms of the cross. The north transept has become obscured by the north aisle and Lady Chapel, but the south transept remains and is exceptionally large. Several other churches had transepts at some stage, one of the pair later becoming incorporated into a second chancel or nave. At St. Laurence the north transept has been thus swallowed, while the south transept remains distinct. In it is the Roman pillar that was mentioned in Chapter Three (p. 52). St. Saviour, Jersey, also has a south transept with some small upper windows, perhaps to light an upper storey. The Castel church, Guernsey, retains a north transept, now used as a vestry.

At the crossing, beneath the bell loft, will be found in most churches the only true groining in the building. In most cases the groining is plain, but sometimes it is ribbed. The ribbed vaulting in the Town Church, Guernsey, is exceptionally fine and dates from the 14th century. The Castel church also has some fine ribwork under the crossing. In both churches the four pillars which support the tower are impressive in their sheer mass. In Jersey the groining under the crossing of the Town Church has both diagonal and ridge ribs, while that of St. Saviour's has heavy diagonal ribs but no ridge ribs. St. Laurence also has diagonal ribs, but the vaulting is marred by some incongruous raised pointing. St. John's church has no ribs, but the vaulting has the advantage of being painted blue, with gold moon and stars.

In every parish church of Jersey the steeple or tower is in a central position, over the crossing between the nave and the chancel. This is also the case in most Guernsey churches, which thus show the influence of mainland Normandy rather than of England. The exceptions are the four churches of St. Michel du Valle,

St. Saviour, St. Pierre du Bois, and St. Andrew, which have their steeples at the west end. In the case of the Vale this may have no significance other than that the tower was the last part of the church to be built—the spire itself is the same type as St. Mary's. St. Andrew's, St. Saviour's, and St. Pierre du Bois each have square towers of dressed stone at the west end, giving them something of the appearance of typical English country churches.

St. Helier, St. Peter Port, and St. Saviour, Jersey, also have square towers, but in the central position. The battlemented tower of St. Peter Port is surmounted by an octagonal steeple of timber with lead covering, which was added to the 15th century tower in 1721. An inscription in raised lead lettering, with St. Peter's keys and the names of the dean, churchwardens, carpenter and plumber, can just be made out from the ground.

The remaining steeples are of highly distinctive design and certainly qualify for the adjective 'vernacular'. The simplest are the low, saddle-back steeples of St. Sampson and St. Brelade. With their rough, rubble construction they have an air of enormous antiquity, and they are indeed almost certainly the oldest steeples of all. St. Laurence also has a saddle-back steeple, but it is taller and less ancient, having been heightened in 1890.

The most characteristically 'Channel Island' steeple is the octagonal spire with spirelets of the St. Mary type, usually covered in cement in an attempt to exclude the weather. The four spirelets are a happy solution to the problem of filling the corners where the eight-sided spire meets the four-sided tower. Guernsey has four such steeples, all in commanding positions. St. Michel du Valle surmounts a hillock overlooking its former northern island; Le Pont Colliche, the dryest way across the west end of the Braye du Valle, led to its foot. Ste. Marie du Castel stands on the brink of the escarpment where the southern plateau ends and the low-lying north begins. The Forest church, on the summit of the plateau near the airport, presides over the ancient settlement of Le Bourg and the church of St. Martin is on the same plateau, surrounded by the houses of La Bellieuse.

In Jersey the church of St. Martin has a spire of the St. Mary's type which was rebuilt in 1837 after being destroyed by lightning. Before lightning conductors were fitted the church spires were extremely accident-prone—Trinity church was struck no fewer than three times between 1629 and 1648—so that most of the spires we see today have at least been rebuilt in comparatively modern times. St. Martin's, Jersey, lacks the four spirelets, though vestigial plinths are visible which suggest that they may once have been there.

The remaining spires of Jersey are tall, four-sided pyramids. That of St. Peter, near the airport, is 123 feet high, the tallest in the island, and is topped by a red light to warn aircraft of its presence. It was built in the late 15th or early 16th century, the upper section being of dressed granite. St. John has a similar spire, the upper part of dressed stone, which was freed from its casing of cement in 1972.

After the Reformation, and particularly in the 18th century, the parish churches became increasingly cluttered with box-pews and galleries erected haphazardly in order to raise money by the sale of pews. The corbels which supported the older galleries can still be seen. Many churches had three-decker pulpits—the only survivor, at St. John, Jersey, has been cut down to reasonable proportions but still has its sounding board. As the only large buildings in most parishes, the churches were used for meetings and for many secular purposes. The Militia kept their artillery in the naves of many churches and the St. Peter Port fire engines were kept in the north transept of the Town Church. The large doorway by which they gained access is now a window, but traces of the opening can still be seen in the outer wall.

All this was swept away in the tide of restorations which swept through the churches of the British Isles in Victoria's reign. Visually the change must have been almost as great as the Reformation.

Chapels and Crosses

Besides the parish churches there were in the Middle Ages scores of chapels. Most of these were chantry chapels, for everyone who could possibly afford to do so, erected and endowed a chapel where Masses were said for his and his family's souls.[4] At the Reformation the chapels were either destroyed or put to secular uses. Many were so unsubstantial that they have not survived, but a few have been restored. St. Apolline, Guernsey, and the 'Fishermen's Chapel', St. Brelade, have already been mentioned. Notre Dame de la Clarté on the summit of La Hougue Bie is another example. On Herm St. Tugual's chapel, said to be of monastic origin, has been well restored and is used for non-denominational Sunday services. On Lihou Island the priory of Notre Dame de Lihou is in ruins; the last piece of vaulting fell in December, 1979. There were also several seigneurial chapels, of which the best preserved, in beautiful surroundings, is at Rozel in Jersey.

Another medieval feature of the islands was the wayside cross. This was a simple granite cross with an octagonal shaft and a heavy octagonal base—the type is still to be seen on the mainland of Normandy. Those in the islands were all thrown down at the Reformation, but some fragments survive, mainly in Jersey. The head of such a cross, mounted on a pillar which is almost certainly the one removed from St. Mary's church in 1867, may be seen in the lane immediately to the north of St. Mary's church, at the entrance to Meadow Court. There is an excellent reproduction of a medieval cross at Elizabeth Castle, marking the site of St. Helier's abbey.

The former existence of numerous crosses is indicated by place-names: La Croix au Maitre, La Croix Besnard or simply La Croix. In Guernsey, de Guérin found evidence for over fifty crosses.[5] The number has risen to about sixty. An example is a field named Le Courtil de la Croix Rompue, next to the former St. Saviour's School. In Jersey, Charles Stevens found 69 place-names containing Croix.

Besides free-standing crosses, many were simply incised in stone. Such a stone is built into a pillar outside the *Hangman* inn, at La Croix au Baillif, St. Andrew's. It is associated in folklore with Gaultier de la Salle, who was hanged in 1320, but where the Bailiff comes in, nobody is quite certain.

Domestic Architecture

Although 21 medieval churches, a few chapels and two castles have survived from the Middle Ages in excellent repair, no medieval dwelling houses have survived in anything like their original condition. Joan Stevens considers that 1500 is probably the earliest date that can be claimed for any house now standing in Jersey, and even then much of the fabric is probably a later addition.[6] The same is doubtless true of Guernsey. At least part of the reason for this is the lack of lime in the islands. Church and State could afford to import lime to make mortar for their buildings; the private householder could not. He used clay, reinforced with chopped straw, cow dung or cow hair as a bedding and filling material for his thick stone walls. Sometimes the clay was mixed with sea sand, which never dried completely and so did not crack. This construction was adequate as long as water was excluded from the walls. When once the thatched roof was allowed to fall into disrepair the building very quickly collapsed.

Those medieval houses that have survived are of stone, which, unlike timber, has always been in abundant supply. There are no 'Tudor' timber-framed buildings, except possibly a few of the houses in the medieval heart of St. Peter Port. Jettied houses and narrow lanes once jostled right up to the walls of the Town Church. Many were cleared in the last century after an outbreak of cholera and to make room for the markets. The last houses, on the harbour side of the church, were not demolished until the beginning of this century. A few jettied houses remain in Church Square, High Street, and Berthelot Street, their overhanging storeys supported on granite corbels. The upper storeys of one or two of them look as if they may be constructed partially of timber, with wattle-and-daub filling. But it was in the country, rather than the town, that the typical Channel Island house came into being.

During the 16th and 17th centuries a type of house evolved in Jersey and Guernsey that is so characteristic that anyone who is familiar with the islands, looking at the photographs of properties for sale in, say, *Country Life*, can pick out the Channel Island houses at a glance. They were not architect-designed, but developed by a process of evolution, determined partly by history and partly by the materials that were available. The evolution continued in the 18th and 19th centuries, and the result was a happily-proportioned, dignified family house, not pretty in a chocolate-box sense, but mature and beautiful. There are island differences but these are trivial—Jersey and Guernsey houses are basically the same.

It is tempting to suppose that the Channel Island farmhouse evolved from the long-house, a dwelling in which people and cattle lived side by side under one roof, with internal access between the dwelling and the byre, and a common external door for man and beast. Long-houses are typical of the Celtic parts of the British Isles and are also common in Brittany, but they have recently been found further east in France than Celtic-speaking Brittany, and thus may have been in Europe before the Bretons arrived.[7] In Guernsey a long-house, thought to be of the 10th century, was excavated in a sand pit near Cobo in 1967, and in Jersey the foundations of one were found after the demolition of a row of houses in Old Street, St. Helier. It was excavated in 1975 and dated to the 13th century.

Two-roomed houses on the same plan, the rooms open to the thatched roof, continued to be built until perhaps the 17th century, though by then the cattle had been banished either to a specially built stable, or to an older house, no longer fit for use as a dwelling. One of the few single-storey cottages to survive from the 17th century or earlier is Le Ménage ès Feuves in La Rue des Landes, St. Ouen, whose *bergerie* was described in Chapter Five. The oldest inhabited dwelling in Guernsey is thought to be part of a single-storey cottage which now forms a wing of a house at Le Gron, St. Saviour's. It stands by the roadside a few yards to the north of the road junction, and may date from Elizabethan times.[8]

The next stage was to build a loft over one room, so that the house was partly of one storey and partly of two. Les Pièces, on the Forest Road, Guernsey, is such a house, but it has recently been extensively restored. Finally the upper storey was extended so that the whole house could be covered by one roof, and the result was the two-storey house which, with additions and local variations, is the basis of the typical farmhouse we see today. The additions almost always include a lean-to extension at the back, originally serving as a store or scullery, but now used as a kitchen so that the original kitchen can become a living room.

The traditional Channel Island farmhouse is a plain, rectangular gabled building of local stone bonded with clay. It is usually sited in a sheltered place and faces south, with blank gables presented to the east and west and with one of the gables bordering the road. The gable walls are extremely thick, commonly 4 feet in the older houses, while the front and back walls are usually about 2 feet 6 inches thick. Each gable wall has a fireplace either upstairs or down. A great deal of trouble has been taken over this feature, which in all but the humblest dwelling is of carved granite. The stone lintel is supported by a pair of long stones which pass right through the wall and can be seen projecting slightly on the outside of the gable. On the inside each supporting stone has a carved corbel below it and below this again is one or more upright stones, usually with a chamfered inner corner. The fireplace stones projecting slightly from the outside wall are not to be confused with the stones known in Guernsey as *témoins* (witnesses) which project several feet from the walls of some buildings in that island. Their function is to remind the owner of the next property that a strip of land as wide as the *témoin* belongs to the owner of the building. This is so that he can repair his wall or roof from the outside if necessary.

The two rooms on the ground floor, kitchen and parlour, are separated by a hall into which front and back doors open. The front door, in the south facade, often has a round arch. Projecting from the back of the house is a stair tower or *tourelle*, usually semi-circular, but occasionally in Jersey square, containing the staircase to the upper floor. This opens on to a landing along the back of the house, separated from the bedrooms by studwork panelling. The main bedroom is over the parlour; another is over the kitchen, and there is a small room, the *cabinet*, between.

The depth of the house from front to rear has remained remarkably constant from the days of the long-house, having been limited by the useful length of an oak tree when made into a beam—commonly 15 or 16 feet internally. The main beams, which support the first floor and act as tie-beams for the roof, always run from front to back, parallel with the gable walls. At right-angles to the beams, and mortised into them, are smaller joists, across which the floorboards are laid. There are no ceilings to hide the joists, which often have an ornamental chamfer.

The length of the house is not so limited. In Guernsey virtually all the houses built between 1680 and 1750 conform to one or other of two plans, which have been called the small and large parlour house.[9] Both have a large kitchen with two windows in the facade, but the parlour is either large, with two front windows, or small, with one. The fenestration upstairs is usually the same, with an extra window over the door. Thus a small parlour house has seven front windows and a large parlour house, nine.

Jersey houses of the same period also vary in size, but the windows are nearly always symmetrical, with the same number on each side of the door. Thus, with the one over the door, there are either five or nine windows. Where there is a round-headed doorway the window above it is sometimes off-centre to avoid cutting into the arch. In Guernsey also this was done, but sometimes, as at Les Piques, St. Saviour's, the outer part of the arch still has a piece cut out.

Until glass became generally available at some time in the 17th century windows were very small, with wooden mullions and sometimes iron bars. The stones forming the window were often chamfered, and, in Jersey particularly, the lintels were often carved in an ornamental pattern. The Governor's House, Elizabeth Castle, which was built in the style of a farmhouse, has small, square, chamfered windows which were formerly protected by iron bars. During the 17th century windows gradually enlarged, but were still small and square by modern standards, with casement openings. Many houses still exist with these small windows, particularly in the back wall and the *tourelle*. They were irregular in size, shape and position—uniform windows only became fashionable in the 18th century. Le Rât Cottage, in the lanes half a mile to the north-west of St. Laurence's church, is a beautifully preserved example of a small 17th-century house with simple square windows. It belongs to the National Trust for Jersey and nestles in the head of a little valley which runs down to join the St. Peter's Valley at Tesson Mill. In the lane just around the corner from the cottage is an *abrevoir,* a place for watering cattle, and across the lane from the *abrevoir* is La Fontaine de St. Martin, one of the old sacred springs said to have healing properties. And to complete the riches afforded by this green corner of Jersey, on the damp side of the hedgebank grows Cornish moneywort.

In the 18th and 19th centuries windows were enlarged further, particularly vertically and were nearly always fitted with 12-pane sashes. Sash windows were introduced in the 18th century, but it was not until the 19th that they were almost universally adopted in the islands. Although belonging to a far later age than the houses to which they are fitted, these 12-pane sash windows add enormous grace to the mellow stone facades. It is only when the sash-bars are misguidedly removed and replaced by staring plate glass that the windows look wrong.

The main bedroom, besides having windows to the south and sometimes the north, often has a small window in the gable wall, to one side of the chimney flue. In several Jersey houses, the main bedroom has an attractive ornamentally-carved sill projecting on the outside of one of the windows in the facade. In Guernsey there is one of these sills in a gable bordering the road in King's Mills.

All the farmhouse roofs were originally thatched. This accounts for their steep pitch, and also for the attractive raised coping which caps the gables at the end of the roof. The thickness of the thatch would have been such that the surface was level with the coping stones. In Jersey there is often a 'gable stone', a corbel projecting from the facade immediately under the coping, bearing a date and initials. Unfortunately, many of the original dressed granite chimneys were replaced by brick at a time when granite was considered only suitable for peasants. Those stone chimneys that survive (and even some brick chimneys) have drip-stones projecting from three sides, or four if the chimney is in the middle of the roof. The thatch was tucked under these stones, which prevented rain from running down the chimney under the thatch. They are usually referred to as witches' stones, in the belief that they were intended as resting places for witches on their nocturnal flights.

Some thatched roofs remained in both islands until comparatively recently, but already in the 17th century slates were being imported for the grander buildings. A slate roof needed far less maintenance than thatch, and those householders who could afford this new, prestigious roof-covering made the change. At the same time some extra room was sometimes gained under the eaves by reducing the pitch of the roof, for a steep pitch is unnecessary with slate.

Tiles were also in use by the end of the 17th century, especially in the towns. The type used was the pantile, shaped into an S-bend so that each series, from ridge to eaves, has a continuous channel for rainwater, well away from the joint between one tile and the next beside it. The pantile originated in the Low Countries and has an interesting distribution around the North Sea and Baltic, which would not lead one to expect it in the Channel Islands.[10] It was introduced into Britain in the 17th century and is found in a narrow strip along the east coast of Scotland and a broader belt of eastern England, as far south as Ipswich. Where pantile and granite areas coincide, as in some east coast towns of Scotland, the architecture resembles that of the Channel Islands remarkably closely. The houses of St. Monans, Fife, with their 12-pane sash windows, could easily be mistaken for island houses. The only obvious difference is the coping of the gables, which are stepped in the usual Scottish manner. Another point of similarity is the medieval church, which has a steeple of the St. Mary's type.

On the Continent pantiles extend down the North Sea coast as far as Calais. Completely separated from this main area are the Channel Islands and also the port of Bristol. The strange distribution has not yet been explained. Perhaps pantiles were imported cheaply into these two seafaring centres as ballast in ships which traded with the Low Countries.

Whatever the manner of their coming, pantiles were a happy addition to the island scene. When used in farmhouses and outbuildings they blend perfectly with the local stone, particularly with the red granite of Mont Mado or Cobo. The steep pitch of the roofs, originally constructed for thatch, suits them, but a disadvantage is their weight, which requires sturdy roof timbers. Because they were cheaper they were not such a useful status symbol as Welsh slates. The author's own roof has slate at the front, where it is visible from the road, and pantiles behind. On a practical note, pantiles are not nailed, but hook over the laths, and the distance between laths is extremely critical. If they are too close a piece has to be removed from the corner of each tile, and if the laths are too far apart gaps appear at the corners. To make matters worse, pantiles vary in size and curliness. They are proof against steady rain, but driving rain, hail and snow penetrate between the tiles. This can be cured nowadays by fitting roofing felt under the laths. Pointing the tiles with cement does more harm than good, as water is drawn inside the roof by capillary action.

Many writers have commented on the delightful roofscape of St. Peter Port, particularly as seen from the mailboat at dawn, as the red tiles reflect the rising sun. The town owes its pantiles to a law which was passed in 1683, after a disastrous fire in the medieval centre of the town. The law forbade the use of thatch within the *Barrières de la Ville.* These are stones marking the position of gates in a wall which Edward III ordered to be built round the town in 1350. Whether the wall was ever built is doubtful, but the *Barrières* were maintained because some laws, particularly those of inheritance, differed between town and country. The present *Barrières de la Ville* date from 1700 and bear the names of the parish constables of the time, Nicolas and James Carey, One stands in Smith Street by the entrance to the main Post Office; others are in Cornet Street, Fountain Street, and the Pollet, while another stands sadly outside the north-east corner of the Town Church between a telephone box, a pillar box, and an advertisement stand.

As might be expected from their history, most of the tenement houses of Sark are typical Jersey farmhouses, while a few are of the Guernsey type. The first dwellings built by the Elizabethan settlers were single-storey cottages such as may still be seen at right-angles to Le Manoir, or at L'Ecluse. Helier de Carteret's later and grander south-facing house at Le Manoir is a symmetrical two-storey Jersey house, whose windows were enlarged and fitted with sashes in 1810. The central part of La Seigneurie is of the same type. Le Port à la Jument, again facing south, is a symmetrical Jersey house with a single-storey 'Granny's house' extending to the east. The dressed stone of the facade was imported from Jersey. The plate-glass downstairs windows demonstrate the unfortunate effect of removing the 'Georgian' sash-bars. La Ville Farm is a Guernsey small-parlour house, built in the 18th century at a time when Sark was coming increasingly under the influence of Guernsey.[11] The last thatched roof in Sark, at Le Fort, disappeared in the 1960s.

In Alderney the old farmhouses are clustered in the town of St. Anne, and although cows are no longer seen regularly in the streets and there has been much

Georgian and Victorian infilling, the narrow roads radiating from Le Marais Square retain a delightfully rural atmosphere with cobbles, whitewashed walls, the occasional sleeping dog and the odd stray hen.

The Round Arch

Perhaps the best known feature of Channel Island vernacular architecture is the round-headed or 'Norman' arch which embellishes the front door of many of the old houses. The round arch arrived in the Islands from France at some time before 1550 and evolved in different directions in Jersey and Guernsey, reaching perfection in the 17th century. After 1700 tastes changed and doorways became square.

Jersey has by far the largest number of round arches, with many variations on a semi-circular theme. Mrs. Joan Stevens has made a thorough study of them, and has managed to devise a chronological system of classification.[12] In its fully developed form the Jersey arch is a most graceful and satisfying structure. The arch itself is formed from three shaped stones or *voussoirs*. The outer pair of these have shoulders which project sideways to key into the surrounding masonry. The arch is supported on each side by three base stones—where there are more it will be found that either the floor has been lowered or the head of the arch raised. An ornamental chamfer runs round the inner corner of all nine stones. The chamfer does not quite reach the ground, but finishes with a decorated chamfer stop. The varied chamfer stops provide a fascinating study in themselves. The height of the arch is about 6 feet 3 inches and the width varies between 3 feet and 3 feet 4 inches. The curve of the arch is slightly less than a semi-circle; for some reason a perfect semi-circle appears to be over-curved.

A good example of such an arch, from La Fosse, Trinity, may be seen at the Jersey Museum. It bears the date 1686. Another is in a garden wall by the roadside at Roseland, Grouville. It bears the date 1636 and probably came from a previous house on the site. The earliest known example of this type is the front door of the Governor's House, Elizabeth Castle, which is known to have been ready in time for Sir Walter Ralegh when he took up residence as Governor in 1600. Before this date Jersey arches had a second, outer ring of *voussoirs*. Joan Stevens suggests that it may have been Paul Ivy, an engineer sent by Elizabeth I to work on the castles, who discovered that with Jersey granite the outer ring was unnecessary.

In addition to these small domestic arches Jersey has over 20 large farmyard arches. These magnificent structures are usually double, with a small arch for pedestrians, and a large one, about 9 feet high, for vehicles. A fine example is at Morel Farm, St. Laurence. This beautifully-preserved farm, complete with farmhouse, stables, pig sties, cider press, and cobbled yard, is not far from Le Rât Cottage, and like it is the property of the National Trust for Jersey. To the right of the small arch, on the outside of the wall, is a mounting block. The main arch bears the date 1666 and the initials RLG for Richard Langlois. Jersey and Guernsey share a highly eccentric system of initialling, to be seen on arches, lintels, gable stones and pump boxes, in which syllables are given their initial letters. Thus at Les Augrès, Trinity, the home of the Jersey Zoo, the second of the two arches one passes under has a stone above it with the date 1741 and the initials EDM and EDC for Elie Dumaresq and Elizabeth de Carteret.

In a few cases the head of the larger arch has been removed, perhaps to permit the passage of carts loaded with hay. This may be the explanation for the unusual gateway at La Fosse, Trinity, on the bend of the hill in the lanes just south of the Zoo. A similar open-topped gateway is at the entrance to Le Groignet, towards the King's Mills end of the Talbot Valley in Guernsey.

The earliest Guernsey arches, like those of Jersey, had an outer ring of small *voussoirs,* but while these disappeared in Jersey, in Guernsey they grew to the same size as the inner ring, giving the Guernsey arch a much heavier appearance. The *voussoirs* are not shouldered; instead, the upper of the three base stones is extended outwards to key into the surrounding masonry. Typical examples are at La Maison de Haut, St. Peter's, Les Mauxmarquis, St. Andrew's, and Les Piques, St. Saviour's. The Cohu family house, Les Câches, down a drive opposite Les Landes Baptist church, has a fine arch inscribed ICH 1758, this late date may, of course, have been added to an older arch. Guernsey also has some shouldered arches of the Jersey type, including the doorway of the old house at Les Poidevins, St. Andrew's (two shouldered inner *voussoirs* and an outer ring) and Les Grands Moulins, another Cohu house which forms the corner in King's Mills. Guernsey has three large double arches, not leading to farmyards, but associated with private estates. One of these arches, the Ivy Gates, belongs to the National Trust of Guernsey, who have caused it to be de-ivied. It stands by the roadside at the top of the Rohais and is of the Jersey shouldered type. Both the carriage and pedestrian arches are considerably lower than was intended because the ground level has been raised by successive layers of road metal. The arch leads into the estate of Les Granges de Beauvoir. The old manor house, an exceptionally fine three-storey house of 1685, is at the bottom of a long drive and can best be seen from La Route Isabelle, together with a magnificent *Pheonix canariensis,* a German hut, and an assortment of ponies, donkeys and pigeons. Among the trees on either side of the drive between the Ivy Gates and the manor are some large houses built in about 1860, but in the Regency style.

The other double arches are at Les Blancs Bois, Castel (now the *Whitewoods* hotel) and the St. Peter Port hospital. This arch, formerly at the entrance to a private estate near Cambridge Park, was embellished with a pelican when it was moved to the 'Town Hospital' at the junction of Hirzel Street and Hospital Lane. It leads into a rather fine courtyard surrounded by Georgian-style 18th- and 19th-century buildings, at present a geriatric hospital.

The round arch has never been a feature of the smaller islands. In Sark there is a typical Guernsey arch standing at the corner of a field near the Seigneurie. It was removed from a Guernsey house in 1835. In Alderney one of the houses in La Trigale, an attractive lane leading from the town to the Blaye, has an arch which appears to be of an early Guernsey type. Apart from this the doorways of Alderney and Sark are square-headed and functional.

Chapter Eight

THE ARCHITECTURAL LANDSCAPE: (2) THE ARCHITECTS MOVE IN

La Ville de Saint-Pierre-Port est fidéle à la reine, à la bible, et aux fêntres-guillotines. —Victor Hugo, 1802–85.

THE VERNACULAR STYLE of the Channel Islands, having evolved over many years to suit local conditions and materials, was extremely long-lived, and houses continued to be built in it well into the 19th century. (Indeed, with the encouragement of certain official bodies, houses in a rather self-conscious vernacular style are still being built today.) However, at the beginning of the 18th century taste underwent a sudden change. Small, irregularly-spaced windows, round arches, and *tourelle* stairways were out. Symmetrical facades, large, regularly-spaced windows, square-headed doorways and internal wooden staircases were in. Ornamental stonework, particularly chamfers around windows and doorways, also fell out of favour though marriage stones continued to be popular, particularly in Jersey, throughout the 18th and 19th centuries. These usually take the form of lintels over doorways, carved with the syllabic initials of the couple and a date, which is not necessarily the date of the house or of the marriage. The husband's initials are on the left and his wife's, by her maiden name, on the right. Many marriage stones are illustrated in the second volume of Joan Stevens' *Old Jersey Houses.*

Privateering had begun to bring wealth to some families, but for most islanders the first half of the 18th century was not particularly prosperous, and houses dating from this period are not nearly as numerous as those from later in the century. St. Helier was still virtually without a harbour, but a pier had been built at St. Aubin's Fort, which attracted merchants and sea-captains to build at St. Aubin. An example of a house of this time is La Maison Le Maistre, on Le Mont Les Vaux which climbs from St. Aubin's harbour. The marriage stone reads I L P   A D   1796. The couple were Jean Lemprière and Anne Durell. Some of the town houses built at St. Aubin at this time were two rooms deep from front to back. This fashion did not spread into the country until much later in the century.

St. Helier at the opening of the 18th century was still little more than a village of narrow streets clustered round the Town Church and the Market Place (now Royal Square). This would have been full of stalls of every description. Fish was laid on slabs where George II now stands, the butchers' stalls were on the site of the National Westminster Bank, and the corn market was in the arcaded

108

ground floor of the building now occupied by the United Club. This had been built in 1668. The granite arches are still there, though obscured by later additions. (Royal Square ceased to be the market place in 1803, when the States bought a site in Halkett Place, which was then being laid out. The present market buildings date from 1882.) The only wide road in the town was La Grande Rue, now Broad Street. La Rue du Dierrière (King Street) and La Rue du Milieu (Queen Street) formed the main thoroughfare; beyond it, to the north, were fields and orchards. To the south-east, beyond La Rue des Trois Pigeons (Hill Street) was Le Mont de la Ville, where Fort Regent stands, its grassy slopes grazed by sheep. To the west, beyond Charing Cross, were sand dunes, commemorated today by names such as Rue des Mielles and Sand Street. Beyond the dunes stood Mont Patibulaire (West Mount), part of the semi-circular escarpment which surrounds the saucer of St. Helier. E. T. Nicolle has compared this low-lying area of dunes, backed by hills, with the present-day hinterland of St. Ouen's Bay.[1]

The building of a pier under Le Mont de la Ville, near the present *La Folie* inn had been begun in 1700, but it was not in use until the middle of the 18th century, and even then it was highly dangerous—a map of 1737 refers to it as 'Town Peer not finished and very unsafe'. There was no road where the present Commercial Buildings stand, and cargoes had to be unloaded at low tide and carried across the beach to the town. Later, Pier Road was built, climbing the lower stopes of Le Mont de la Ville to reach the pier.

Some early 18th-century houses survive in the centre of the town, though most are heavily disguised by subsequent embellishment. One of the more fortunate is the town's first public library, an austere early Georgian three-storey brick building in Library Place, whose cistern head gives the date 1736. One of the first brick buildings in Jersey, and one of the first public libraries anywhere in the world, it was saved from demolition a few years ago by the various pressure groups on the island. Until recently there was a nucleus of run-down early 18th-century houses immediately to the north of Charing Cross. Old Street and most of Hue Street have been demolished to make way for a new development, but a few survive in the neighbouring Dumaresq Street. No. 1 may even date from the 17th century. It is now a restaurant but retains an attractive double shop front. At the time of writing there are still a few anxious survivors on the west side of Hue Street; the row is terminated by the rebuilt *Post Horn* pub, a sympathetic and successful reconstruction in the Regency style.

Hill Street contains some well-disguised houses of the early and mid–18th century. No. 16, now lawyers' offices, was probably the *Hotel des Trois Pigeons* which gave the road its original name.[2] Although it bears the date 1748 the facade is not original, having been rebuilt in the last century in line with its neighbours. The shutters of the ground floor windows are a characteristic feature of St. Helier. The next two houses below this, Nos. 12 and 14, have plain but attractive facades of Regency stucco. Further up the hill, No. 35 is an example of a house that would benefit enormously from sympathetic restoration. It is a tall, narrow town house with basement and three storeys, a flight of stone steps leading to the front door and date-stone of 1737. A photograph published in E. T. Nicolle's *The Town of St. Helier* shows that by 1931 the windows had already lost their Georgian glazing bars. More recently most of the stonework has been obscured by cement rendering, the first floor has acquired a box-like picture window and the basement a bogus bow-fronted window.

Perhaps the finest house of the early 18th century in the islands is Sausmarez Manor in St. Martin's, Guernsey. Although the manor contains elements of five periods, it is the beautiful Queen Anne facade that can be seen from Sausmarez Road, facing a croquet lawn and an imposing gateway surmounted by heraldic beasts. The court house by the gates has been described (p. 57). The manor house is of three storeys plus dormers, of dressed grey granite with string courses and red granite quoins. The sash windows are of a very early type, with 24 panes and only one section opening. The hipped roof is surmounted by a gazebo and balcony.

Traces of the original medieval manor house are to be seen across a courtyard at the back, and the 16th-century manor is still standing behind the present house. The Queen Anne house was built in 1714. A Regency wing was added later which was replaced in 1873 by a Victorian extension whose fine, large rooms are linked to the Queen Anne house by an entrance hall. The house is open to the public on certain days and is well worth a visit. Among the most interesting features are the paintings, which include a series of portraits with the strong de Sausmarez features running firmly through them.

In Sark La Seigneurie, formerly La Perronerie, became the residence of the Seigneurs in 1730, when the fief was bought by a leading Guernsey privateer owner, Nicholas Le Pelley. The facade of the house dates from 1732, when the windows were enlarged, using granite imported from Jersey.

As might be expected, the manor houses of Jersey have parts dating from every conceivable period, though in most cases the facades are comparatively modern. Some, for instance the plain classical facade of Vinchelez de Bas (*c.* 1820), the much grander late-18th-century facade of La Hougue Boëte or the French château of Trinity Manor (1910) are extremely fine. The senior manor, and the one most steeped in Jersey history, is that of St. Ouen. The house is full of interest but has been heavily restored.

In the second half of the 18th century the flow of money into Jersey and Guernsey derived from seafaring increased to a flood. Some came from fishing and some doubtless from smuggling, but the real wealth came from legalised piracy. The boom years were from 1778 to 1815, when islanders were not slow to take advantage of the American and French wars. The vast fortunes derived from privateering during these 37 years had an immediate impact on the landscape. Harbours were improved; warehouses, villas and mansions built. Numerous farmhouses were enlarged or rebuilt at this time, for many farming families held shares in the privateers. For the design of their new buildings islanders looked beyond their own shores, and particularly to England. It is fortunate for us and for posterity that these 37 boom years coincided with one of the greatest periods of English architecture.

At the opening of this prosperous period the condition of the roads was still such that it was impossible to commute daily between the more distant country districts and the towns of St. Helier and St. Peter Port. Those merchants and shipowners who could afford to run two establishments retained their roots in the country but built themselves town houses as well. In St. Peter Port these Georgian town houses were built on the outskirts of the medieval town, and particularly in High Street, Smith Street, and the Pollet. One of the finest of the survivors is *Moore's* hotel in the Pollet, once the town house of the Saumarez family. It is a substantial six-bay house of three storeys, plus dormers, with a severely formal facade of dressed grey granite, built in about 1760 by the father of the famous admiral. It was here that the Duke of Gloucester, brother of George III, finally found a bed on the unfortunate occasion in 1765 when he came ashore unexpectedly at 2 a.m. and was turned away, first by the only inn in the town, and then by the Lieutenant-Governor himself.[3]

Slightly smaller, but more satisfying architecturally, is the town house of the Le Marchant family, now the Constables Office in Lefebvre Street. This was built by the Bailiff of Guernsey, William Le Marchant, in 1787. It is another formal three-storey house of dressed grey granite with segmental-headed windows, but it has a Doric porch with Venetian windows above it. The entrance to Lefebvre Street from High Street is still through the carriage arch which formed the main gateway to the Le Marchant house.

Near the archway is the junction of Smith Street, High Street, and the Pollet; the spot was formerly known as Le Carrefour, the crossroads, but is now generally referred to as 'outside Boots'. The ground floor of the Guernsey branch of Boots the Chemist is exactly like any other Boots, but on looking up one sees a pair of semi-detached Georgian houses of dressed granite, each of four storeys and a dormer, built in about 1780. One was the town house of the Brock family and the childhood home of General Sir Isaac Brock, who died in the act of saving Upper Canada for the Empire at the Battle of Queenstown Heights. The practice of looking above the shop-fronts to the buildings themselves is a rewarding one which is (understandably) not often indulged in. In this case it is not too hazardous as traffic is banned from this part of the town.

In St. Helier town houses of this period are more difficult to find, partly because the town was still without a satisfactory harbour, and partly because many of the houses that were built have since been either demolished or altered out of all recognition. No. 9 Castle Street, now the *Castle House* private hotel, is a relatively unspoilt town house of the period. It belonged to the Néels, a ship-building family, and contains some fine mahogany fittings, perhaps made in their own shipyards.[4] A photograph in Nicolle's *St. Helier* shows it as a two-storey house with hipped pantile roof and a fine fanlight over the front door. The fanlight is still there, but the hipped roof has since been replaced by a third storey. At the time it was built the house must have stood on the sandy outskirts of the town. Soon afterwards a new nucleus was established further to the north-west when the original hospital was built in 1768. Almost immediately the intervening land, to the south of the Parade, was developed. The present General Hospital building is a Victorian one of 1860.

The finest example of a merchant's town house in St. Helier is No. 9 Pier Road which is now, very fittingly, the museum and headquarters of the Société Jersiaise. It is a severely formal four-storey house of dressed granite, built in 1817 or slightly earlier by Philippe Nicolle who, among his other interests, established a ship-building yard in what is now the garden on the seaward side; the sea came right up to the foot of the garden. The facade facing the sea is rather forbidding, but the severity of the facade facing Pier Road is greatly relieved by a well-proportioned classical porch with Tuscan columns, and a fanlight over the door. A life interest in the property was presented to the Société by one of its founder members, Jurat J. G. Falle, in 1893; it has been its headquarters ever since.

An example of a country house of the period is La Haule Manor, now a hotel, which stands at the foot of a little wooded valley, Le Mont au Roux, and looks across the coast road to St. Aubin's Bay. The seigneurial dovecote has already been mentioned (p. 58). The present house was built in 1796 by Philippe Marett and his wife, Ann Janvrin. It is a three-storey house of five bays; the pedimented middle bay has a fanlight over the front door, a handsome doorcase, and a Venetian window. Not far away Le Bocage, near the top of Le Mont au Roux, is an example of a cottage built in the 'Picturesque' style. Originally thatched, it was built by Sir John Le Couteur (already mentioned in connection with agriculture) for his marriage in 1818.

Alderney, too, was permanently enriched by some fine Georgian buildings during the privateering boom. A jetty had been built at Braye in 1736 by Henry Le Mesurier, and his family subsequently brought much wealth to the island by their successful privateering. The first buildings encountered by the traveller who arrives by sea are a row of 18th-century pubs and houses in Braye Street, backing on to the sandy harbour formed by the Le Mesurier's jetty. Across the road are some warehouses of the period. Unfortunately, the view of the group from the direction of the new harbour is spoiled by an unsightly modern extension to the most northerly of the houses, the *Sea View* hotel.

In 1763 the Le Mesurier family rebuilt Government House, facing what is now Royal Connaught Square, as a three-storey, five-bay house with an imposing facade of dressed stone. The rather heavy porch and side wings are later additions. Today, as the Island Hall, the building contains, among other things, an excellent public library.

In 1779 the Le Mesuriers built Mouriaux House across the road, and this became the family home. It is a well-proportioned house of two storeys and dormers, with almost contemporary side wings. The facade was stuccoed and a portico and mouldings round the windows were added in the last century. The house still has its Georgian glazing bars, and the stucco has lately been removed to reveal the attractive random stonework.

A more modest Georgian residence is Sauchet House, in one of the *venelles* leading off to the south of High Street. Built of pink, dressed stone it is perhaps the only Georgian house in the town to have survived in an unaltered condition.[5]

The Regency Building Boom

Apart from the large houses built in the high Georgian style, the buildings of the 18th century remained basically vernacular, with their facades modified by the new fashion for large, regular windows and square-topped doorways which had reached the islands in about 1700. In the early 19th century a more fundamental revolution in building style took place. In their new-found prosperity the islanders enthusiastically embraced the English Regency style, and for the first time the architecture of the towns began to differ markedly from that of the neighbouring parts of France.

Although the houses continued to be built of local stone, this was no longer acceptable for the facade, which was covered with stucco—a smooth, cream-coloured cement which was scored at intervals in order to simulate large, regular blocks of stone. It was most definitely never deliberately roughened, as is regrettably to be seen in some modern buildings, in an attempt to resemble random stonework. Facades were embellished by pilasters and doorcases, pillars and porticoes which followed with varying degrees of correctness the various classical orders. Ornamental ironwork burgeoned in the form of area railings, balconies and canopies; the islands are fortunate that their ironwork survived the last war, unlike the Regency towns of England, where the railings were removed for scrap. Today the railings are falling prey to a more insidious process and are being removed, little by little, to provide parking spaces for cars.

The whole emphasis of the Regency facade was vertical and the roof, much reduced in pitch, was hidden by a parapet, topped sometimes by urns, acorns or pineapples. Windows became larger still and were invariably of the sash or guillotine type, except in a few cases where the tall, narrow casement windows of France were consciously copied. The sliding sashes almost always contained six panes each, making a 12-pane window, though some houses, particularly in Guernsey, and later in Alderney, had triple windows with extra lights flanking the central sashes.

In England, 12-pane sash windows were popular in the second half of the 18th century, and continued to be built until about 1830, when they changed to four panes, and finally in 1850 to two.[6] The Channel Islands were more conservative and 12-pane 'Georgian' windows continued to be fitted until the end of the 19th century. Victor Hugo remarked that 'the town of St. Peter Port is faithful to the Queen, the Bible and guillotine windows'. These windows are still among the most characteristic and important visual features, not only of Guernsey, but of Jersey and Alderney as well. Louvred shutters are common, and are particularly characteristic of St. Helier.

In St. Helier, work on the Quai des Marchands began in 1811, to form the east side of what was to become known as the 'New Harbour' (now the inner harbour). At first the quay could only be reached by a slipway from the beach, but eventually the land between it and the town was made up and St. Helier at last had a harbour that was accessible from land at any state of the tide. Trade increased enormously, and the growth of the town was accelerated, aided by the ease with which goods and materials could now be imported. The fine range of merchants' houses and warehouses, known today as Commercial Buildings, was built on the Quai des Marchands between 1818 and 1831. Although some have been altered out of all recognition, those that remain have dignified, three-storey pink granite facades of very fine workmanship. The ground floor contained the offices of the merchant or shipowner, with comfortable living accommodation above. The height of the terrace was limited so as not to interfere with the line of fire from the newly-completed Fort Regent. Each of the 31 units originally had a lintel carved with the number of the property and in some cases the date, in raised lettering. Only five of these lintels have survived in situ; others may be encountered elsewhere in the island.

The Quai des Marchands was such a success that between 1829–35 the Esplanade was built along the beach to the west of the harbour, as far as Patriotic Street. From 1858 it was widened and extended as far as West Park. The original warehouses and hotels on the landward side of the Esplanade have fared worse than Commercial Buildings, and many have been replaced by developments of a different scale.

St. Aubin's harbour was completed in 1819; goods, which hitherto had had to be unloaded at the Fort and carried across the beach at low tide, could now be unloaded straight on to the quay.

Jersey's deep-sea fishing industry, which had begun as long ago as the 16th century, now reached its height. Jerseymen would set sail in the spring for the fishing grounds of Newfoundland and the adjacent coasts of North America, then carry the salted fish to the Catholic countries of Latin America and the Mediterranean, and return to Jersey with the exotic goods they had traded for the fish, in time to help with the winter ploughing. Besides the general prosperity which this traffic brought to the island, huge fortunes, based on cod, were made by the shipowners—so much so that the mansions they built themselves became known as cod houses. Many farmhouses were extended and embellished in Regency-classical style during the same period of prosperity, but a cod house can be distinguished because, although it may be in the midst of a country estate, there are no true farm buildings.[7] One of the most ostentatious is Melbourne House, in the Rue de la Mare Ballam near St. John's church. It is a large, square Regency villa with classical pilasters at the corners, shuttered windows and a heavy parapet concealing the roof. On the south side is a verandah supported by pillars of a different, rather indeterminate classical order. Because its owner, Carcaud, bankrupted himself in his entirely successful attempt to built a grander house than his neighbours, it became known as La Folie Carcaud.

After the close of the Napoleonic wars there was an influx of English residents into Jersey, and this, coupled with the islands's prosperity from seafaring, created a huge demand for superior houses on the outskirts of St. Helier. The result was a wealth of villas and terraces, which continued to be built in the Regency style until well into Victoria's reign. Queen's Road contains some excellent examples, including on the west side a terrace of eight large stuccoed houses climbing up the hillside, with curving steps and railings to their porches. The windows, French below and Georgian above, are fitted with Jersey louvred shutters. The section of Rouge Bouillon between Queen's Road and Midvale Road has several fine stuccoed terraces on both sides of the road; many more are to be found in side streets in various parts of the town, particularly on the northern and eastern outskirts and at Havre des Pas, where there are some lacy Regency wrought-iron balconies. Of particular interest is Almorah Crescent, occupying a magnificent but highly exposed site on the hill above Rouge Bouillon, overlooking the harbour and bay. The crescent consists of 10 houses, each of two bays and four storeys. Although it was not begun until 1844 it is fully Regency in every detail. The ground floor is plain, with no ornamentation. The first floor has French windows with shutters and a balcony, covered by a curving lead canopy, which extends the whole length of the terrace. The second floor windows are Georgian 12-pane sashes, each with a frilly canopy, and the top floor windows are Georgian and square. Joan Stevens[8] considers Almorah Crescent to be the most distinguished piece of Regency architecture in the Channel Islands, and I must agree with her, though yielding to none of my admiration for Regency St. Peter Port.

St. Peter Port, which had had a reasonably good harbour since the Middle Ages, had already grown to fill the narrow belt of low-lying land around the harbour, and extended up the tributary valleys, by the opening of the 19th century. The Regency development took place in two directions; outwards, up the steep slopes and on to the plateau overlooking the harbour, and inwards, to replace the medieval houses and alleys which were demolished during the first 30 years of the century to make way for more hygienic markets and wider roads.

The market stalls had previously been clustered round the Town Church, while the butchers operated in Cow Lane, the alley beside Le Lievre's shop. At high tide the sea washed up the narrow *venelles* between the building on the front, removing the garbage, and in the case of Cow Lane, the debris from the butchers' activities. When a quay was built along the west side of the old harbour, an arch was left so that animals for slaughter, which had been unloaded on to the bed of the harbour, could be driven up Cow Lane. The cobbled lane, the overhanging jettied houses, and the arch can be seen in a number of old prints.

An arcaded market, now known as the French Halles, was built originally for the butchers, in 1780. Above it were the Assembly Rooms, which now form part of the Guille-Allès Library. In 1822 a new meat market, in Grecian style with blank arcading and two Doric porticos, was built the other side of Market Square. The architect was John Wilson.

Guernsey owes more to John Wilson than to any other single architect. He was equally fluent in the neo-Greek style, in Regency Gothic, and in a kind of mock-Tudor. His known work includes St. James-the-Less church, Elizabeth College, and Fountain Street, but many other buildings in the town bear his stamp. He also built Torteval church, and presided over the first of two 19th-century restorations of the Town Church. Besides having a wide private practice he was Surveyor to Guernsey's Board of Works. He appeared in Guernsey in 1816 and disappeared in 1830, and nobody knows whence he came or whither he went; his life and work could provide a challenging thesis for an architectural historian.

In 1830 Wilson built the States Arcades as a fish market. When viewed across Market Square from the French Halles it is a splendid composition with a flag-paved first floor balcony, with balustrade and wrought-iron canopy. Beyond the Arcades is Fountain Street, designed by Wilson as part of the same development. The south side of this street is extremely fine, particularly Barclay's Bank which curves round the corner into Cornet Street. This and the shops further up Fountain Street have a facade unified by a series of fluted Doric columns. The unity of the terrace is destroyed by one shop, Rediffusion, which has abolished its Doric columns and replaced them by a plate-glass shop-front.

While Wilson's market and Fountain Street development was taking place, a Jerseyman, George Le Boutillier, was laying out an ambitious scheme for the shopping precinct which is known today as Commercial Arcade. The scheme involved the removal of a hill, covered with terraced gardens, which stood between the High Street and the markets. One hundred and twenty-five thousand cart-loads of spoil were dumped on the beach to form the South Esplanade, where the bus station now is, before the excavations were brought to a halt by an outcrop of solid granite, and the bankruptcy of Le Boutillier. The whole area was originally intended to be covered—hence the level roof-line. Although the full plan was never carried out, the paved pedestrian precinct and plain Regency buildings form an extremely pleasant shopping area.

The outward expansion of St. Peter Port during the early 19th century mainly took the form of what today would be damningly described as 'ribbon development' along the main roads out of town. Fortunately, the design and quality of the buildings was such that they enhance rather than detract from the character of the town. Hauteville, the steep road leading out of town to the south, had been partially developed in the late 18th century, and now the remaining spaces were filled by Regency villas. All command splendid views across the Russel. The most famous, because it later became the home in exile of Victor Hugo, is Hauteville House. Many others are of architectural interest, particularly May Trees, which C. Brett describes as 'splendidly formal pyramidal composition in restrained neo-classical stucco'.[9] Despite its Regency appearance it was built as late as 1845.

The Grange, the main road from town to the west, was transformed from a country lane into a street of opulent dwellings. Many have lately been transmogrified into banks and offices; others have been sub-divided into flats. Some are large piles whose plainness is relieved by Doric or Ionic porches. Grange Lea is a fine neo-classical villa reminiscent of May Trees in Hauteville. Grange Lodge, now a hotel, is a battlemented Tudor edifice almost certainly designed by John Wilson. The ochre-coloured stucco, known as Roman cement, was much loved by Wilson, who used it also on St. James-the-Less church, Elizabeth College, Castle Carey, and many lesser buildings.

Elizabeth College was built in 1826. Wilson was in his Tudor, battlemented mood, but in spite of the turrets, loopholes, Tudor hoods and Gothic glazing the building is basically a symmetrical Georgian one. The porter's lodge, by the roadside, is in the same style. The entrance to the courtyard was through the arch, now filled in, in the centre of the lodge. The main building replaced an older schoolhouse of 1760, now known as the Ozanne Building, which itself replaced the Elizabethan college which was in the vicinity of the science laboratories in the Rue des Frères.

Opposite the college and facing up the Grange is Bonamy House, almost certainly by Wilson, and one of the finest neo-classical buildings in the islands. The facade, covered in Virginia creeper, has three-light windows flanking a bowed central bay with Ionic columns. The front door opens into a circular ante-room with niches for statuary. The focal point of this sector of the town is the disused church of St. James-the-Less, designed by Wilson, and bearing the date 1818. It is described on p. 121.

Regency terraces and villas are to be seen in many other access roads to the town, particularly Candie Road, Doyle Road, Les Gravées and Queen's Road. A more modest, but highly intriguing thoroughfare is Victoria Road. This is lined on both sides by houses of the early 19th century, in a variety of styles. This street demonstrates how completely the appearance of a house can be transformed by comparatively trivial details. Of a pair of basically identical houses, one may have Georgian-glazed windows and a classical door-case, while the other has an elaborate Gothic doorcase, pointed glazing and 'icicles' hanging from the eaves. The atmosphere created by the two houses is totally different.

In 1792 Peter de Havilland, later Sir Peter, and Bailiff of Guernsey, bought four fields to the south of the rural lane which was to become the Grange. Later, a fifth field gave him access to Lower Vauvert. The object was to develop the area so that he would have something to leave his children. This piece of speculation, which would with some justification be frowned upon today, resulted in the New Town; a grid of streets and Regency terraces on the plateau above Clifton, and one of the finest pieces of provincial Regency development to have survived anywhere in the British Isles. Saumarez Street, St. John Street, and Havilland Street are linked by Union Street, which connects with Vauvert by George Street and Allez Street. Battle Lane, an alley connecting St. John and Havilland Streets, contains two extremely comely small houses. No. 2 has what appears to be an original shop window. The name of the lane commemorates the original name of the fields, La Bataille. The battle took place in 1372 between a defending garrison and Evan of Wales, who had landed at Vazon with a force of French mercenaries.

The New Town was laid out and the houses built between 1792 and 1843 by Sir Peter de Havilland and his various relatives. Sir Peter's own house is thought to have been No. 8 Saumarez Street, now the Brentford guest house. Most of this street consists of large, terraced houses of three or four storeys, with a variety of Doric and Ionic porches and doorcases. The houses of Union Street are more modest, but at the west end, facing Havilland Street, is a terrace of four tall houses of four storeys, basements and dormers, with fanlights over the doors and large 18-pane drawing-room windows on the first floor. The blue pantiles covering the roofs of this terrace are unusual in that their provenance is known: Sir Peter's account books record that they came from Rotterdam. Behind the railings on the opposite side of the road is one of the earliest pillar-boxes in the British Isles, installed in 1853. Havilland Street, round the corner, contains more modest houses, some beautifully maintained, and others in need of a coat of paint. Of particular interest is No. 21, whose original shop-front is urgently in need of sympathetic restoration.

The amenities of the Island of Sark do not include Regency architecture; the small amount of building that took place in the early part of the 19th century was in the traditional style, which continued in use until it was overtaken by the shanty development of the present century. In Alderney, too, traditional building continued in the 19th century, but with a strongly local flavour which does not seem to have been in any way compromised by the influx of troops and workers who descended upon the island later in the century to build the fortifications. Most of the houses are of local stone—mainly the sandstone—and often white-washed. Sash windows are almost universal, but a characteristic Alderney variation is the segmental-headed window with curved glazing bars and 'Gothic' pointed upper panels. Triple windows are common. Such houses are to be seen in plenty in High Street, between Le Huret and Longis Road. Individually the houses are unremarkable, but as a whole they form a street of great charm and character.

Victorian Exuberance

The chaste good manners of the Regency style continued in Jersey and Guernsey well into Victoria's reign, particularly in domestic architecture. Many private clients were content to leave the details of their new houses to the builder, who chose the style he knew. It is perhaps in public and commercial buildings that the exuberance of Victorian architecture is best seen. The quarrying industry was now in full swing, and finely-carved stonework returned to favour. Motifs that would elsewhere have been executed in brick or plaster were in the islands wrought in granite; scrolls, cornices, oculi and the contrasting textures and colours of different granites were combined to produce a kind of Channel Island municipal style which may be seen in its full glory in the harbour buildings, slaughter houses, and markets of St. Helier and St. Peter Port.

Before the days of refrigeration meat had to be imported on the hoof, and in both islands the slaughterhouses were situated conveniently by the quay. In Jersey the abbatoir is the first building to greet the traveller as he leaves the Albert Pier. It consists of an impressive series of gables and arches, inscribed 'Bétail Etranger, 1888'. It is at present used as a parking lot and general dump, and badly needs a new use more in keeping with its dignified appearance. Nearby are the Harbour Office of 1863 and the Tourist Office, originally a railway station, but much altered in the years that have elapsed since it was possible to travel from the town to La Corbière by rail.

1.   Part of Jersey's rugged north coast. On the right is the Ile Agois, site of a Dark Age settlement. The headland immediately behind is Col de la Rocque.

2.   Pleinmont Point, Guernsey, looking west. In the distance Les Hanois lighthouse guards the remains of a vanished island.

3. Les Autelets, the Altar Rocks, on the west coast of Sark. Beyond is the wild northern extremity of the island.

4. La Coupée, the precipitous causeway connecting Little Sark with Great Sark. The steps on the left lead down to La Grande Grève.

5. A main road in Sark. The carriage, the tractor, the dusty road and the overhead wires all contribute towards Sark's special atmosphere.

6. (*above*) Rocquaine Bay, Guernsey, viewed from the 'fossil' cliff of a former shoreline. The reclaimed marshland in the foreground is occupied by glasshouses and fishermen's cottages. Beyond are Chateau de Rocquaine, L'Erée Peninsula and Lihou Island.

7. (*below*) A hedgerow of elms on the plateau, St. Saviour's, Guernsey. The erect trunks and upturned twigs are characteristic of the Guernsey elm.

8. The Great Menhir, Blanches Banques, Jersey. This photograph was taken soon after the menhir had been re-erected in 1922. Behind are the dunes of the Quennevais.

9. La Longue Rocque des Paysans, the largest menhir in the Channel Islands, stands 11ft. 6ins. high on the plateau above Rocquaine Bay, Guernsey.

10. Le Trépied, a megalithic burial chamber on Le Catioroc near Perelle, Guernsey, was mentioned in the witch trials of the 17th century.

11. Detail of the Richmond Map of Jersey, 1795. The portion shown corresponds approximately with the parish of St. Brelade, only 36% of which had been enclosed by 1795. The largest unenclosed area is the Quennevais. There were few houses near the parish church, the largest settlement being at St. Aubin, where a pier had been built at the Fort in 1700. The south pier of St. Aubin's Harbour is shown; the north pier had yet to be built, as had the coast roads in St. Ouen's and St. Brelade's Bays.

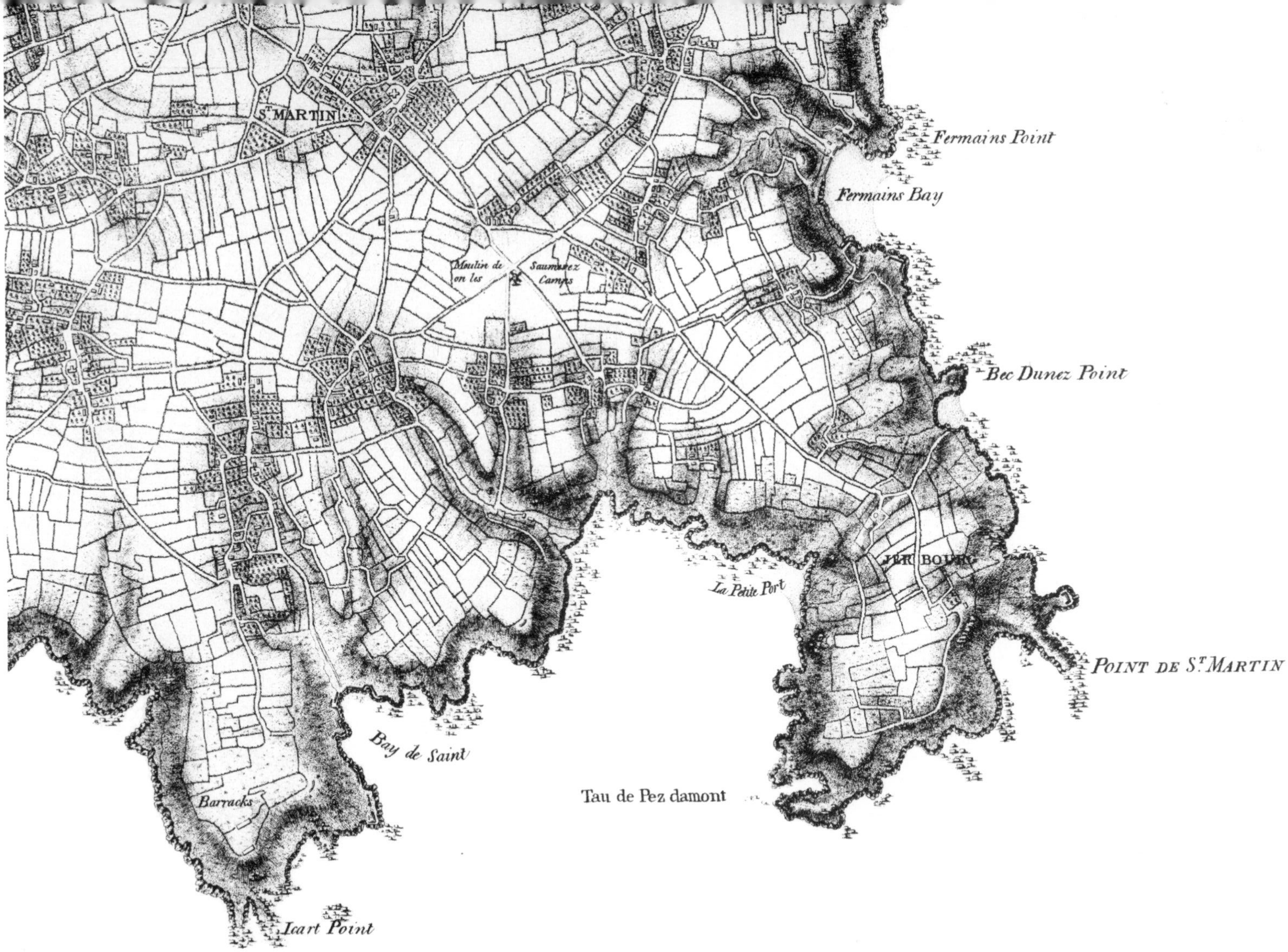

Fermains Point
Fermains Bay
Bec Dunez Point
POINT DE S.T MARTIN
S.T MARTIN
Moulin de on les
Saumarez Camps
La Petite Port
Bay de Saint
Tau de Pez damont
Barracks
Icart Point

12. Detail of the Richmond Map of Guernsey, 1787, corresponding approximately with the parish of St. Martin. Apart from the cliff land, the parish was completely enclosed by 1787 except for Les Camps, where the Old Mill stood at the centre of an area of open fields. A nucleated settlement, La Bellieuse, is clustered round the parish church, each farm having its cider orchard.

13. Preparing the soil for carrots, Sark. In the background is the 16th-century seigneurial windmill, now a souveni shop.

14. Open fields at Pleinmont, Guernsey. A rare survival of the medieval system of strip cultivation. Note the unfenced road and the low balks of earth between the strips.

15. Gathering vraic in St. Ouen's Bay, Jersey. Tractors and loaders are usually used today, but horses are less adversely affected by salt water and may still sometimes be seen.

16. Piles of vraic left to dry on the sandy plain behind St. Ouen's Bay.

17. Slipway at Torteval, Guernsey, built for collecting vraic. The granite setts are cut so as to afford a grip to horses' hooves when pulling loaded carts up from the beach.

18.   Jersey cows on the move. In winter they spend the night in the stable, and are led out to graze during the daytime.

19.   Guernsey cows at Les Vauxbelets, St. Andrew's. Small herds of tethered cows are still to be seen in the Island, but the milk cans beside the road are a thing of the past—milk is now collected in bulk by tanker.

20. Field wellhead, St. Peter's, Guernsey. Water was winched up in a bucket and tipped into the stone trough for the animals.

21. *Farmyard Scene* by Edmund Blampied, 1945. Blampied, the son of a Jersey farmer, captured the essence of rural life in Jersey. The gabled cottage, the pump manure heap, lopped trees, horse and boxcart are all typical.

22. St. Helier's Hermitage, Jersey. An oratory built in the 12th century on the traditional site of the martyrdom of St. Helier, and now connected by a breakwater to Elizabeth Castle.

23. St. Sampson's, Guernsey, from the south-west. The church is first mentioned in a charter of 1060 and was enlarged in stages during the middle ages. Behind are the crane jibs of St. Sampson's Harbour.

24. St. Brelade's, Jersey, from the south-west. Like St. Sampson's, the church dates from before the Conquest. To the right is the 'Fishermen's Chapel' containing medieval murals.

Guernsey's slaughterhouse, one year older than that of Jersey, is a more restrained edifice—a long, low building with rounded ends, standing at the landward end of the Castle Pier. Originally adjacent to the Albert Dock, it now overlooks a marina. It is still used for its original purpose, and there are those who would have it moved, but an alternative site has yet to be found. Prison and slaughterhouse have this in common, that while everybody agrees they are necessary, nobody wants to live near one.

Reminiscent of the slaughterhouse, and almost certainly by the same architect, is Guernsey's fish-market. Completed in 1877, it ingeniously fills a rather awkward triangular site. Externally it is a long, low building of plain red granite below, and ornamental grey granite above, with an attractive roof of patterned slate. Within, it is the timber roof, carried on cast-iron columns, that catches the eye. C. E. B. Brett describes the fish-market as 'A wholly magnificent building by any standards; indeed, one of the most satisfying High Victorian buildings known to me anywhere—not excluding Balthard's Halles in Paris.'[10] The architect was John Newton of London, whose only other recorded work seems to be St. Paul's Church, St. Leonard's, Sussex.

The final stages in the development of Guernsey's market complex was the grandiose Lower Vegetable Market, completed in 1879. This was laid out by Newton but, after a disagreement with the authorities, the building was finished in vastly different style by another London architect, Francis Chambers, who also designed the hall of the old Ladies' College (now the Spencer Gerhold Hall of the Education Department). Both buildings have elaborate Dutch gables. The facade of the market building faces the west door of the Town Church, and, in its great bulk and fussiness, dominates the space between the two. But the Guernseyman, having grown used to it, would defend it with his life. The bronze tobacco plants, one at each end of the roof ridge, commemorate the tax on tobacco which partly paid for the building. The ceiling inside the lower market is supported by columns whose capitals are embellished with carved ormer shells and a variety of fruit and vegetables.

Jersey's market in Halkett Place, in contrast to Guernsey's, is all of a piece, having been built in 1882 to designs by T. W. Helliwell. The large, square, covered space is bounded by arcaded walls of finely-dressed granite. The arches are filled by a wealth of decorated iron gates and railings. Within, the focal point is a central pool with a splendidly ornate fountain.

The commercial centre of St. Helier is rich in Victorian buildings, many occupying important corner sites. Key buildings include the solidly classical Lloyds Bank, the more ornately classical Midland Bank, and the National Westminster Bank in St. Pancras Gothic.

In St. Peter Port Lloyd's Bank occupies a particularly important site at the corner of Smith Street and the Pollett, closing the view from the High Street. The facade follows the curve of the corner and is topped by a green dome and cupola.

The finest piece of Victorian nonsense in Guernsey, completely useless except as a site for radio aerials, is the Victoria Tower. This splendid folly, which commemorates Her Majesty's first visit to the island in 1846, stands between the Arsenal and the ex-*Odeon* cinema, overlooking Candie cemetery. The site was formerly occupied by a windmill. The tower, of pink granite, tapers to a crenellated superstructure with four towerlets and a central octagonal lantern. It commands unrivalled views of the town and archipelago and, together with the towers and steeples of St. Barnabas, St. Joseph, St. James-the-Less, Elizabeth College, and Lloyd's bank, it forms the skyline which Guernseymen in exile dream about.

Private houses in the High Victorian style are comparatively rare: two examples are Le Chatelet, Victoria Street, St. Helier, and Newlands, Prince Albert Road, St. Peter Port. Numerous houses were built in the late 19th century with Victorian details such as gabled attic windows, decorated barge-boards, and fancy ridge tiles, but the use of granite gives these houses a distinctly local flavour. The standard of masonry at this time was extremely high.

Sash windows continued to be used throughout the century, but by late Victorian times large sheets of glass were easy to obtain and the sliding sashes were usually made with a single, large pane. To compensate for the strength lost by abolishing glazing bars, these Victorian sashes had a pair of spurs projecting downwards, one on each side of the frame. Georgian 12-pane sashes never had these spurs, though modern reproductions are usually incorrectly equipped with them.

Dormer windows were popular—indeed, both in number and variety, they are a feature of the islands. The gabled dormers with decorated barge-boards which embellish many otherwise plain 19th-century workmen's cottages are particularly attractive. Besides the original Regency and Victorian ones, dormer windows have since been added to numerous houses in order to make use of the roof-space. In recent years many new houses have been designed with dormers to obtain an extra storey while retaining a low, cottage-like appearance. This tendency has received the encouragement of the planning authorities, but in many cases the dormers are too many and too large, giving a crowded appearance which was never the case in earlier buildings.

The Post-Medieval Churches

Besides the medieval parish churches, the islands are richly endowed with a variety of churches and chapels built during the last 200 years. Many are still in use as places of worship; others have been converted into banks, youth hostels, furniture stores, garages, and private houses.

The only civil parish in Jersey or Guernsey to have lost its medieval church is Torteval, Guernsey. The old church had been allowed to become so ruinous during the 18th century that it was demolished and the foundation stone of the present church was laid in 1816. Designed by John Wilson, it is not perhaps his most distinguished building, though the tall, round tower surmounted by a circular spire is a major landmark in the south-west of the island. Like Wilson's other church, St. James-the-Less, Torteval is an 'auditory' church with an apsidal east end. But while St. James-the-Less has a neo-classical stuccoed west end, Torteval is entirely of grey granite. The rather cumbersome semi-circular buttresses are perhaps made necessary by the construction of the roof, which lacks heavy tie-beams.

St. Peter's, Sark, is another plain granite building, this time with a square west tower. The church was begun in 1820 to replace the outbuilding at Le Manoir which had been used for worship since the Elizabethan settlement of the island. The chancel was added in 1880.

St. Anne's church, Alderney, was completed in 1850 to designs by Sir George Gilbert Scott, and is thus one of the few Channel Island buildings by an internationally recognised architect. Although Scott later became famous for his exuberent Gothic buildings (St. Pancras Station hotel and the Albert Memorial, for instance), he designed for Alderney a dignified church with a distinctly Norman flavour, in the transitional style between Romanesque and Gothic. The building is of local stone with dressings of Caen stone, built on a cruciform plan, with apse and square central tower. The pyramidal spire is a conspicuous landmark from the sea. Internally the church is sturdy, but light and spacious.

In both Jersey and Guernsey the 19th century saw a resurgence of church buildings, such as had not been known since the Middle Ages. This was the result partly of the rapid spread of Nonconformity and the return of the Roman Catholic Church to the islands, and partly of the increase in population, which demanded places of worship in the new areas of settlement. With the ending of the Napoleonic wars in 1815 there was an influx of British settlers, largely retired army and naval officers with their families, who required Anglican churches, with services held in English, in the new suburbs of St. Helier and St. Peter Port. In addition, in Guernsey at least, there had been friction between the garrison and the town, which it was felt would be reduced if the garrison had a church of its own, instead of having to attend the Town Church, whose services were held in French. The neo-classical church of St. James-the-Less, built in 1818, was the result.

St. James-the-Less has been described by Bryan Little as Wilson's masterpiece.[11] It occupies a key position in the apex between College Street and St. James Street, within a stone's throw of Elizabeth College and the prison. The outside of the nave is plain and not particularly attractive, but the western facade, facing the main road as it curves round the college grounds, is extremely fine and forms an integral part of the Regency development of the Grange and New Town. The pedimented portico, massively built in the Doric order and correct in every detail, is surmounted by an Ionic cupola which forms part of the familiar skyline of St. Peter Port when seen from the harbour or sea. The contrast between the solidity of the Doric portico and the elegance of the Ionic cupola illustrates Wilson's mastery of the classical orders. Something of this mastery is shown by the unknown architects of the doorcases of the large houses further up the road—a facility which is not shared by the badly-proportioned and incorrectly-detailed doorcases tacked on to so many banks, offices and 'neo—Georgian' houses. St. James-the-Less, no longer in use as a church, became the property of the States in 1972. Plans were drawn up for its conversion into a cultural centre, but in 1980 the States, with almost unbelievable Philistinism, reversed its previous decision and resolved to demolish all except the façade and tower, and to build instead a police station.

In Jersey the garrison church is another St. James, in St. James' Street in the eastern part of St. Helier. It was completed in 1829 in the Gothic style with twin western towers whose crocketed pinnacles have sadly had to be abbreviated as they were unsafe. C. E. B. Brett much admires the slim, vertical detailing, but has some astringent comments to make on the way the building has been treated.[12]

As the 19th century progressed the populations of St. Helier and St. Peter Port increased to the point where further Anglican churches had to be built, each with a parish carved from the original civil parish. In Guernsey, St. John's church, serving the north of the town, is a simple, unfussy building of grey granite with a square pinnacled tower, begun in 1836. Ten years later Holy Trinity church, Trinity Square, formerly a Nonconformist chapel, was reconstructed as an Anglican church. Dating originally from 1789 it is a handsome building with Dutch gables and oeils-de-boef flanking a Doric doorcase. Not far away the steep, red-tiled roofs and pyramidal granite spire of St. Barnabas overlook the Bordage from the summit of Tower Hill. The church was built in 1874 on or near the site of *La Tour de Beauregard,* one of the forts that defended the medieval town. The architect of the church was Sir Arthur Blomfield, whose nephew, Sir Reginald Blomfield, re-designed Trinity Manor, Jersey, in the form of a French château. Like St. James, St. Barnabas forms an important element in the town's skyline. And like St. James it is redundant. From 1938 to 1970 it housed the Lukis archaeological collection, and now, with an unsafe roof, it stands derelict.

Jersey and Guernsey each have a church by G. F. Bodley, a pupil of Sir G. G. Scott, and an important figure in the Gothic revival. Unlike his contemporaries, who were using 'Gothic' features indiscriminately for effect, Bodley studied the Gothic styles academically and favoured the comparatively plain Early English style. Among his first churches were St. Stephen's, Guernsey (1862), and St. Simon's, Jersey (1865). St. Stephen's, in Les Gravées, is built of red granite with courses of grey. A steeple was planned for the east end, but because of the exposed site on the plateau to the west of St. Peter Port it was never built, for which the present churchwardens are duly thankful. The interior is lit by narrow lancet windows below and round clerestory lights above. Some of the stained glass windows are by William Morris's firm of Morris, Marshall, Faulkner and Co., which had just been founded when the church was built. Particularly fine is the west window, behind the organ loft, which represents the Tree of Jesse. The scenes in the east window have the appearance of being the early work of Burne-Jones.

The red granite of St. Stephen's church came from a quarry, now filled in, at Cobo. The same quarry provided the stone for St. Matthew's, Cobo, built in 1852 to serve the fishing community centred on this part of the west coast.

Bodley's other church, St. Simon's, Great Union Street, St. Helier, like St. Stephen's, is of granite with pointed internal arches and columns of Caen stone. Also like St. Stephen's it lacks a steeple; funds did not permit this or a planned north aisle to be built.

In Jersey a William Morris window, designed by Burne-Jones, has recently been identified in the Lady Chapel of St. Aubin's church.[13] The church, on St. Aubin's Hill, was built in 1889 to replace an earlier one which stood on the site of the car park to the north of the present building. It serves the settlement that has grown up round St. Aubin's harbour, at some distance from the parish church of St. Brelade. Proceeding from St. Aubin towards town, on the northern of the two parallel roads at Millbrook stands the famous 'Glass Church' of St Matthew. Externally the church is an unattractive cement-rendered box, built in 1840 to serve the residential area that was springing up around St. Aubin's Bay. In 1934 it was restored as a memorial to Lord Trent, formerly Jesse Boot and founder of Boots the Chemists. The interior was embellished by his widow with Lalique glass in such profusion that the church is unique. Altar, Cross, candlesticks, Communion rail, screens, and even the Font are all of glass.

The skyline of any town which has not succumbed to tower blocks will be dominated by church steeples. One of the landmarks of St. Helier is the slender hexagonal spire and weathercock of St. Mark's, David Place. The church, begun in 1842, is in a later Gothic style than most Victorian churches, with a battlemented parapet and a square western tower bearing the spire.

Another landmark is the dormered spire of St. Thomas's Roman Catholic church, Val Plaisant, whose Cross is 196 feet from the ground. Roman Catholicism, long absent from the strongly Protestant Channel Islands, returned at the end of the 18th century with an influx of French royalist refugees, particularly into Jersey. Several churches were built in Jersey, of which St. Thomas's is the finest. Begun in 1883 it is built of dressed pink Jersey and grey Breton granite. The details are Gothic, but the external proportions are rather strange, with a very tall, slender tower supporting the spire. Not far to the east is the church of St. Mary and St. Peter, designed by Joseph Hansom, inventor of the cab, but never completed to the original design.

Guernsey's main Roman Catholic church, St. Joseph's, La Couperderie, was begun in 1846 to the design of A. W. N. Pugin, one of the best-known Victorian architects and part-designer of the Houses of Parliament. As befits the work of an architect who held that the only Christian architecture is pointed Gothic, St. Joseph's is a fine Gothic building of grey granite, with dressings of a much softer white stone. The tall, copper-clad spire was added in 1885 by Pugin's sons, P. P. and S. P. Pugin. The summit, 150 feet from the ground, was given a weathercock when the spire was restored in 1980. The spire is a major landmark of the town, and is much used by fishermen to mark their favourite hunting grounds. Not far away in Burnt Lane, one of the delightful alleys on the hillside above Vauvert, is a new landmark: the elegant, slender campanile built for Notre Dame du Rosaire in 1980. Notre Dame serves Guernsey's French community, and is one of the most successful modern reconstructions in the islands. The original building, dating from 1829, had its roof in the shape of an upturned boat. This was taken as the theme for the new church, whose interior is furnished in a most delightful and imaginative manner.

Methodism was introduced into Jersey in 1774 and into Guernsey slightly later. At first it met with considerable opposition, but in 1787, at the age of 84, John Wesley visited Jersey, Guernsey and Alderney. His preaching had a profound long-term effect, and by the 1820s chapels were springing up all over the islands; some are simple buildings in the Channel Island vernacular style, others are Gothic and some of the more ambitious resemble Greek temples. In Jersey 18 Methodist churches are still in use.[14] One of the most important in St. Helier's townscape is Wesley-Grove, whose idiosyncratic but pleasing and well-preserved classical facade faces down Halkett Place. In Guernsey, St. Andrew's Methodist church at Four Cabot has a Greek portico of gigantic proportions—an unexpected feature of the view across the fields from La Brigade Road. A fine example of a Gothic Methodist church is Six Rues, St. Laurence, Jersey. A typical example in Guernsey, though only mildly Gothic, is Deslisles Methodist church, sturdily constructed in Cobo granite. Facing it across the road is the original *Chapelle Wesleyenne,* now the Sunday school—a plain whitewashed stone building with hipped pantile roof.

20th Century Housing

While much has been written about the churches, manor houses and major buildings of the island, very little attention has been given by local authors to modern domestic architecture. Yet the dominant feature of the landscape, in all but the most rural parts of the island, is comparatively modern housing.

The sheer number of detached dwellings scattered over the countryside is enormous, and can hardly be said to improve the landscape. The alternative would be large blocks of flats, but these have been firmly and rightly rejected both by the planning authorities and by the islanders themselves. Although he lives in a densely-populated archipelago, the Channel Islander is by nature too independent to take kindly to high-density housing. He likes his detached house and his garden, whether he cultivates it or simply covers it with gravel and keeps his car or his boat in it. The problems of planning and the way the islands have attempted to solve them will be discussed in Chapter Twelve.

Ribbon development is not a product of the 20th century; it had existed on the outskirts of the towns for hundreds of years. However, in the early part of this century improved transport, coupled with the lack of any form of control, allowed the ribbon development to extend along the main roads, deep into the countryside, especially in Guernsey. Also, the increasing interest in beaches and bathing resulted in some particularly unfortunate ribbon development along the coast roads. Fortunately the cliffs of north Jersey and the south of Guernsey were saved from this fate by the absence of a coast road.

Quite apart from ribbon development, there is a scattered pattern of houses throughout much of the landscape of the islands. This scattering is particularly marked in Guernsey, where it can be attributed to the glasshouse industry. A typical holding of glass covers a very small area of land compared with other types of farm unit, yet each unit typically includes the grower's dwelling. If it dates from the beginning of the century this will be a small but sturdily-built stone house of two storeys plus dormers, rendered in front, with slate roof and Victorian sash windows. If it was built between the wars it is more likely to be a bungalow, still with a slate roof and with a verandah over the front door. The front door itself is never in any circumstances used.

The period between the two world wars was perhaps the low-point of architecture, when numerous cheaply-built bungalows, often little more than asbestos or corrugated iron shacks, appeared in Jersey, Guernsey and Sark. The better-built houses were in a style completely alien to the islands, with flat roofs and windows with a horizontal emphasis, in contrast to the vertical ones which had hitherto been universal. Fortunately money was scarce and such houses are not common.

The styles exhibited by the islands' stock of 20th-century housing are as diverse as they would be in a developing residential area in any part of the British Isles. Until about 1700 the appearance of a house was determined by two factors: the wealth of the owner, and local tradition, which itself was determined by the climate and the materials to hand. In the 18th and 19th centuries tradition was still a powerful factor, but it was increasingly modified by English ideas, brought back to the islands by merchants and seafarers or introduced by new settlers. Most of the houses were not individually designed by architects, but were taken from builders' pattern books and adapted to suit local materials and conditions.

In the first half of the present century tradition was abandoned and houses were built in whatever style was in vogue elsewhere, without regard to the surroundings. Today, when every home, however humble, is designed by an architect, there are potentially as many styles as architects. At the same time, increasingly severe planning control ensures that only certain styles have a chance of actually being built. The appearance of a house is now a compromise between what the planning, housing and health authorities will allow on the one hand, and what the funds of the owner or his bank will allow on the other.

The Island Development Committees of Jersey and Guernsey now have far-reaching powers and highly qualified staffs whose job it is to ensure that such development as does take place is of the highest standard and in a style that will blend in with the surroundings. One way of doing this is to encourage the use of local stone. This has had the enormous advantage of keeping alive the mason's craft, but in Guernsey, at least, it has had some unfortunate results. A number of houses, otherwise rendered and whitewashed, have pieces of stone self-consciously distributed over the surface like currants in a bun.

The more expensive modern housing falls largely into two categories. First the ranch-style bungalow, with shallow-pitched tile roof, panels of local stone and picture windows from which the salt spray has to be cleaned every day; this type is to be found mostly in a rural or coastal setting. The second category is the 'neo-Georgian' house which is burgeoning in the towns and suburbs. If it is sympathetically designed and executed there is much to be said for 'neo-Georgian' architecture; the proportions are well-tried, both from the point of view of comfort and appearance, and it blends reasonably happily with the genuine article. It is frequently marred, however, by details that are completely alien to the spirit of the age it is striving to recapture. The worst of these is a kind of rough-cast rendering which attempts, without success, to resemble whitewashed granite. The stucco with which late Georgian houses were rendered was smooth and only faintly scored to resemble large, dressed blocks of stone—rough stone would have been considered a peasant material. The other pitfalls are doors and windows. Doors would have been pannelled and painted, not varnished and decorated with medieval studs and hinges. Unsuitable doorcases have already been mentioned. Windows contained sliding sashes with panes separated by slender wooden glazing bars, not flat aluminium strips, and the sashes were certainly not hinged at the top. Carpentered bow windows would only have been seen in shop-fronts.

An example of a highly successful reproduction is the *Post Horn* pub, built in 1976 at the end of the surviving portion of Hue Street in St. Helier. It is a plain, three-storey building, pantiled and stuccoed, and the wooden 12-pane sash windows are just right. It is in this kind of position, next to existing houses of the period, that neo-Georgian architecture is at its best. It is less successful in new estates where small, detached houses are clustered together with little space between. The age would have demanded either terraced houses or isolated stately homes, surrounded by space and standing aloof from other buildings.

A shortage of housing is endemic in the islands and estates offer the best alternative to ribbon development or to buildings scattered throughout the countryside, particularly if, as in Jersey, use can be made of former industrial sites. But in such estates plain contemporary architecture looks more comfortable.

Chapter Nine

THE MILITARY LANDSCAPE

*These two islands are the despair of France at the beginning of
every war by their very active privateering.*—Général Charles Dumouriez,
1739–1823.

IN THE YEAR 1202 King Philip of France invaded Normandy and began to
'liberate' the duchy from the unpopular John of England. By the middle of 1204
the only parts of Normandy left to John were the Channel Islands. As English
possessions on the hostile Norman side of the Channel, commanding the
maritime route to those parts of southern France that were still held by John,
the islands immediately assumed an immense strategic importance.

Fortifications had existed in the islands before. The Nunnery in Alderney is
probably a coastal fort of late Roman age and mention was made in Chapter
Three of the Iron Age earthworks at Câtel de Rozel and Câtel de Lecq in Jersey,
and at Jerbourg in Guernsey. Also in Guernsey evidence has recently come to
light which suggests that Vale Castle was built on the site of an Iron-Age hill
fort. Apart from these early defences, all the fortifications with which the
islands are endowed, from Gorey Castle and Castle Cornet to Hitler's bunkers,
owe their existence to the separation of the Channel Islands from Continental
Normandy in the time of King John.

John never acknowledged the loss of Normandy, and it was not until 1259
that his son, Henry III, finally did so. In the meantime the islands had been
invaded on more than one occasion, but such was the importance attached to
them by the English Crown that strenuous efforts were made to regain them, and
on each occasion the French were evicted. Some of the fortifications that were
hurriedly erected, perhaps mainly as places of refuge for the islanders, are still
to be seen.

Grosnez Castle occupies a headland in the extreme north-west corner of Jersey,
protected on nearly every side by steep cliffs, and on the landward side by a
ditch. The keep, which contains the foundations of a number of small buildings,
was formerly surrounded by a roughly circular wall, with perhaps five bastions.
All that remains of the castle today are the ruined gatehouse and the ditch. It
is possible that Les Câteaux, an enigmatic earthwork a few hundreds yards to the
south west of Les Augrès Manor, may also date from this time.

Excavations in Guernsey have shown that the Iron Age promontory fort at
Jerbourg was equipped with higher turf ramparts at some time in the 13th
century, perhaps to provide a refuge for the people of southern Guernsey at the

troubled time of the separation from Normandy. Château des Marais, otherwise known as Ivy Castle, probably also dates from this time. Here a hougue which projected from the marshes inland from Belle Grève Bay was enlarged by removing many tons of material from the centre and dumping it round the edge. The central area, levelled and protected by a ditch, formed an inner bailey, while the dumped material formed an outer bailey, protected by a bank. A causeway, also built in the 13th century, crosses the march to the south of the castle and connects it with the Grand Bouet. The ivy-covered walls, which give the castle its English name, date from the Napoleonic wars. It is difficult to imagine that Château des Marais, wedged as it is between a go-kart track and several large blocks of flats, was once in the centre of a desolate marsh, subject to periodic flooding by the sea. Further residential development is planned for the area, making use of the castle as a focal point and a green oasis in a rather featureless district.

For the inhabitants of the Clos du Valle, then a separate island to the north of Guernsey, an obvious place of refuge would have been the hill now occupied by the Vale Castle, immediately to the north of St. Sampson's harbour. Unfortunately, no medieval remains have been found, but this may be because the hilltop was levelled before the present walls were built in the 18th century. An excavation in 1980 did, however, produce evidence of an Iron-Age hill fort.

The two major military installations of the Channel Islands are Mont Orgueil and Castle Cornet. Both date from the separation from Normandy in 1204 and both have been re-fortified in every subsequent century, culminating in the German occupation of the present century. Because of their long history the layout of the walls and buildings is complicated, but each castle basically consists of a hill encircled by a series of independent concentric walls, founded on bed rock and supplemented in many places by sheer rock faces.

Mont Orgueil, or Gorey Castle, occupies a magnificent site on a rocky eminence overlooking Gorey harbour and the Royal Bay of Grouville. The hill is an outlier of the northern plateau of Jersey, whose southern escarpment runs inland from St. Helier towards the east, returning to the coast at Gorey. By the 13th century there were already two chapels on the rock, and the first fortifications are likely to have been centred around that of St. Mary, which still stands near the summit of the castle. The earliest defences to be seen today are in the area of the middle ward, where soon after the loss of Normandy a plateau of rock was encircled by a wall, at the base of a natural cliff upon which the keep now stands.[1] Beside the middle ward was the second chapel, dedicated to St. George. The chapel itself has since collapsed, but the 12th-century crypt remains and has been restored.

Throughout the turbulent Middle Ages the castle was extended and rebuilt repeatedly, each advance in the technique of warfare being met by new defence works at Mont Orgueil. To mention but a few features of this magnificent monument: immediately to the left of the main entrance as one enters from the castle green is the Harliston Tower, dating from the reign of Edward IV. The second gate opens into a large outer ward, now gardens. Overlooking the outer ward from the far end is a machicolated bastion dating from the 14th century. A flight of steps lead through the third and fourth gates into the middle ward. Soaring above this is the Somerset Tower, built in the 16th century to support a gun battery and provide it with a clear line of fire. Until the coming of artillery the precipitous walls and cliff faces had remained almost impregnable, but the castle was now within the range of cannon mounted on St. Nicholas Mount, facing it on the landward side. It appeared to have outlived its usefulness, and was replaced as Jersey's main strongpoint by Elizabeth Castle. Fortunately for posterity Mont Orgueil was saved from demolition by Sir Walter Ralegh, who advised Queen Elizabeth that it would be a pity to cast down so stately a fort.

Today the various buildings of the keep contain a museum and tableaux illustrating the history of the castle and island. Topping the entire pile are German observation towers.

Castle Cornet, though in many ways similar to Mont Orgueil and dating from the same period, had a different function. It was not primarily to protect the island of Guernsey, but to keep open the sea route between England and her possessions in the south of France.[2] Although the castle is now connected to Guernsey by the south arm of the Victorian harbour, it was built on an islet which could only be reached on foot at low spring tides. It commanded the Russel, and its protective presence immediately off St. Peter Port must have exerted a powerful influence on the development of the harbour. As in the case of Mont Orgueil, the medieval fortifications were concentrated near the summit. Fragments of the 13th-century curtain wall, built of rubble masonry with narrow buttresses similar to those of the medieval churches, can be made out here and there around the present citadel, and on the east side of the so-called 'Prisoners' Walk', which was made into a narrow passage about a century later. The intention was to render an assault through the gate more difficult and a new gateway, the attractive Barbican, was added at the outer end of the 'Prisoners' Walk', together with a pit, drawbridge and portcullis. It has been suggested that the Barbican was built by the French, who occupied the castle between 1338 and 1345, and that the small size of the stones is due to the fact that the quarries of Guernsey were not available to the builders, who had to make use of what they could find on the beach.[3]

The castle was repaired and extended again in the 15th century; the Carey Tower dates from 1435 and the machicolations surmounting the Barbican are of a similar date. Immediately to the south-west of the Carey Tower is the Mewtis Bulwark, one of several emplacements built in the reign of Henry VIII for the cannon which were then coming into use. It commanded the approach to the castle from land, while the Well Tower, built at the same time, guarded the seaward side.

By Elizabeth's reign artillery had made such advances that the castle would have been within the range of cannon mounted on the old south pier. Stronger walls were necessary and these were built outside the medieval walls, on an 'ivy-leaf' plan with projecting bastions. The present main gateway, the gun ports above it, and those facing it, are of this date. The gate was designed to face away from the town, so that the entrance would be protected from gunfire from that direction. At the same time it is covered by the gun-ports opposite. The rounded projections from the corners of the bastions to east and west of the gateway are orillons, designed to protect the gun-ports from distant fire. Most of the outer walls on the southern side of the castle are also Elizabethan.

From the outbreak of the Civil War in 1643 Guernsey supported parliament, but for eight years Castle Cornet held out for the king. Supplies could reach it from the seaward side as long as the royalists had command of the sea, but finally in 1651 the castle was forced by Admiral Blake's fleet to surrender—the last fragment of the British Isles to do so. During these eight years St. Peter Port was constantly under fire from the castle and the castle received a severe battering from the town. Among the works that probably date from this time is the high wall between the inner and outer baileys, to which have been fixed the bronze plaques in memory of Admiral de Saumarez, which formerly embellished an obelisk at Delancey Park, felled by the Germans.

Hitherto Castle Cornet had been surmounted by a tall, round medieval keep. It appears in a number of contemporary drawings and gives the castle a pyramidal outline very different from its present squat but impressively brooding silhouette. The change came 12 years after the Restoration of the Monarchy when, on 29 December 1672, the powder magazine was struck by lightning, killing seven people and demolishing the keep, the chapel and all the medieval buildings in the inner courtyard. These were never replaced, but several sturdy barrack buildings were built during the 18th century to house the garrison. The fine hospital building, now a military museum, is dated 1746 and the main guard and married quarters also date from the mid-18th century. In the Napoleonic wars Castle Cornet was armed with more than 70 guns, fortunately never called upon to fire in anger, and in the present century a number of concrete pillboxes and gun emplacements, part of Hitler's Atlantic Wall, were added to the historic document that is Castle Cornet.

Military Place-Names

Although our sketch of Mont Orgueil and Castle Cornet brought us briefly to the present century, we now return to the Middle Ages to mention some place-names which have a military significance. Between the separation from Normandy in 1204 and the Battle of Jersey in 1781, numerous attacks were made on the islands by the French, by mercenaries employed by them, and by pirates operating on their own account. Apart from the fortifications made necessary by them, these attacks have left little imprint on the landscape, and are commemorated only by place-names.

The word *rouge* occurs in several places in Jersey and Guernsey, and is usually taken to imply a battle with its consequent bloodshed. La Rouge Rue, leading down the hill to the west of St. John's church, Guernsey, is said to have run with blood after a skirmish during the invasion of 1372 which has already been mentioned (p.117) in connection with Battle Lane in the New Town. The invaders landed at Vazon and not far inland a stretch of the road now known as Les Eturs was formerly called Rouge Rue. A few months later Sark was raided with such havoc that the island was abandoned until the 16th century. This accounts for the scarcity of pre-Elizabethan place-names in that island. Jersey suffered some particularly vicious attacks, and was completely occupied by the French from 1461–68. An engagement which took place at the top of Grouville Hill in 1406, when the island was invaded by 1,000 Frenchmen and Castilians, is commemorated by La Croix de la Bataille. There is a National Trust property near the site, containing an old well-head. Blood is said to have flowed down the hill towards Grouville church, giving the name Blood Hill to the older and narrower of the two parallel roads. (Rouge Rue, near Victoria College, and Rouge Bouillon, owe their names to the red clay soil rather than to a battle.)

A common place-name is *Les Buttes* or *La Butte.* In the Middle Ages every parish had its archery butts, on a piece of level ground close to the parish church. When archery gave way to musketry the association with the parish church persisted; guns and military equipment continued to be kept in the churches until the Militia arsenals were built in the 19th century. In Jersey, the butts of St. Mary's parish were to the east of the church, where there is still a Rue des Buttes. In St. John, Les Buttes are a quarter of a mile due south of the church. In St. Martin there is a Route des Buttes to the south of the church, and in St. Saviour the butts were on the south side of the churchyard.

In Guernsey La Butte, between Elm Grove and Amherst, is on level ground but some distance from the Town Church, while La Butte, Vale, is just to the east of Vale Mill and neither level nor near the church. The other butts, as in Jersey, were near the churches. Les Buttes, St. Saviour's, are a quarter of a mile east of the church; in St. Andrew's they were to the south-west of the church, near the *Last Post* pub; in St. Peter's they were immediately behind the church, and in Torteval a few yards to the west of the church. Butes, in Alderney, is a magnificent site on the plateau overlooking Braye harbour, and is now a playing field—perhaps it is the nearest of any of the medieval archery grounds to its original use.

Tudor Fortifications

The introduction of firearms, and particularly of cannon, brought about a revolution in the technique of warfare that is reflected in the fortifications which still figure in the landscape. At Castle Cornet, as we have seen, Henry VIII began a programme of reconstruction, continued in Elizabeth's reign, which completely altered its appearance by surrounding it with a heavy, battered outer wall with projecting bastions. Although the castle could be reached by cannon fire from St. Peter Port harbour there was no vantage point from which it could be dominated, and it remained the tactical centre of the island until the 18th century. Other fortifications existed around the coast, but these have been almost entirely obliterated by later, mainly Napoleonic defences. An example is le Château de Rocquaine, alias Fort Grey, alias the Cup and Saucer, which stands on a tidal islet in Rocquaine Bay, near the south-west corner of Guernsey. The present building dates from 1804 and is one of the 'true' martello towers to be described later in the chapter. It replaced an earlier Château de Rocquaine which had a much more medieval appearance and lacked the outer curtain wall. The fort is run by the States Ancient Monuments Committee as an excellent little maritime museum. At Vale Castle fragments of the 16th-century bulwarks were found beneath the massive 18th-century walls during excavations in 1980; doubtless other 16th-century fortifications remain to be discovered.

Essex Castle in Alderney was begun by Henry VIII in 1546. The site was chosen to command Longis Bay, then the main harbour of the island, but for some reason the project was abandoned in 1554 and the present building is largely Victorian. The surviving Tudor parts are the outer walls on the north and west sides. The round, pointed-roofed gazebo, which can be seen from many parts of Alderney, was built in Regency times. The castle was converted into flats shortly after the last war.

The fortifications begun by Henry VIII in the other islands did not extend to the abandoned isle of Sark. The result was that it was occupied intermittently by the French, who built themselves three small forts. Le Grand Fort was sited to cover the landing places of L'Eperquerie and La Banquette in the north of the island; the tenements of Le Fort, Le Grand Fort and La Tour were built on or near the site. Another was on the Hog's Back, overlooking Dixcart Bay, and the third was at La Vermondaye in Little Sark, guarding the Coupée. The forts were demolished by a party from Jersey some 10 years before the island was finally colonised by Helier de Carteret.

The defences of Sark after the Elizabethan colonisation consisted of the tenements themselves; we have already seen how they were sited to cover the various possible landing places. When after his successful colonisation the queen formally conferred upon Helier the fief of Sark in 1572, she presented the island with six brand-new pieces of ordnance: two demi-culverins, weighing 29 cwt. each; two sakers, weighing 16 cwt. each; and two falcons, weighing 9 cwt. each.[4] A brass cannon at La Seigneurie, in the garden to the north of the house, bears the inscription 'Don de Sa Majeste la Royne Elizabeth au Seigneur de Sercq AD 1572'.

By far the finest of the 16th-century fortifications of the Channel Islands is the Upper Ward and Keep of Elizabeth Castle, Jersey, the main part of which was built during the last decade of the century on the summit of l'Islet, a tidal island in St. Aubin's Bay, close to the Hermitage Rock where St. Helier is said to have lived. A new castle was necessary because advances in gunnery had rendered Mont Orgueil too vulnerable to bombardment from the landward side. The nearest dry land to l'Islet was over half a mile distant, and the new fort was purpose-built for the new style of warfare. The architect was Paul Ivy, an accomplished military engineer, who was sent by Elizabeth I to bring Jersey's fortifications up to date. Ivy has already been mentioned (p. 106) in connection with the round Jersey arch. His keep is now surmounted by a round tower of German concrete.

Within the walls and bastions of the Upper Ward were two houses, the Captain's and the Governor's. Of the Captain's house only half remains. The Governor's house is intact and in an excellent state of repair. It can be dated fairly closely as it was just ready for Sir Walter Ralegh when he was appointed Governor of Jersey in 1600. At some stage the house was covered with plaster. This was removed early this century to reveal the excellence of the masonry, with chamfers around the small, square windows and the doorways. The front door has a rounded arch which Joan Stevens considers to be the prototype for the typical Jersey arch with a single row of voussoirs.[5] Another doorway in the facade has a straight lintel, whose chamfer shows it to be contemporary. It is interesting that this house, which was considered a suitable residence for Sir Walter Ralegh and later for King Charles II, is basically a normal Jersey farmhouse of its period.

Access to the Upper Ward is by Queen Elizabeth's Gate, one of the finest pieces of masonry in the Channel Islands. The round arch has a single row of voussoirs and a crocketed hood. The arch over the front door of La Maison Maret, near Trinity church, is so similar that one must have been copied from the other.

At the foot of the eminence upon which the Tudor fort was built was the priory of St. Helier, founded originally as a monastery in 1155 and dissolved by Henry VIII. During the years between the death of Elizabeth and the Civil War, the remains of the priory were enclosed by a defensive wall to form the Lower Ward, while a separate outpost, Fort Charles, was built at the extreme northern end of l'Islet, to protect the castle from surprise attack from the landward side at low tide.

During the Civil War Elizabeth Castle was the last strong-point in Jersey to hold out for the king. It survived a siege of 50 days and only capitulated when a bomb, fired from a huge mortar set up at the foot of the hill where Fort Regent now stands, crashed through the roof of the priory church and detonated 12 barrels of gunpowder. The church was completely destroyed and so were the garrison's food supply and ammunition. Today the site of the priory is marked by a reproduction of a medieval wayside Cross (see p.100). It stands in the middle of the barrack yard and around it are an 18th-century barrack block, an 18th-century gymnasium (now a Militia museum) and officers' quarters (now a café) dating from the 19th century.

The remaining part of l'Islet was fortified after the Restoration of Charles II when, in 1668, the Green was enclosed by a curtain wall linking Fort Charles with the rest of the castle, thus forming the Outer Ward. Of particular interest are the small sentry boxes which project from the walls in an almost medieval manner. Elizabeth Castle remained of strategic importance until the present century, as is testified by the large number of German fortifications it contains.

The Castle Breakwater, which links Elizabeth Castle with the Hermitage Rock and continues for some distance to the south, was part of an ambitious scheme to enlarge St. Helier's harbour. Started in 1872, it was abandoned five years later when storms had washed part of the project away. (See p. 168.)

The west side of St. Aubin's Bay had been guarded since Tudor times by St. Aubin's Fort. Like its larger sister, Elizabeth Castle, it stands on a tidal islet, and under its protection the harbour and town of St. Aubin have grown up. Its history is typical of the fortifications of Jersey and Guernsey. The original fort, consisting of a low, round tower, was begun in 1542. It was heightened and the outer ramparts were added in the Civil War, it was reconstructed in Georgian times and again in the 19th century, and finally the Germans added their usual bits of concrete. The pier extending from the north-east corner of l'Islet was completed in 1700 and was the only place at St. Aubin where a ship could lie alongside until the harbour was begun in 1754.

Not far from St. Aubin, at the foot of Beaumont Hill and a familiar landmark to every visitor who is driven from the airport to the town, stands the St. Peter's parish field piece. It is a bronze falcon and dates from the reign of Edward VI.

Georgian Fortifications

During the reign of the first two Georges the only strife in the islands was political, and the only fortifications to figure in the history of the time were the dungeons of Mont Orgueil and Castle Cornet. In 1760 George III began his long reign. During much of it England was at war with France, and Guernsey and Jersey were transformed into island fortresses by a chain of coastal towers and batteries that still feature prominently in the landscape. Fort Henry, on Grouville Common near the centre of the bay, dates from the beginning of George III's reign. This interesting fort consists of a square tower (to which the Germans appear to have added two projecting balconies), surrounded by a rectangular wall with steeply-battered sides. Half a mile to the north, towards Gorey harbour, is Fort William, dating from about the same time.

Between 1780 and 1814 a considerable number of fortifications were built in both Jersey and Guernsey, most of which survive. They include Fort George, Fort Regent, and many round towers, of which each island has its own particular variety. Besides these larger fortifications there are numerous small coastal batteries, often consisting simply of a paved area bounded on the seaward side by a low wall. A Jersey example is Le Coleron, on the little headland immediately to the south of St. Brelade's church. The site belongs to the National Trust for Jersey, and is reached by a footpath from the harbour below. In Guernsey an example may be seen at the extreme tip of Pleinmont. It is reached by walking from the Pezeries car park, past La Table des Pions, and through a gap in the rocks, presumably cut for the purpose of reaching the battery. This is a splendid vantage point from which to view the fury of the sea when a westerly gale is blowing.

Beside many of the towers and batteries will be found a structure resembling a small cottage or large dog-kennel, with a solid roof of vaulted masonry. This was a powder magazine. A prominent example in Jersey, known as The White Cottage or La Caumine à Mary Best, stands on the shore of St. Ouen's Bay, opposite the southern end of St. Ouen's Pond. It was whitewashed as a sea-mark. Larger cottage-like buildings with vaulted roofs were built as watch-houses on coastal eminences. An example in Guernsey stands on the brink of the quarry at Le Guet, near Cobo.

Fort George, on the clifftop immediately to the south of St. Peter Port, was built as the main strongpoint of Guernsey and the home of the garrison when advances in artillery had rendered Castle Cornet too vulnerable. It was begun in about 1782, although the main gateway, one of the few parts of the fort to have survived intact, bears the date 1812. The heart of the fort was a star-shaped citadel of brick, with a dry moat. There were several outlying batteries on the cliff top, with lines for the garrison, and the whole considerable area was enclosed by a substantial granite wall. Parts of this may be seen from the road at the top of the Val des Terres. Apart from an Allied bomb attack in 1944 the fort never saw any action. The garrison remained until 1939 and after the war the site was offered by the War Office to the States of Guernsey, who sold it to a private developer. The citadel was bulldozed away. The main gateway near the top of the Val des Terres, with its dressed-stone arch, was spared, but the attractive guard-house, just inside the archway, was demolished by the developers, despite a public protest. Today the site is an up-market housing estate. The walls of the Charlotte Battery have been retained, and a house of modern design built upon them. The outlying Clarence Battery, on Cow Point, has escaped development and is a pleasant vantage point within walking distance of the town. Access is by the cliff path which begins near the aquarium. The Picquet House, now the offices of the bus company, near the foot of Cornet Street, was built in 1819 as a guardroom where erring soldiers from Fort George were rounded up.

During the 1780s fifteen round towers were built on Guernsey's coastline. They were of a design peculiar to the island, and 13 of them remain as a highly charac-teristic feature of the landscape. They are small, vertical-sided towers with a diameter of about 20 feet, and two storeys of loopholes. The parapet has no battlements but is bevelled; a well in the roof was intended for a gun, though these were never mounted. The towers cost £100 each.

Tower No. 1 was built on an outcrop of rock, Hougue à la Perre, near the *Red Lion*. It was demolished in 1905 when the hougue was levelled to make way for the tramlines between the town and St. Sampson's. All that remains today is the name of the road which leaves the coast at this point, First Tower Lane. Tower No. 2, a quarter of a mile further north, was demolished for no very clear reason in 1959. The remaining round towers happily survive. No. 3 is on Mont Crevelt, a hillock surrounded by reclaimed land to the south of St. Sampson's harbour. No. 4 is on the Fort Le Marchant headland, and the next five are distributed around L'Ancresse Bay. These towers are particularly attractive, standing as they do on the shortly-grazed turf of the common. Towers No. 10, on the Chouet headland, and No. 11, at Rousse, guard between them the entrance to Grand Havre. No. 12 is at Vazon and the remaining three guard the possible landing beaches of the south: Petit Bôt (13), Saints (14), and Fermain (15).

These early round towers are usually referred to as martello towers, but this is a misleading name. The martello towers of the Kent and Sussex coast were designed after an engagement in 1794 between two British warships and a gun-tower at Mortella Point, Corsica. Guernsey's towers are of a different design and were built some years before the Mortella Point incident. Fortunately, they were never called upon to defend the island, for they would have been inadequate to withstand the artillery that had already been developed at the time they were built. Guernsey has three fortifications built in the early 19th century that may be regarded as 'true' martello towers: Forts Grey, Saumarez, and Hommet. They are broader in relation to their height than the earlier towers, with steeply-battered sides and a much more solid construction. Fort Grey (the Cup and Saucer) has already been mentioned (p. 131). Fort Saumarez, on L'Erée peninsula, has been capped by a German concrete tower whose beetling observation slits brood over Lihou Island. Fort Hommet, on the peninsula between Vazon and Albecq, was obscured by a later square fort. This was demolished after the last war, to reveal the beautiful red granite tower.

In 1779 there was an attempted invasion of Jersey, when a party of French under the Prince of Nassau arrived in St. Ouen's Bay. The landing was repulsed, but it demonstrated the need for more effective defences, and hastened the building of a chain of coastal towers. Thirty towers had, in fact, already been planned, for an estimate received in 1778 put the total cost at £4,680.[6] (Jersey's towers were to be more expensive than those of Guernsey, costing all of £156 each). Twenty-three towers were built between 1779 and 1801, of which 17 survive.[7] These 'pre-martellos' are larger and more elaborate than those of Guernsey, and are a highly characteristic feature of the Jersey scene. First Tower, a well-known landmark standing on the seaward side of St. Aubin's Road at its junction with Mont Cochon Road, is a typical example. Like the Guernsey towers it has loopholes on two floors, but it is larger, having a diameter at the base of about 24 feet, and a height of 36 feet, and the walls have a pronounced batter, the diameter at the top being some four feet less than the bottom. Projecting from the parapet are four turrets with loopholes directed downwards. Today First Tower serves as a gigantic sewer vent.

Second Tower, at Bel Royal, was demolished by the Germans, and Third Tower stands opposite the bottom of Beaumont New Road. In St. Brelade's Bay the numbering begins again with St. Brelade No. 1 on Ouaisné Common, and No. 2 near *L'Horizon* hotel. Most of the towers in St. Ouen's Bay are of a later date, but La Rocco, on an outlying rock towards the south of the bay, was the 23rd and last of the 'pre-martello' group to be completed, in 1801. Although this was seven years after the Mortella Point engagement, La Rocco conforms in design to the earlier Jersey towers. It was used as a target by the Germans, who aided by the sea, left it in a ruinous condition. After the war it was restored by the States, with the help of funds raised by a public appeal.

The tower in the middle of the car park at Grève de Lecq dates from 1780. The barracks nearby were built at a later date, in about 1815, and were used by the British regiments stationed in Jersey. The buildings, consisting of two outer barrack blocks flanking a central officers' block, were bought by the National Trust for Jersey in 1972, and are being restored. The remainder of the north coast was considered to have sufficient natural protection and there are no further towers until we reach Fliquet, where Telegraph Tower is so-called because it was once used as a terminal for a submarine cable. At some stage the top of the tower has been removed and replaced in concrete. In St. Catherine's Bay are St. Catherine's Tower, painted white as a sea-mark, and a little further to the south Archirondel Tower. This is painted red and white and is surrounded by a battery designed for four guns. At the time the tower was built, in 1792, the rock on which it stands was 200 yards offshore. In 1847 Archirondel Rock was joined to the shore to form part of a huge new harbour which it was proposed to build in St. Catherine's Bay. The northern arm was completed, but the southern arm was abandoned at a point just beyond the tower. (See p. 169.)

A group of five towers in the Royal Bay of Grouville are numbered from south to north, beginning with No. 1 at La Rocque. Another tower is at Platte Rocque, a little further to the west. This is where a party of French under the Baron de Rullecourt landed in 1781. The island was taken by surprise, not expecting a landing on such a rocky and inhospitable shore, and the invaders reached St. Helier before being defeated in the famous Battle of Jersey. The ease with which the French had landed caused a considerable fright and the following year Seymour Tower was built on a tidal islet called L'Avarison, about a mile and a quarter out to sea from La Rocque Point. Unlike its contemporaries Seymour Tower is square. The tall, gaunt structure replaced a Tudor fort that had previously stood on the islet. In 1979 some German shells which had been found at Gorey Castle were exploded at low tide at L'Avarison, as this was the only place in Jersey far enough from a populated area.

The remaining 'pre-martello', at Le Hocq, was built in about 1780.

Jersey's first three 'true' martello towers were erected between 1808 and 1814. All are squat round towers with sloping sides. The first is on the Ile au Guerdain in the centre of Portelet Bay. Half a mile to the east, at the foot of the cliff at the tip of Noirmont Point, is La Tour de Vinde. In common with many coastal features it is used as a sea-mark and it is painted black and white. The third tower, Icho, is on a rock a mile and a quarter to the south-west of Platte Rocque, where it guards the approach to St. Helier's harbour.

While these small towers were being built, a large fort was erected on Le Mont de la Ville and named after the Prince Regent. The beautiful granite ramparts of Fort Regent encircle the hill, with projecting bastions covering the town and harbour. The considerable area enclosed by the walls has been imaginatively converted into a leisure centre, whose roofs are just visible above the ramparts. On the glacis to the south of the fort is an ugly covered swimming pool.

Victorian Defences

In the peace which followed Waterloo there was a pause in defence work until the 1830s, when renewed international tension, coupled with the advent of steam navigation, made it necessary to revise the islands' defences. Jersey's four remaining martello towers, built on the English pattern, date from this time; the last of their kind to be built in Europe. Two border the Five Mile Road at St. Ouen's Bay: Kempt Tower to the north of the *Cutty Sark* restaurant, and Lewis

Tower near Les Laveurs slipway. The others are La Collette Tower, Pointe des Pas, to the south of Fort Regent, and Victoria Tower on the spur of land overlooking Geoffrey's Leap. Victoria Tower was built in the first year of the queen's reign and is a true defensive tower, complete with dry moat and drawbridge, unlike Guernsey's extravagant folly of the same name, built 11 years later.

Although Great Britain and France were at peace there was still much suspicion on both sides, and the islands were subject to yet another round of fortifications from about 1845 to 1860. In the days of sail the islands had to some extent been protected from attack by their strong tides and treacherous reefs, but with the advent of steam navigation they became far more vulnerable. Unease was increased by a huge fortified harbour that was being constructed at Cherbourg, though this clearly threatened the south coast of England more than the Channel Islands, and Portland harbour was built as its counterpart. The 'harbours of refuge' (a euphemism for naval bases) which were partially built and then abandoned in Alderney and Jersey will be described in Chapter Eleven. Jersey has comparatively few Victorian fortifications, Guernsey has a few, and Alderney positively bristles with them.

The forts of the mid–19th century are typically very like a child's toy fort— square, battlemented buildings with projecting corner turrets and loopholes for rifle fire. They have a medieval air about them and would have been totally useless against the field-guns that were already in use when they were built, yet those of Alderney, in particular, are beautifully constructed with dressed granite cornices and arches, and many of the surviving forts have been converted into flats and houses. In Guernsey, Fort Richmond at the western end of Vazon Bay, and Fort Doyle, in the extreme north-east corner of the island, are survivors of this period. (Forts Hommet and Le Marchant have been demolished since the last war, in each case revealing the Napoleonic defences behind.)

Bréhon Tower, in the Little Russel, was built in 1856. The oval fort stands on a rock midway between Guernsey and Herm. Landing is difficult and it is seldom visited, but the tower is an important sea-mark used by ships approaching St. Peter Port from the north.

At some stage in the 19th century arsenals were built for the Militia in most of the parishes of Jersey and Guernsey. They are beautifully constructed buildings of dressed granite with large, arched doorways for the parish artillery, hitherto kept in the churches. Today the arsenals of St. Peter Port and St. Helier are used as fire stations, while many of the country arsenals have been converted into flats.

Alderney was considered to be the key to the Channel Islands. In a forceful letter to the British government in 1848 the Lieutenant-Governor of Guernsey, General Bell, expressed the view that the harbour of refuge, then under construction, contributed nothing to the defence of Alderney, while adding incalculably to the temptation to attack it. If Alderney fell, she could never be recovered, and Jersey and Guernsey would follow; if Alderney could be held, the other islands could be re-taken, even if temporarily held by the enemy.[8] The government concurred, and a chain of forts was built to cover the entire coast, excepting only the precipitous cliffs of the south and west.

The Victorian forts of Alderney are so distinctive a feature of the landscape that it is worth recording their architect. He was Captain William Jervois, a young engineer who was only 30 years of age when he was sent to Alderney in 1852.[9] He was unusual among military architects in having a strongly developed aesthetic sense, which sometimes seems to have over-ridden mere military considerations. His forts are embellished with such medieval features as machicolations and arrow slits, but he also made modern innovations, such as floors supported by brick vaulting springing from iron tie-beams.

Jervois's largest and most impressive creation is Fort Albert, on the hill overlooking Braye Bay and designed to protect the 'harbour of refuge' which would have taken in most of the bay. The ramparts, built into the hillside, include artillery positions and enclose a number of barrack buildings. Château à L'Etoc, between Saye and Corblets Bays, is a handsome fort now converted into flats. Fort Corblets, on the next headland, is a private house. The inhospitable eastern coast of Alderney was guarded by three small forts, all now abandoned: Fort Les Homeaux Florains on an off-islet opposite the lighthouse, Fort Quesnard on the headland, and Fort Houmet Herbé on another off-island looking out over the Race of Alderney to Cap de la Hague.

Longis Bay was defended by Frying Pan Battery, below Essex Castle and opposite Queslingue and by a fort on the island in the entrance of the bay, Ile de Raz. This was reached by a causeway which was later repaired by the Germans and still serves the fort, now a private house. Essex Castle was extended and used as barracks.

Alderney's southern cliffs are too precipitous to need fortifying. The martello-like tower above Telegraph Bay is not a fortification but was used early in the 19th century for signalling Guernsey, and to Jersey via Sark. On an off-islet below the cliffs overlooking the Swinge lies Fort Clonque, reached by a causeway from the base of the cliffs. This is Jervois at his most romantic; rounded bastions full of loopholes, with an isolated gun emplacement on a separate rock, reached by a brick arch. The fort has been restored by the Landmark Trust and converted into holiday flats.

The next headland is guarded by the much larger Fort Tourgis. An extensive barrack block, parts of which are still used by visiting military units, is surrounded by a network of gun emplacements, high walls and stabling. The whitewashed cone outside the southern wall is a sea-mark to help shipping in the Swinge, the turbulent channel between Alderney and Burhou. Fort Platte Saline, a small battery in the middle of the bay of that name, is used as a sand and gravel depot. The fine-graded pebbles from this area are exported for use as aggregate and for surfacing paths, while the finer grit is used in birdcages. Fort Doyle, with German additions, overlooks Crabby Bay, and Fort Grosnez stands at the base of the breakwater, where it was intended to guard the 'harbour of refuge'. A long glacis on the landward side was once paved, but is now overgrown with grass. Grosnez was the first of the Alderney forts to be built, having been started in 1847, before the arrival of William Jervois. The rather austere fort has for some time been used as a depot by the Department of the Environment, whose unending job it is to maintain the breakwater.

The building of the Victorian defences had a profound effect upon Alderney's landscape, quite apart from the appearance of the forts themselves. Hundreds of labourers were brought in, mainly from Ireland, for quarrying and building, and this more than doubled the population. Houses were built, only to be left derelict when the work was done and the labourers had departed. Numerous quarries were opened, including York Hill, from which the electricity generating station draws its cooling water, and Battery Quarry, inland from Braye Bay, now used for water storage. The largest quarry was Mannez, at the eastern end of the island, which provided sandstone for much of St. Anne, many of the forts, and for the breakwater. A railway was constructed to carry stone from the quarry to the breakwater, a function it has continued to perform to this day.

German Fortifications

In the 18th and 19th centuries it was essential for strategic reasons that the Channel Islands should remain British; the number of Georgian and Victorian fortifications testify to the importance attached to the islands by successive British governments. In 1940 the situation was entirely different. With the fall of France Churchill's government decided that it had no alternative but to demilitarise the islands, leaving them to the mercy of the Germans, but saving them from becoming battlefields.

Hitler attached immense importance to the islands and insisted that they be transformed into impregnable fortresses, not simply for present needs, but for all time. By 1944 there were concentrated in the islands 11 heavy batteries and 39 other strongpoints, besides numerous bunkers and control towers. By contrast the thousand kilometres of coastline from Dieppe to St. Nazaire had the same number of batteries and one less strongpoint.[10] The fortifications had used 484,000 cubic metres of concrete, compared with 6,100,000 for the whole of the rest of the Atlantic Wall.[11]

The most heavily fortified island, as in Victorian times, was Alderney. The population had been evacuated just before the arrival of the Germans, who at first planned to farm the island to supplement Guernsey's food supply. However, at the end of 1941 the foreign workers of the Organisation Todt arrived to put into practice Hitler's extravagant plans, and the island became simply a fortress. The landscape is still haunted in an indefinable way by this unhappy period. The site of the labour camp at Saye still has an air of desolation; at the road junction nearby is a memorial to the foreign workers who died, with inscriptions in Polish, Hebrew, Russian, French, and Spanish. More tangible are the concrete fortifications that the workers built. Gun batteries were dug into the cliffs. Pillboxes and bunkers were added to the Victorian forts. The east end of the island is still brooded over by the immense tower on Mannez Common, designed to control the fire from the various batteries deployed around the island. The ugliest German legacy, though useful, is the water tower at Les Mouriaux, a hideous concrete affair with protruding iron rods which spoils every view of St. Anne.

By far the heaviest guns in the Channel Islands were those of the Mirus Battery at Le Frie Baton above Perelle in Guernsey. The four 12-inch guns came originally from a Russian battleship that had been broken up in 1935. These gigantic weapons had a range of 50 kilometres and controlled the Gulf of St. Malo. The guns are no longer there, but the circular emplacements and underground barracks remain. One of the emplacements is included in the amenities of La Houguette primary school.

As in all the islands, many of the German fortifications in Guernsey are superimposed on earlier works. At Castle Cornet several gun emplacements may be inspected. Some have thumb-nail sketches giving the ranges of the landmarks in the field of view. Most important in the landscape are the various observation and fire control towers around the coast, such as the one at Chouet, standing on the brink of a quarry. The tower at L'Erée, which uses as a base the martello tower of Fort Saumarez, supplies a focal point in the attractive view of the headland from the escarpment inland, and although not in itself a thing of beauty, it would be missed. For the first time in history the Germans found it necessary seriously to fortify the cliffs; one of their largest structures is the look-out and range-finding tower at L'Angle, to the south-east of the television aerials at Pleinmont.

Sark, always the least fortified island, suffered little outward change during the Occupation, except that many trees and even some wooden bungalows were sacrificed for fuel.

In Jersey, as in Alderney and Guernsey, gun positions were grafted on to existing fortifications and dug into the cliffs, while the skyline was punctuated by huge observation towers which controlled the fire from the batteries around them. The landscape was further altered by the removal of earlier structures, including some martello towers, which interrupted the lines of fire.

Mont Orgueil, always of strategic importance, was fortified yet again and topped by an assortment of concrete towers. Elizabeth Castle was heavily armed and the keep surmounted by a round concrete control tower. Though hideous in itself, this does provide an apex to the silhouette of the castle when viewed from the distance. The headlands of Noirmont and La Corbière were honey-combed with batteries; the screes of excavated rock which extend down the cliffs from these and other coastal strongpoints have yet to be covered by vegetation. On the clifftop on each of these headlands stands a control tower. The one at La Corbière is particularly large and was camouflaged (not very effectively) to resemble granite. It is now used as a radio navigation station. Its five observation slits, one above the other, scowl down on the St. Helier-bound mailboat immediately she has passed the lighthouse.

At St. Ouen's Bay, where the escarpment retreats some distance from the coast, there were two lines of defence: a coastal line, including the re-fortified Lewis, Kempt and High Towers, and a second line on the heights inland. The Germans believed that St. Ouen's Bay would be the most likely beach for an Allied landing. Besides the gun batteries they built an anti-tank sea wall, and canals extending north and south from St. Ouen's Pond to act as a moat.

Another prominent German landmark is the fire-control tower near the rifle range at Les Landes, in the north-west corner of the island.

After the liberation the islanders naturally wished to remove all traces of the Germans and the suffering they had caused. The concrete fortifications, however, were built to last, and only a small proportion were destroyed. Gradually, as the distance in time widened, the Occupation was seen as part of the islands' long history, and the towers, batteries and bunkers were accepted as a permanent part of the landscape.

Chapter Ten

THE INDUSTRIAL LANDSCAPE

Jersey never kept all its eggs in one basket.—G. R. Balleine, 1951

ALTHOUGH THE CHANNEL ISLANDS have no heavy industry, the landscapes of Jersey and Guernsey do contain a large number of industrial buildings. Fortunately most of them are concentrated in well-defined areas. Some light industry is producing goods for export, but most is servicing the dense population of the islands, and their agricultural and horticultural industries. The other major industries, tourism and finance, do not involve buildings that would normally be described as industrial, though some hotels nearly qualify for this adjective.

In all the islands the countryside contains small industrial remains which have mellowed with time to become attractive parts of the scenery. Among these are the *lavoirs,* communal washing places where a stream runs through a paved area, sometimes surrounded by a wall. In Jersey, which has the largest number, they are known as *douets à laver.* The right to use a particular *lavoir* was jealously guarded. A beautiful example in the parish of St. John has a stone by the entrance inscribed with the names of those who were allowed to use it in 1813. This *lavoir,* in a beautiful setting at St. Cyr, now belongs to the National Trust for Jersey. An example in Guernsey, in less attractive surroundings, is outside the service department of the garage at the bottom of Colborne Road, at Pont Renier. In Alderney there is one near the top of Le Petit Val, below a bend in the road and shaded by trees.

Rather similar are the *abrevoirs* or drinking places for cattle, often to be found where a stream (*douet* in Jersey, *douit* in Guernsey) crosses a road. In Guernsey the *douit* is often also a parish boundary and the opportunity has been taken at some time to embellish the *abrevoir* with an elaborate piece of masonry marking the exact position of the boundary and bearing the names of the constables of the two parishes. Judge Barbenson's Fountain of 1913 is an exuberant example in Alderney. It stands beside the road to the north of the airport.

Windmills and Watermills

Although none are working commercially, mills still exist in all the islands, and the sites of many more can be made out. Watermills are perhaps the islands' earliest industrial buildings. The first was probably the mill at Le Port du Moulin in Sark, belonging to the monastery founded in 565 by St. Magloire. The dam of

143

the millpond, further up the valley, gave its name to the property still known as L'Ecluse. Many island mills date from the early Middle Ages, but they have been rebuilt on several occasions and few of the present buildings are more than 300 years old. All the watermills and most of the windmills belonged in the Middle Ages to the seigneur of the fief on which they stood, who thus ensured for himself the revenue from the milling of the corn grown by his tenants. Sometimes the seigneur was the king himself, as was the case at King's Mills in Guernsey.

The greatest possible use was made of the small streams of the islands, particularly those that have carved themselves steep-sided valleys in their descent from the plateaux to the sea. The main valleys of Jersey and Guernsey each contained a series of mills. The Talbot Valley in Guernsey contained six within the space of a mile. In Jersey St. Peter's Valley had five, and Waterworks Valley seven. Joan Stevens[1] has plotted the sites of 38 watermills in Jersey; doubtless others remain to be discovered. The valley mills were of the overshot type, water being directed from above on to the top of the waterwheel. In order to obtain the necessary head of water the natural stream, in the valley bottom, was diverted into a man-made mill stream. This followed a contour along the side of the valley until the natural stream had fallen a sufficient distance below it. Above the mill an artificial millpond was constructed, which collected the water from the mill stream and stored it until it was needed to turn the wheel. The factor that controlled the minimum distance between mills was the length of valley needed to obtain sufficient vertical distance between the millpond and the natural stream. The steeper the fall of the valley floor, the closer the mills could be.

Mill streams may still be seen in many of the valleys of the Channel Islands. One of the most obvious is in the Talbot Valley in Guernsey, where it can be seen from the road as it follows a contour on the other side of the valley. This example is in unusually good repair. In most cases the banks have collapsed in a number of places so that the water returns to the floor of the valley. Near the head of the Talbot Valley were two mills, Les Moulins de l'Echelle, one immediately above the other. Much of the machinery of one of the mills remains, though the wheel has gone. The millpond which supplied these mills was at the bottom of the lane running from St. Andrew's church to the head of the Talbot Valley—the lane is still called L'Ecluse, the dam. A little below L'Echelle is another mill, Les Niaux. This has been restored by its owner and equipped with a new waterwheel. Below Les Niaux there is a longer distance while the mill stream gains enough head for the three mills of Les Grands Moulins, King's Mills. The stream follows approximately the 125-foot contour, making a detour round a side valley before passing under Candie Road and entering the mill pond above Le Moulin de Haut. This mill was still in use between the wars, and water still cascades over the broken wheel. Le Moulin du Milieu, now a dwelling house, is beside the Rue a l'Eau near King's Mills. The site of Le Moulin de Bas is now occupied by a water pumping station whose appearance has already been adversely commented upon. The position of the waterwheel may be seen to the left of the building.

At Petit Bôt there were at least two mills, one on the site of the tea-room, and the other just across the road at a higher level. During the last century the lower mill was used for a time to make paper from rags and old rope.[2] The upper mill continued to grind corn, but access was too difficult—the road from Le Bourg had not yet been built and the mills had to be approached from the St. Martin's end or down the steep, muddy lane from Le Chêne—and both mills had stopped work by the beginning of this century. They were demolished during the Occupation, but the position of the upper millwheel is still indicated by the waterfall which cascades from the mill stream at this point.

In St. Peter Port there was a chain of mills along the stream which ran down the Charroterie, Bordage and Fountain Street. Today the stream is piped out of sight below the streets and the original mills are no more, but a string of industrial buildings in the valley owe their siting and their names to the mills from which they grew. Pheonix Mills, immediately below the *lavoir* at Pont Renier, are now a depot for States vehicles. A short distance down the hill are the Charroterie Mills, lately a sawmill, but now the site of various commercial enterprises. Further down and on the other side of the road are the Town Mills, until very recently a bakery. The main stream continues down the Bordage, but a mill stream was diverted into Mill Street, named after the mill that it operated. The last mill was by the Town Church. Finally the water ran down Cow Lane into the harbour.

Of the numerous watermills which formerly existed in Jersey, a fair number survive, though only a few have retained their wheels. In the Grève de Lecq valley Le Moulin de Lecq, now a pub, has been restored and the revolving gear used as a feature in the bar. More recently Quetivel Mill has been restored to full working order by the National Trust for Jersey; corn is ground, which sells as fast as it can be produced.

The mill, one of the chain in St. Peter's Valley, stands at the foot of Mont Fallu. The wooded côtil to the north of the mill is one of the Trust's finest properties, Le Don Gaudin. The mill stream runs along the lower boundary of the wood, with a meadow between it and the natural stream in the valley bottom. The other mills of St. Peter's Valley, like Quetivel and indeed most of the watermills of the Channel Islands, are in a characteristic position on the side of the valley, a little way up from the bottom, at a point where a steep lane plunges down the valley side to cross the stream.

Most of Jersey's valleys, like St. Peter's, are remarkably unspoilt, but Bellozanne Valley, running inland from St. Aubin's Road at Ville ès Nouax, is highly industrialised and Friquet Mill, still in its typical position on the valley side, is wedged between a coal depot and a sewage processing plant.

One of Jersey's most secluded beauty spots is Queen's Valley. From the disused Moulin de Haut, near St. Saviour's hospital, it runs south, cutting deeply into the plateau and opening out when it reaches the low-lying land half a mile north of Grouville church, near Le Moulin de Bas. The white farmhouse in the most beautiful middle stretch of the valley is Le Blanc Moulin. Here there were two mills and a brewery; one of the mills was for wheat, the other milled malt for the brewery. In 1976, the year of the great drought, there was a proposal to flood this beautiful valley to make yet another reservoir. The scheme met with vigorous opposition and was shelved, only to be put forward again in recent months.

Alderney's watermill is at the foot of Le Val de la Bonne Terre, a delightfully secluded wooded valley leading down from Rose Farm to Fort Tourgis. The mill, surrounded by farm buildings, stands between Fort Tourgis and Platte Saline. The wheel, 17 feet in diameter, remains with much of the machinery, though the building itself has been partially demolished since it stopped work early in the present century. The millpond is some distance up the valley. The stream descending Le Val de la Bonne Terre must have proved inadequate, for an additional mill stream was dug along a contour, to capture water from another stream further to the east. Traces of this channel may still be found—it is marked on the Ordnance Survey map as 'Drain'.[3] The mill now belongs to the Alderney Society, who are restoring it.

Windmills have never been as numerous as watermills, but standing as they do on the most exposed sites, those that do exist have become well-known land- and sea-marks. Most of the present buildings date from the 19th century. None are still working; some are in ruins, while others have been converted for other uses. In Jersey four are still standing. St. Ouen's Mill, to the west of the parish church, is surrounded by traces of the open fields which once supplied it (see p. 62). The present building, now a Scout headquarters, dates from the early 19th century, with alterations by courtesy of the Germans. St. Peter's windmill, built in about 1870, a little to the west of St. Mary's church and on the watershed between the Grève de Lecq and St. Peter's Valleys, has been equipped with a new set of sails and incorporated into a restaurant. Rozel Mill, painted as a sea-mark, stands at the head of the Vallée de Rozel. Grouville Mill, near the summit of Grouville Hill, stands amid traces of open fields.

A major land- and sea-mark in the north of Guernsey is Vale Mill, on the Hougue du Moulin above Bordeaux harbour. A windmill was built here in 1771, to mill the corn grown in the northern island, Le Clos du Valle. The present building, probably slightly younger than this, was increased in height by the Germans and now has a forbidding and top-heavy appearance. On the main island of Guernsey four windmills survive. Le Hêchet Mill, near the top of the Ruettes Brayes, was built in 1825 and was still grinding corn, using only two sails, in the 1920s. It has been converted into a private house. Not far away, across the Colborne Road valley, Les Vardes Mill was used for making cement. It, too, has been converted into a dwelling. Another cement mill was at Mont Saint, on the spur overlooking Perelle. Again it has been converted into a house, this time with castellations.

Sausmarez Mill, St. Martin's, usually referred to as 'The Old Mill', stands at Les Camps du Moulin, not far from Sausmarez Manor. The Richmond map of 1787 shows the mill in the centre of an extensive area of open fields, at the intersection of five unfenced roads. This was almost the last part of Guernsey to be enclosed, and it is tempting though unprofitable to imagine the scene in

1787 and compare it with that of today, when the mill is wedged between a busy road junction and the Old Mill Housing Estate. The last vestige of the open fields is a tiny triangular traffic island. The mill itself, though gutted, is still sound.

The seigneurial windmill of Sark stands at the highest point of the island, beside Mill Lane, which has to make a kink to avoid it. The weathervane bears the date 1571, and Helier de Carteret's arms are on the lintel over the door. Much of the machinery survives, but the sails are gone and today the mill is used as a tourist shop. The remains of a smaller private mill stand in a field to the north of La Sablonnerie in Little Sark. Alderney, though an eminently suitable island for windmills, does not seem to have possessed one since the Middle Ages, when the king owned a mill on the Blaye.

The Quarrying Industry

All the islands are blessed with excellent building stone and this has been used from the earliest times for the more permanent buildings. In numerous places on the coast and inland, often overgrown with ivy and brambles, may be found small quarries which have supplied the stone for some nearby building. Sometimes, on steep sites, the quarry supplied both the stone and a level platform on which the cottage or stable was built. The best building stone was not the easiest to extract from the ground, and usually these local quarries provided only irregular stone or rubble for walls. Lintels were either of wood or of dressed stone from further afield, and quoins were very often of brick. Examples of this in Guernsey may be seen in the old houses of the coastal parts of St. Martin's, whose rubble construction is of Icart gneiss from small quarries on the cliffs. In Jersey many walls in the north-east corner of the island are of 'pudding stone' or Rozel conglomerate, which again is unsuitable for lintels and quoins, as it cannot be trimmed. In the western half of Jersey the sedimentary shales which form a broad band from St. Ouen's Bay to St. John's Road were much used as a local building stone in the days before steel tools were available that could cut the harder igneous rocks.

For those who could afford a better building stone for corners and lintels, or even for the whole building, a considerable choice was available. Diorite ('blue' or 'grey granite') was extensively used in northern Guernsey and also in Jersey and Alderney. In Jersey some beautiful granites were available. Particularly highly esteemed was that from Mont Mado, near Frémont Point in the parish of St. John. The quarry, now filled in, yielded a fine-grained stone varying in colour from pink to almost white. Another much-used granite came from La Rosière, near Corbière Point. Rosière granite is a coarser-grained stone which, nevertheless, can be dressed to produce a fine edge.

The Minquiers, a reef of islets lying between Jersey and St. Malo, were extensively quarried and their stone may be seen in a number of places in Jersey and Guernsey. The main islet, Maîtresse Ile, yielded the stone for Fort Regent. There is a story that at one stage the fishermen collected up all the quarrymen's tools and dumped them in the sea to preserve the very existence of the island.

A considerable amount of blue stone from Chausey and yellowish stone from Les Ecréhous was also used in Jersey.

In Guernsey red granite was quarried in Albecq and Cobo; a large quarry at Cobo has been filled in, but there are smaller ones among the pine trees at Le Guet, besides the much larger one below the watch house. In Alderney full use was made of the hard sandstone in the building of St. Anne, and later in the breakwater and fortifications.

The effect on the landscape of quarrying for local needs was as nothing compared with the effect of the huge export industry that sprang up in Guernsey and some of the smaller islands and reefs in the 19th century. St. Sampson's harbour and the industrial landscape around it, although now mainly concerned with the import of oil and the generation of electricity, owe their existence to the stone industry.

The export of stone from Guernsey began in the late 18th century, the stone being carried by boxcart to the ships, stranded at low tide on the beach which is now St. Sampson's harbour. The ships had to be flat-bottomed and extra sturdily built to withstand the stone being tipped into the hold. The industry grew enormously in the peace that followed Waterloo. Besides the demand for paving setts and kerbs, the invention of the macadamised road surface at about this time created a huge market in England for road metal, and the diorite and gabbro of the Vale and St. Sampson's proved to be ideally suited to this purpose. The intensely hard gabbro from the area to the south of St. Sampson's harbour in particular was unrivalled for roadmaking.

When the creek leading into the Braye du Valle became St. Sampson's harbour, the stone boats could lie alongside and the stone could be tipped directly into the holds from the quay; the boats still needed to be able to take the ground as the harbour is tidal. The yards grouped around the harbour, now used for a variety of purposes, housed stone depots and crushing plants.

The stone trade continued to increase throughout the 19th century, and up to the First World War, when 400,000 tons were being exported each year. The north of the island became pock-marked with huge holes; a total of 268 quarries have been counted in Guernsey.[4] Since 1914 exports have steadily declined, until today only a handful of quarries is working, producing almost entirely crushed stone for the local market. It is used as an aggregate for concrete-making, and as a road metal.

The legacy of huge holes in the ground left by the quarrying industry has proved a boon to Guernsey, which has used them for two main purposes—water storage and refuse disposal. Unworked quarries fill naturally with water to a certain level, and many such quarry pools lie darkly among the greenhouses and bungalows of northern Guernsey, fenced off more or less safely from wandering children and dogs. Some of the larger quarries, not subject to seepage from the sea, are used as reservoirs by the water board, who fill them in times of surplus and pump the water out when it is needed. One such quarry is Juas, down a lane opposite the Vale Methodist church, from which the steps of St. Paul's cathedral are said to have come. Another is the mighty gabbro quarry near St. Sampson's church.

Refuse disposal is a serious problem in a small island whose population is growing all the time, but whose area is strictly limited. Guernsey has been extremely fortunate to have so many disused quarries, though the supply of suitable holes to be filled is now coming to an end. Many small coastal quarries have been filled and either grassed over or made into car parks; one such park is on the headland between Portinfer and Port Soif. The level of refuse in the present tip, a huge diorite quarry at Bordeaux, is now nearing the top. Filling is hastened by the fact that for health reasons each layer of refuse has to be sealed by a layer of hardcore. In 1980 a refuse baling plant was installed at Bulwer Avenue, This will make more economical use of the remaining quarries, as less hardcore has to be used, and the bales may also be used for land reclamation.

The Channel Islands yacht marina, in the extreme north-eastern corner of the island, was created by blasting a channel to connect the diorite quarry of Beaucette with the sea. Approaching down the narrow, winding lane to the quarry a small forest of masts appears unexpectedly amid the little fields, stone walls and greenhouses. A smaller quarry a quarter of a mile to the south is used for rearing oysters. Another unusual use for a quarry was as a dump for crude oil washed ashore in 1967 from the *Torrey Canyon*. This was the fate of a small quarry on the south side of the Chouet peninsula.

Jersey, with fewer disused quarries and a larger population, has a more acute refuse problem even than Guernsey. When the available holes had been filled, large-scale dumping took place in the sandpits of St. Ouen's Bay. This, with its attendant piles of backfilling materials and heavy traffic, threatened to destroy the maritime turf and rather special atmosphere of the sandy plain at the foot of the Quennevais. More recently refuse has been used as filling material in an ambitious reclamation project at La Collette, to the south of St. Helier harbour. This has provided space for the oil storage tanks for the new power station, a tanker berth and a yacht marina, together with an area of potential building land. There is also a resources recovery plant in Bellozanne Valley, where as many materials as possible are recovered for recycling.

Alderney was extensively quarried to provide stone for the Victorian fortifications and breakwater. The sandstone quarry at Mannez, which had already yielded much of the stone for St. Anne, was enormously extended in the process of building the breakwater, to which it was connected by a railway. The quarries at York Hill, Battery and L'Etoc provided diorite. When the fortifications had been completed an important export trade built up, which continued until after the First World War. The stone was carried by the railway to crushing-machines near the present power station, and the chippings were exported from Braye Jetty. Another diorite quarry was at Cachalière, on the south coast midway between Telegraph Bay and Essex Castle. Here a concrete pier was built at the beginning of the present century, from which stone was exported until about 1918.

Mannez, Battery, and York Hill quarries were still in use between the wars; the last of the stone crushers, a monstrous concrete box near Braye Jetty, reinforced by the Germans as part of their defences, was demolished with much difficulty in 1972. Sandstone is still carried by the railway from Mannez to help in the unending task of protecting the breakwater from the force of the waves.

The granite of Herm had a reputation for great density and hardness, and the face of that small island was permanently changed by the export trade which grew up in the first half of the 19th century. There were three main quarries, all facing Guernsey. The Monku quarry bit into the hill behind Fisherman's Cottage, near the Common; La Chausée quarry, now very overgrown, is behind the hotel, and Rosière quarry, a deep one used today as the island's refuse dump, is just north of the landing steps. Rubble from all these quarries litters the shore from Monku to Rosière. A large harbour was built, enclosing all the water between Hermetier (Rat Island) and the present jetty. The piers were connected to the quarries by railway lines; the broad, level path along most of the west coast of Herm owes its existence to these mineral lines. The north pier joined Hermetier to Herm. A contemporary print shows it as a broad pier with two railway lines, a train of four trucks drawn by two horses, and a sailing barge lying alongside. This pier has long since been washed away; all that remains today is a slightly raised causeway, visible at low water, between Herm and Hermetier. The south pier was maintained, and is the pier used today when there is sufficient water to enter the harbour. The small, round building beside the tennis court in front of the hotel was built as a lock-up; the population had been increased to about 400 by imported labour, and it was necessary to have somewhere where drunks could be safely deposited.

In the second half of the 19th century, in order to secure a supply of granite for various projects, particularly the new harbour of St. Peter Port, the States of Guernsey took the lease of Jethou and Crevichon. The most impressive quarry is on Crevichon, a once conical islet north of Jethou, which has been half quarried away. Crevichon has the distinction of being the earliest recorded quarry in the Guernsey bailiwick, for in 1564 it was mentioned in the accounts of Castle Cornet as having supplied stone for the castle.[5]

Veins containing silver, lead and copper exist on Herm, and various unsuccessful attempts have been made to extract these minerals commercially. The remains of a mine shaft may be seen by the cliff paths near Rosière Cottage.

Quarrying in Sark seems to have been confined to supplying local needs, and even these have been met to some extent by importing stone from Jersey. There have, however, been strenuous attempts to exploit the mineral veins of the island, and the remains of mining still figure in the landscape of Little Sark. Mineral lodes containing silver, lead and copper run diagonally across Little Sark from Port Gorey in the south-west to Le Pot, a great, cauldron-shaped natural cavity in the cliffs of the east coast. The richest silver lode, known as Sark's Hope, runs north-east from a gully immediately to the south of Port Gorey, to intersect the road near the bend to the west of the barracks. This lode was extensively mined, but although the spoil heaps are full of silver-rich minerals, it never yielded silver in economic quantities. Mining ruins, desolate and ivy-clad, still mark the line of the lode. A shaft near the road to the barracks is used as a

25. (*above*) St. Mary's, Jersey, from the north-west. The north chancel, just visible on the left, may date from the 11th century; the south nave, on the right, was begun in 1838, shortly after the spire had been added to the medieval tower.

26. (*left*) St. Mary's, Castel, Guernsey, from the north-west. The north chancel, just visible on the left, contains some 13th-century wall paintings.

27. St. Saviour's church, Jersey. As in all Jersey's medieval churches, the tower is over the crossing and not at the west end. The two east windows—one reticulated and the other flamboyant—are particularly fine.

28. (*above*) Le Colombier, Torteval, Guernsey, is named after the seigneurial dovecote which still stands on the property.

29. Morel Farm, St. Laurence, Jersey. The house, largely dating from the early 18th century, is the property of the National Trust for Jersey.

30. Mont Orgueil Castle and Gorey Harbour, Jersey. The castle was begun in the 13th century and last added to during the German occupation. The pier was built for the oyster fishery in the early 19th century.

31. Roofscape of St. Peter Port. Beyond the vast Victorian harbour is Castle Cornet, with the islands of Herm, Jethou and Sark in the distance. On the right is the tower of the Town church; in the centre, the obtrusive summit of the Woolworth's building.

32.   The church of St. James-the-Less, Guernsey, built in 1818 for the English-speaking community. Described as 'Wilson's Masterpiece', the neo-classical church is under threat of demolition.

33. High Street, Alderney. Though the houses, dating from the 18th and 19th centuries, are not remarkable in themselves, they add up to a street of enormous charm and character.

34. Regency villas in the Grange, St. Peter Port. The iron railings survived the war but are now disappearing to provide parking places.

La Seigneurie, Sark. The facade was altered in 1732, when the windows were enlarged, using Jersey granite. ...hind is a Victorian wing, including a Dutch gable and an ornate tower intended for signalling to Guernsey.

6. Sausmarez Manor, St. Martin's, Guernsey. The main house was built in the reign of Queen Anne. The wing ...n the right is a Victorian addition.

37. Round arch of the standard Jersey type at Robin Place (Gas Lane, off David Place) St. Helier. The late date, 1726, may account for the unusually generous head-room afforded by this arch.

38. Tower No. 6 near Fort Le Marchant, Guernsey. Fifteen of these small towers were built in the 1780s to defend the island against the French. Beyond is L'Ancresse Bay and the German fire-control tower at Mont Cuet.

39. Le Hocq Tower, Jersey. Built shortly after the French had attempted to invade the island in 1779, the tower is of the characteristic Jersey pattern with four projecting turrets.

40.   Kempt Tower, St. Ouen's Bay, Jersey, as it was before the war. A 'true' martello tower built on the English pattern in about 1832, and one of the last to be built in Europe.

41.   Fort Les Homeaux Florains—one of Alderney's many Victorian fortifications.

42. Lavoir, Bouley Bay Hill, Jersey. On the stone trough are the initials HNC, IGLC and ILBTL for H. Nicolle, J. Gallichan and J. Le Boutillier, and the date 1834.

43. (*left*) Between the parishes of St. John and Trinity, Jersey.

44. (*below*) Between St. Martin's and St. Peter Port, Guernsey. At Les Hubits the *douit* which forms the parish boundary is channelled through a *lavoir* behind the stone and a drinking trough in front.

ISLAND OF HERM GRANITE QUARRY

(CHANNEL ISLANDS.)

45. The export of granite from Herm. In this 19th-century print the artist appears to have been standing on Hermetier, which was joined to Herm by the north pier of a large harbour. This pier has since been washed away. The south pier still exists, but there is no trace today of the jetty which seems to have extended from the beach opposite the hotel.

46. Lane near St. Peter's church. One of the few remaining lanes that have not been surfaced and thrown open to motor traffic. The high earth banks, ivy and pennywort are typical.

47. L'Erée Road at Les Adams de Haut. One of General Doyle's military roads, built in 1810. Note the footpath which extends the whole length of the military roads; the straight stretch in the foreground is another characteristic feature.

48. North-eastern Jersey from the air, with St. Catherine's Breakwater. The entire bay as far as Archirondel Tower, on the right, was to have been a 'harbour of refuge'. Note the ravine produced by quarrying near the base of the breakwater

49. Fine masonry at the end of St. Catherine's Breakwater, completed by the British Government in 1855. The States of Jersey finally accepted the breakwater, useless for everything except angling, as a gift.

50. The Admiralty Breakwater, Alderney. Molly the engine and a grouting machine engaged in the endless task of repairing the thousand-yard breakwater. The arched niches are for shelter when the sea breaks over from the left.

51. Creux Harbour, Sark, from Les Laches. The tunnel which gives the harbour its name was driven through the headland to the bottom of Harbour Hill in 1588.

rubbish tip. Further down the valley are the remains of an engine house, with another shaft beside it. Two mine chimneys stand a little way up the slope to the east, and further down the hill, near Port Gorey, are more shafts. Most have been filled in, but their positions are indicated by whitish spoil heaps.

Mining has also taken place in Jersey and Guernsey, though with little impact on the landscape. Readers who would like to pursue the matter further are referred to the *Transactions* of La Société Guernesiaise for 1933.[6]

Other Exporting Industries

The agricultural and horticultural crops which have played such an important part in the economy of the Channel Islands have been dealt with in Chapters Five and Six. Since the produce must be exported, and the raw materials imported, through the harbours, the service industries connected with agriculture and horticulture have tended to be concentrated near the ports. The warehouses of fertiliser and sundries merchants are still to be seen, for instance, along the esplanades to the west of St. Helier, and the north of St. Peter Port. The tendency today is for these town sites to be re-developed as offices and shops, while the box factories, packing sheds, seed and fertiliser warehouses move to less valuable sites out of town, where their asbestos-clad roofs can cover a greater area. The coming of palletisation has complicated the issue further. Guernsey tomatoes used to be packed in wicker baskets at the vinery and then carried by horse and van directly to the White Rock. Today three-quarters of the crop are not packed in the vinery, but are taken to one of several packing and grading stations before being moved to the huge depot of Bulwer Avenue, where the wooden trays are loaded on to pallets. Finally the pallets are transported by lorry and trailer to the White Rock.

Shipbuilding was formerly an important industry in Jersey and Guernsey. Ocean-going ships were built in numerous yards, but the valuable coastal sites have been re-developed and very few signs remain of an industry which died with the coming of iron ships. Often the only evidence is a 19th-century print showing ships in the course of construction on the foreshore. St. Aubin's Bay was ringed by yards. One between St. Aubin and La Haule was near the present St. Brelade's parish hall. A large yard at the foot of West Mount is now covered by the Victoria Avenue, and yards in the centre of St. Helier have been completely obliterated by the harbour works and the bus station. Four shipyards at Havre des Pas are now covered by hotels and seven at Gorey by a sea wall and promenade.[7] In Guernsey the brewery and bus station stand on the site of a series of yards: one at La Piette is now the yard of a builders' merchant, and one on the south side of St. Sampson's harbour is now a coal store.

If ocean-going ships are no longer built, yacht and small boat-building is flourishing, using both fibreglass and timber hulls. Since these boats can easily be moved along the roads, boat-building is no longer confined to the coast and takes place in workshops, garages and gardens throughout the islands.

St. Peter Port in the Middle Ages was an important depot for the wine trade between Bordeaux and England. The cellars in Guernsey had a reputation for whatever qualities were necessary for maturing the wine, before it was shipped on to England. The brick-vaulted cellars still exist, particularly on the quay beside the old harbour, where they now serve as restaurants, ships' chandlers, shipping offices and garages. More vaults in the lanes around Le Truchot are used as workshops, car-hire offices, and in some cases still as wine stores. The breweries of St. Helier and St. Peter Port are the flourishing survivors of a host of small breweries and distilleries that once existed in the towns and countryside. Today the breweries have to import all their raw materials, but they survive by producing a high quality, almost hand-made product.

In recent years the authorities of Jersey and Guernsey have encouraged light industry to establish itself in the islands, in an attempt to broaden the base of the economy. Products include electronic equipment, aluminium windows and greenhouses, motor components, knitwear, and pottery. Some light industry is centred round the airports; Guernsey has an oscilloscope factory close to the airport, which it uses both for importing components and for exporting the finished product. In Jersey a relatively huge new development is centred to the south of the airport, but this is mainly residential with shops, school and community centre. New light industry in Jersey is being concentrated at the Rue des Prés industrial estate, opposite Longueville Manor to the east of St. Helier, where it will not affect the amenities of the residential areas. Guernsey has an industrial estate at Braye Road, Vale. Attempts to establish light industry in Alderney have been made at various times, but have failed because of the difficulty of communication. The island is now almost wholly dependant on tourism.

Tourism and Finance

Besides agriculture or horticulture and the developing light industries, the two major money-earners today are tourism and finance. These two industries have vastly different physical requirements and differ greatly in their effect on the landscape. Banks and finance houses employ relatively few people directly, and the service industries required to keep their offices functioning are also on a modest scale. What they do need is a suite of offices, preferably in a prestigious quarter of St. Helier or St. Peter Port. Some of the larger merchant banks have built new office blocks on run-down town sites; others are content to take over large houses in areas of the towns that were previously residential. The Grange, on the outskirts of St. Peter Port, is such an area. The gracious houses, built by wealthy Regency families, were first divided into residential flats, and are now being taken over by finance houses. In most cases care is taken not to change the appearance of the building, the main external manifestation of its new use being the insignia of some international finance corporation in anodised aluminium beside an expensive mahogany front door. There is, nevertheless, a subtle change in the character of these areas from gracious residential suburbs to prosperous financial centres, occupied only during office hours.

The effect upon the landscape of the tourist industry is by contrast enormous. A regular tourist industry was made possible by the advent of steam navigation in the last century. Since then the islands have catered for an increasing number of regular visitors, attracted by the slower pace of life, the beaches and scenery, and the Continental flavour without language problems. Jersey has made the most spectacular growth since 1945, and now caters for nearly a million tourists a year. There are two holiday camps and six registered camping sites, but the great majority of Jersey's visitors are accommodated in hotels and guest houses. Self-catering accommodation is not encouraged because of the acute shortage of housing for permanent residents. There are no caravan sites in any of the islands.

Guernsey's tourist industry is more modest, catering for visitors who are content with fewer amenities. Holiday camps have never been allowed, and there are very few camping sites, the majority of visitors again being accommodated in hotels and guest houses. During the last decade there has been a great expansion in self-catering accommodation, holiday 'chalets' springing up wherever planning permission could be obtained. However, as in Jersey, there is a shortage of houses for local people, and permission to build self-catering units is now more difficult to obtain.

Alderney depends entirely on tourism for its income and has hotels, holiday cottages and a camping site. The attractions it offers are fresh air, space, beaches and hostelries whose conviviality is legendary. Sark has an abundance of natural beauty but less conviviality. Its tourist industry is important, but as a tax-free refuge Sark cannot be said to depend on tourism for its survival. Herm has a hotel, holiday cottages and a camping site, and numerous day trippers from Guernsey.

The great majority of the hotels in all the islands were originally private houses. Some, like Longueville Manor in Jersey, or La Collinette in Guernsey, have retained their original character, but most have been extended and altered so many times since becoming hotels that their original appearance is difficult to imagine. Two of the commonest alterations, done in stages winter by winter, are to add an extra storey covered by a mansard roof, and to throw out a flat-roofed dining-room on the ground floor in front of the house, obscuring the facade. Very few Channel Islands hotels have been built as such.

Gaily painted self-catering units are now a prominent feature of the Guernsey scene. Some are converted barns and outbuildings; more often they are small, box-like bungalows, huddled in groups on the site of an old greenhouse or swampy field.

The number of tourists who can be accommodated in hotels, guest houses and self-catering units is limited by the number of beds, and for this reason yachting has been actively encouraged in recent years. Since there are very few moorings that are not occupied by local boats, marinas have been built to accommodate all but the largest visiting yachts. In St. Helier, a marina has been provided to the south of Victoria Pier, by the power station. In St. Peter Port the old harbour has been converted by the States into a marina for visiting boats, and another has been provided by private enterprise at Beaucette, in the north of Guernsey.

When not occupying their accommodation tourists concentrate in the towns and on the beaches. The effect on the towns is that the shops are more numerous and larger than they would be if they relied upon local custom; there are far more restaurants than there would otherwise be, and the parking problem is even more acute. The effect on the more popular beaches is that the coastal turf tends to wear through to the sand beneath; loos and kiosks have to be provided, and so do refuse bins, for English visitors, unlike those from the Continent, drop litter wherever they go. The design of a beach convenience offers a particular challenge; it needs to be as inconspicuous as possible, yet if it is too inconspicuous it defeats its own object.

Beside the direct impact on the landscape of tourist accommodation and facilities, tourism has a considerable indirect influence, since every major planning decision has to be taken with one eye on the possible effect on the tourist trade. This has tended to produce a pleasanter, more carefully-planned environment than might otherwise have been the case.

Water Supply and Other Services

The large population of the islands, augmented every summer by thousands of visitors, consume a great deal of water, and the maintenance of an adequate supply is a problem. Apart from a sea-water distillation plant at La Rosière, Corbière, which supplies a small proportion of Jersey's needs, all the islands depend entirely on the rain that falls directly upon them. Some of this is caught as run-off, either by constructing reservoirs in the valleys or by pumping directly from the streams. The remainder is supplied by wells and boreholes.

Jersey has five main reservoirs: Grands Vaux in the valley of that name to the north of St. Helier; Handois, Dannemarche and Millbrook in Waterworks Valley, and Val de la Mare above St. Ouen's Bay. All are well kept and enhance the beauty of the valleys. However, the mains supply still covers little more than a quarter of the island, and further reservoirs will be required if it is to be extended.

In Guernsey the demand for water is greatly increased by the glasshouse industry. Both tomatoes and tourists require huge quantities of water in the summer, when rainfall is at its lowest. As much water as possible is therefore caught as run-off during the winter and stored against the summer. Two-thirds of the storage capacity is provided by the disused quarries of the north; the remaining third is stored in the reservoir above Mont Saint in St. Saviour's. This has tongues extending up three valleys and collects water from a large catchment area to the west and north of the airport. Below the dam is the original pumping station which abstracted water from the Rue a l'Or stream before the dam was built. Beside the old pumping station may be seen the remains of the old road from Perelle to St. Saviour's church, as the point where it disappears under the dam. The present road skirting the eastern arm of the reservoir is modern until the bend where it rejoins the old road as it emerges from the water. From here the road climbs straight up the hill to

Mont Varouf School. This section, although it is shown on the Richmond map of 1787, is Le Neuf Chemin, the new road, and it can be seen from the triangular fields on either side that it cuts diagonally across the original enclosures.

Another pumping station and treatment plant is at Kings Mills, on the site of Le Moulin de Bas. Treated water is stored in a covered reservoir which appears as a grassy bank by the water tower on the Forest Road. Most of Guernsey is covered by the mains supply, though there are many private wells and boreholes.

The smaller islands are almost totally dependent on water pumped directly or indirectly from wells. Alderney has the advantage of disused quarries for storage.

The urban areas of Jersey and Guernsey have a mains gas supply. This used to be town gas, made in the extensive gasworks by St. Saviour's Road, St. Helier, and at the Bouet, St. Peter Port. Town gas had to be discontinued as the change to natural gas in the United Kingdom meant that suitable appliances would no longer be available. Butane is now imported; this involves far less plant, and much of the area formerly occupied by the gasworks in both islands has been taken over by a variety of other industries.

The electricity generating stations now run on oil, and are sited near the harbours where this is imported. Jersey's generating station at La Collette, to the south of Fort Regent, was built in 1966. The huge chimney, a hexagonal prism of concrete, dominates the skyline from much of southern Jersey. The oil storage tanks and tanker berth are on land reclaimed from the sea by tipping refuse. The earlier power station, at Queen's Road, remains as a standby.

Guernsey's power station is to the north of St. Sampson's harbour, the port through which all the island's fuel oil is imported. The tanks for storing oil for other purposes are at Bulwer Avenue, to the south of the harbour. Much of the land between here and Mont Crevelt has been reclaimed from the sea and is now an industrial wasteland of scrap yards, warehouses and workshops. As far as possible electricity is distributed by underground cable, reducing unsightly overhead wires to a minimum. This does have the disadvantage of adding to the many services buried under the roads, which all too frequently have to be dug up and attended to. Alderney's generating station is at Crabby, on the brink of York Hill quarry, from which its draws its cooling water. That of Sark is beside the road at the top of Harbour Hill. Even Herm has a central generating station, in the farm buildings at the summit of the island.

The problem of refuse disposal has been touched on in connection with the quarries. Equally important is the disposal of sewage. That of Guernsey still goes into the sea, though not before it has been treated to render it harmless. The position of the main outfall, far out in Belle Grève Bay, is usually indicated by a flock of gulls. There is a smaller outfall and treatment plant at Creux Mahie, on the Torteval cliffs. Jersey's sewage is no longer pumped out to sea, but is treated in the States Sewerage Board plant at Bellozanne. The sludge is sold to farmers as a fertiliser, and enough methane gas is produced to generate the electricity which runs the plant.[8]

Chapter Eleven

THE LANDSCAPE OF TRANSPORT

There are few places so small that take so long to see as the Channel Islands.—E. D. Marquand, 1901

UNTIL THE BEGINNING of the 19th century the roads were narrow, twisting, muddy in winter, and dusty in summer; names like Rouge Bouillon and Rue Poudreuse recall these two extremes. Most of the medieval roads were local tracks connecting the settlement with the church, the fields with the mill, and the nearest suitable beach for collecting *vraic*. Some tracks were wide enough for a bullock cart; others could accommodate only a pedestrian or a donkey. Such lanes can still be found in all the islands. Some escaped forming part of the modern road network by becoming private property at some stage, often because a road was straightened and the landowner received the old road in return for the land for the new. Others are still public paths which have never been surfaced as they are too little used or too narrow for machinery to enter. Most are extremely attractive and searching them out provides an excuse, if one is needed, for a country walk. Two examples near the author's home in Guernsey are La Ruette de St. Germain and La Bissonerie. Both lie on a straight line between King's Mills and the former chapel of St. Germain, whose site is now a large quarry. La Ruette de St. Germain is a steep footpath, just wide enough for a donkey, running from la Rue de la Hougue to the summit of the quarry. La Bissonerie, wide enough for a rather slim cart, runs north from Le Pavé, near King's Mills. It was left as a backwater when the military road was cut from Les Eturs to the bottom of La Houguette Road.

Besides these local names there were wider roads connecting the settlements with central points such as markets and harbours. That main roads existed in Guernsey in the early Middle Ages is proved by the *Chevauchée de St. Michel*, the triennial inspection of the roads referred to in Chapter Four. This colourful ceremony is mentioned as being already ancient in a document of 1309.[1] In Continental Normandy the main roads belonged to the king, and presumably this was also the case in the Channel Islands. Several stretches of road in Guernsey are still known as Chemin le Roi, the king's highway. One of them, the lane running parallel to the Forest Road and a little to the north of it, would have been the route taken by the *Chevauchée* between St. Martin's and Le Bourg. In the Richmond map of 1787 it appears as of equal width to the Forest Road; today it is a quiet country lane, while the traffic hurtles by on the Forest Road, one field away, which was widened for military reasons in the early 19th century.

The narrow, local roads were in feudal times under the control of the seigneurs of the fiefs through which they passed. The function of seeing that the hedges were kept from encroaching on the roads and the surfaces were kept in repair was later taken over by the parish authorities. In Jersey this is still the case, and the parish boundaries thus have a special significance. One of the characteristic details of the Jersey scene is a boundary stone beside the road, inscribed with the initials of parish dignitaries, with a change in the road surface extending across the road, corresponding exactly with the parish boundary and showing where the road surfacing activities of one parish end and those of another begin. A particularly magnificent boundary stone is in La Rue des Haies, the lane running east from Sion, on the border between the parishes of St. John and Trinity. *Branchage*—the cutting of hedges bordering the roads—takes place in June and September.

In Guernsey the parish authorities are no longer concerned with repairing the roads, though they still have to ensure that the hedges are cut. The hedge-cutting is still done by the occupiers of the properties bordering the roads, twice a year in June and September.

Before the fields were enclosed there would have been no hedges bordering the lanes, which could change course from time to time to avoid particularly muddy patches. After the enclosures this became impossible, and the surface of the lanes in winter was often appalling. The repair of the roads, as in France, was by compulsory unpaid labour, or *corvée*. Every man with few exceptions owed six days' labour per year, and horse owners and farmers had to cart the materials. The system was abolished in Jersey in 1938, though for some time payments in money instead of actual labour had been allowed. In Sark *corvée* was not abolished until 1951.

The widths of the ancient roads would provide an interesting subject for study. According to de Gruchy,[2] Jersey had the Norman custom of classifying roads by their width into those of 24, 16, 12, 8 and 4 feet. To get the equivalent in English feet one inch per foot would have to be deducted. De Gruchy goes on to say that those of 24 feet or one Jersey perch were known as *perquages*, and ran from each parish church to the sea, affording a means of escape for fugitives from justice who had taken sanctuary in the church. They were immune from arrest as long as they remained on these roads. Joan Stevens[3] points out that the surviving fragments of these sanctuary paths are nearer four feet in width, and this would seem to be a far more realistic width for a path that was used by fugitives on foot. She suggests that the name *perquage* may refer not to the land measure but to a rod of perhaps four feet used to measure the width of roads, for all the widths mentioned by de Gruchy are multiples of four. There is a strong tradition, supported by very little documentary evidence, that sanctuary paths were used in Jersey in the Middle Ages. The advantage to the island was that it got rid of undesirable characters at no cost to the community. The practice ceased at the Reformation, as it was not in the Puritan character to allow sinners to get away with it.

The courses of the *perquages* have been worked out with some certainty in the parishes of St. Ouen, St. Peter and St. Laurence, and are fairly well established for St. John and St. Mary. Wherever possible, they follow the course of a stream. St. Ouen's *perquage* struck north from the church until it found the stream that flows into St. Ouen's Bay a quarter of a mile north of Kempt Tower. That of St. Peter crossed the land now occupied by the eastern end of the airport runway and followed the stream which descends the valley from Pont du Val to St. Aubin. The same course is followed by the old railway line from La Moye, and together they run immediately to the south of the main road down Mont Les Vaux to St. Aubin. The St. Laurence *perquage* struck west to the stream that runs down a valley to Tesson Mill. Here it was joined by the sanctuary paths from St. Mary and St. John, which are thought to have made use of St. Peter's Valley. The last half mile of the St. Laurence *perquage* may still be followed, as it crosses Goose Green March and emerges at St. Aubin's Bay to the east of Beaumont.

The outlaw who had taken sanctuary in St. Martin's church climbed the north wall of the churchyard by a stile, descended the valley and followed the stream to St. Catherine's Bay. The full course of the St. Saviour's path has yet to be worked out, but recently Mr. R. Cox has established the route of a *perquage* which followed a line west of Le Grand Douet, down the west of St. Saviour's Road behind Hemery Row and along Hilgrove Lane. This will probably prove to have originated at St. Saviour's church.[4] The shortest *perquage* was that of St. Brelade, whose church is by the shore. The sanctuary path consists of a flight of steps from the churchyard to the beach.

If sanctuary paths existed in Guernsey all record of them has been lost; the word *perquage* in that island means a list of feudal holdings.

A brief mention may be made of the farm vehicles which used the old roads, for survivors still form part of the landscape; they are still used, for instance, to carry water to cattle in the fields. They were built locally, and had evolved island characteristics. The boxcart was a sturdily-built two-wheeled vehicle used for collecting *vraic* and carting stone and manure. The hay-cart had a longer body and was fitted with ladders fore and aft to support the load. A winch at the rear was for tightening the rope which held the load. The four-wheeled van was introduced into Jersey in about 1875 and into Guernsey at about the same time. It was used for general farm duties and for carrying barrels of potatoes to St. Helier and baskets of tomatoes to St. Peter Port. The vans built in the two islands were of very similar design, and of lighter build than the boxcart.

The Military Roads

The medieval road networks of Jersey and Guernsey seem to have survived virtually unchanged until the early 19th century, when the threat of invasion by the French made it imperative to improve the roads so that troops and artillery could be moved rapidly within the islands. By a coincidence this was also the time when the macadamised road surface was invented. The improvements in the roads were brought about by the energetic efforts of the two Lieutenant-Governors, Sir George Don in Jersey, and Sir John Doyle in Guernsey.

Between 1806 and 1814 General Don built 19 military roads in Jersey, including most of the main radial roads still in use today.[5] The first direct road from St. Helier to Gorey was built by Don in 1806—the section from Grouville church to Gorey is still known as Rue à Don (or more correctly Route Don). To gain access to the southern end of Grouville Bay he built La Grande Route de St. Clement (St. Clement Inner Road), with La Route des Côtils as a link road between this and Grouville church. Rozel Bay was reached via St. Saviour's Hill, La Grande Route de St. Martin to St. Martin's church, and La Grande Route de Rozel to the bay. St. Martin's church was linked to Gorey by La Grand Route de Faldouet. Trinity Road was built as a direct route to Trinity church and Bouley Bay.

Until 1810 there was no road between St. Helier and St. Aubin; the only direct route was along the beach when the tide permitted. In 1810 the St. Aubin's main road was opened as far as La Haule. One then had to climb Le Mont au Roux and turn left to continue down St. Aubin's High Street. The coast road from La Haule to St. Aubin's Harbour was not built until 1844, when the High Street became the quiet and unspoilt backwater that it is today. La Grande Route de St. Laurent left the St. Aubin's road at Millbrook for St. Laurence's Arsenal, and the new road continued as far as St. John's church, with a branch from Carrefour Selous to St. Mary's church and Grève de Lecq. The next radial road left the coast at Bel Royal for St. Peter's Valley, then up Les Routeurs to join yet another military road, to St. Peter and St. Ouen. This latter road is the one that today serves the airport. It begins as Beaumont New Road, passes St. Peter's church as La Grande Route de St. Pierre and continues to St. Ouen's Manor as La Grande Route de St. Ouen. The military road then turned left to pass the parish church and continued down Le Mont Matthieu to emerge at the coast just south of Kempt Tower. Don's original road passed very close to St. Ouen's Manor, having been built in about 1810 along the line of what had been a private drive. Some years later, in 1878, the seigneur gave the land for the present main road, which passes at a respectful distance to the east of the manor, in return for the old road which became once more a private drive. A military link road ran from St. Peter's church to St. Aubin, via Rue des Landes and St. Peter's Arsenal. The most westerly radial road ran from St. Aubin, up Mont Les Vaux and down Mont Sohier to St. Brelade's Bay, then up again via Red Houses to St. Peter's Barracks, on the site of the airport.

An integral part of the programme of road improvements that was going on at the same time in Guernsey was the draining of the Braye du Valle, the tidal channel that separated the northern part of the island from the rest. Doyle was concerned that the French might land on the broad sands of L'Ancresse Bay and establish themselves on the northern island, Le Clos du Valle, protected by the muddy Braye from attack from Guernsey. He remarked that he did not know whether he should be a general or an admiral, for it would entirely depend on the state of the tide whether the battle would be a military or a naval one. Accordingly he persuaded the British government to pay the cost of draining the Braye, and work began in 1806.

The Braye du Valle ran from Grand Havre in the west to the bay that is now St. Sampson's Harbour. Its northern shore ran from immediately below the Vale church—the present road skirting the south of the church runs along the old shoreline—to St. Sampson's Bridge, the only crossing place that could be used at any state of the tide. The southern shore ran from L'Islet, which was a salt-marsh, south as far as the Brae Side traffic lights. A creek which had formerly run west towards Capelles had been converted into saltpans, bounded by Salines Road, La Rue Sauvage and Basses Capelles Road. Here salt was extracted from seawater. A dam, Le Grand Fort, separated the saltpans from the Braye. It would have contained sluices which allowed the saltpans to flood at selected tides. Le Grand Fort still exists as a raised footpath to the west of the Corbet playing field. To the east of Brae Side was a large saltmarsh, crossed today by the Route Militaire, and beyond this was another area of saltpans which still bears that name.

Before draining this extensive area, substantial barriers had to be constructed at each end. The present coast road across the southern end of Grand Havre can be clearly seen to make use of such a barrier. It is still called Le Pont St. Michel, the name of an ancient causeway, only usable at low tide, across the western end of the Braye. Behind Le Pont St. Michel is the Vale Pond, the last undrained fragment of the Braye du Valle. This expanse of brackish water and saltmarsh—a rare habitat in the Channel Islands—is run on behalf of the owners by La Société Guernesiaise as a nature reserve.

To reach the newly accessible Clos du Valle Doyle built a military road, still called the Route Militaire, from the Halfway to the Vale church and on to L'Ancresse Bay. Another military road followed Belle Grève Bay and Grande Maison Road to St. Sampson's Bridge. Later, this was continued along Vale Avenue, turning left into Braye Road and extending as far as Camp du Roi and Landes du Marché. Braye Road and the Route Militaire cross at right-angles in the midst of the Braye du Valle. The sections built on reclaimed land, with no previous roads to follow or wayleave to be obtained, are notable for their extreme straightness.

The draining of the Braye yielded 732 vergees, or about 300 acres, of useful land. William Berry, author of a particularly pompous history of Guernsey, published in 1815, wrote enthusiastically that 'corn now grows, and cattle graze, where, seven years ago, vessels might have sailed'.[6] The reclaimed land was sold by the government and the proceeds, amounting to £5,000, were given to the States to help pay for two new main roads, from town to Rocquaine, and from town to Vazon. These, like most of Doyle's roads, were to have a main carriageway 14 feet in width, and a footpath four feet wide. Work began on them in 1810.

The Vazon Road ran via Les Gravées, the Castel church and La Houguette to the coast at Vazon Tower. The Rocquaine Road ran by way of Fort George, Sausmarez Manor, St. Martin's rectory, Le Bourg and Les Paysans Road to L'Erée. The construction of these two roads, totalling 11 miles, involved the purchase of 12 vergées of additional land and the bringing in of 35,200 cartloads of hardcore, at a total cost of £8,733.[7]

In 1812, the existing military roads were linked by a road from Longstore to St. Martin's via Amherst, Queen's Road, Mount Row, Ville au Roi and Les Merriennes, and from Mount Row a new road penetrated into the wilds of St. Andrew's. This led to an alarm gun which was placed somewhere between St. Andrew's church and the Hougue Fouque. In an emergency the gun would be fired and the island immediately placed under martial law. The following year the route we call the Cobo Road was built, from the bottom of the Rohais as far as La Planque, near Saumarez Park, and the following year again a road was built from La Planque, crossing the Vazon Road at La Houguette and continuing via King's Mills, Le Mont Saint and Les Rouvets, to join the Rocquaine road near L'Erée.

Grey granite milestones were erected on the main military roads, bearing in raised Roman numerals the distance in miles from the Town Church. Twenty-six of these stones are still to be seen, on seven routes. Some are built into walls, like the two-mile stone in the churchyard of the Castel church, which may be contemplated while one is waiting at the traffic lights. Others, like the five-mile stone at Landes du Marché, are free-standing. The highest numbered stone, opposite Les Adams Chapel near L'Erée, is seven miles from the Town Church.

The military roads of Jersey and Guernsey were not completely new, for wherever possible they followed the course of existing roads which were widened, straightened and levelled to an extent never before seen in the islands. Where no road existed land was bought, or exchanged for a stretch of public road that was no longer required. New sections are easy to see as they were laid out with a line and are perfectly straight, unlike the medieval roads which antedate the enclosures and still wind along their original courses. Often a corner is cut off by driving the road diagonally across a field; this is betrayed by the triangular pieces of field which remain each side of the road. In title deeds and feudal documents the two parcels of land will bear the same name. In many places boundary walls were built for the properties on either side; in other cases hedges were thrown up and planted with trees. In several places, where a stream flowed across the original road, it has been left as an *abrevoir*, together with enough of the old road to give access to it from the new.

Don and Doyle have always been remembered with gratitude and affection in their respective islands for the great improvements they brought about, and indeed it would be difficult to over-estimate the impact of the new roads on the everyday life of the islands, quite apart from their military role. At the time, however, they had to use their considerable persuasive powers to the full to achieve the improvements. The British government paid some of the expenses, but much of the money had to be raised locally by various forms of taxation. Doyle, in trying to persuade Guernseymen to submit to this, had to point out that the island was 200 years behind the rest of civilised Europe. When, despite the opposition, the first few roads were in use, islanders saw the benefits for themselves and road improvement schemes began to be put forward in every parish.

While the military roads were being built in Jersey and Guernsey, the improved method of road surfacing invented by John McAdam was being successfully tried out in England. The first record I can find of macadamisation in the Channel Islands is in 1824, when the constable of St. Brelade, Sir John Le Couteur, introduced the system to the western parishes of Jersey.[8] The first section of road to be treated was near Le Pont du Val. In 1830 the main street in St. Aubin was macadamised, and St. Peter's Valley and many country lanes had already been so treated. The brief day of the horse-drawn carriage had arrived, to be brought to an end early in the present century, in every island except Sark, by motor transport.

The Motor Age

Roadmaking on the scale of the 1810s has never again been seen in the islands; modern roadmaking consists almost entirely of minor adjustments designed to keep a growing number of motor vehicles circulating on the early 19th-century road system. The island of Sark made the conscious decision not to allow motor transport, with the result that horse-drawn carriages are still one of the main attractions of the island. Tractors are, however, permitted for agricultural purposes, and naturally the word agricultural is interpreted fairly broadly. Apart from the tractors, with its quiet, dusty tar-less roads and bicycles leaning against the wall outside shops and houses, Sark retains an atmosphere that has not been experienced in the rest of the British Isles since the beginning of the century.

Alderney's motor traffic has never been on the same scale as the larger islands; it has, however, reached the point where traffic has had to be banished from Victoria Street in the summer, and to proceed up hill only at other times. The streets of St. Anne and the *venelles* leading out to the Blaye are undoubtedly medieval. The main coastal roads were probably built as part of the Victorian defences. The Germans improved some of them, for the same reason.

Since the first motor car arrived in Jersey in 1899, the people of Jersey and Guernsey have taken enthusiastically to motor transport. To cover the relatively short distances within the islands everybody who can possibly drive now has a private car, with the result that snarl-ups are frequent, there is a permanent parking problem, and the motor car has become the most obtrusive and over-bearing item in the landscape. Jersey has attempted to alleviate the parking problem by providing multi-storey car-parks, positioned so as not to intrude upon the skyline. Guernsey has so far resisted the pressure for these, taking the view that the number of cars would immediately increase to fill the available spaces.

Very few new roads have been built in the present century. The most notable in Guernsey is the Val des Terres, which climbs in sweeping curves from the South Esplanade to Fort Road, providing an alternative route between the town and the south of the island. The road was cut through former War Department land, and generously planted with trees. It was opened in 1935. In Jersey La Route du Nord was built largely during the Occupation, with the object of keeping the local work force fully employed and thus not available to the Germans. This imaginative road opened up for the first time a section of Jersey's north coast, previously shut in by private property. The original plan was to build a coast road from Les Mouriers to La Saline, in St. John's parish. The first stage was completed round La Saline and foundations were laid as far as Sorel, but no progress could be made further to the west, which was inside the German's military zone. Today the road runs from Frémont Point to Ronez point, through some of Jersey's most magnificent coastal scenery.

Trams and Railways

The railways of Jersey and the trams of Guernsey have long disappeared, but traces of them remain in the landscape in the form of cuttings, embankments and converted station buildings. Only in Alderney is a railway still running. Jersey formerly had two railways, running east and west from St. Helier. The Jersey Railway, running round the bay between the town and St. Aubin, was opened in 1870. The town terminus was the grey granite building at the Weighbridge, now used as a tourist information office. In 1899 the line was extended to La Corbière. The Jersey Railway stopped running in 1936, killed by the motor bus and a disastrous fire which destroyed the St. Aubin's station. The only building to survive was the station hotel, now the parish hall of St. Brelade. Today the site of the station is a garden. The four miles of track from St. Aubin to Corbière have since been transformed into an extremely pleasant walk. The Germans re-laid the lines for building their fortifications, but they have again been removed. From St. Aubin's station the line, now the Corbière Walk, ran up Mont Les Vaux to the south of the road, plunged under the road at the hairpin bend, and continued up the valley to the Quennevais. It then ran past the golf club house and over the fields of La Moye to the station at Corbière, now a house and cafe.

The Jersey Eastern Railway Company opened a line from town to Gorey Village in 1873, and in 1891 the line was extended to Gorey Pier. Trains ran until 1929, when the company could no longer compete with motor transport. The town terminus was at Snow Hill, immediately under the north cliff of Fort Regent. The line ran to the coast just east of Le Hocq Point, followed the St. Clement Coast Road as far as Le Bourg, then turned inland to pass the church of St. Peter, La Rocque, as it turned north to cross Gorey Common. The line of the railway as it approached Gorey Harbour is now occupied by gardens; the terminus station was near the present bus shelter.

In Guernsey a steam tramway was opened in 1879, running between the harbours of St. Peter Port and St. Sampson. The town terminus was opposite the Picquet House and the line ended at St. Sampson's Bridge. It was a single line, with loops to allow passing at the Salerie, Les Banques and Bulwer Avenue. Electric trams were introduced in 1892. The tram sheds at Hougue à la Perre are still in use as warehouses; the tramlines can be seen in the concrete floor of the doorway. Opposite the sheds, on the seaward side of the road, was a hillock, Hougue à la Perre, over which the tramlines ran. The trams had difficulty in negotiating the gradient, and steam trams sometimes had to retreat to level ground and raise steam before making a second attempt to surmount it. The hougue, with Martello Tower No. 1 upon it, was demolished in 1905.

The trams stopped running in 1934 and the lines were removed, only to be replaced in 1943 by the Germans, who built a railway to carry the materials for their defences. The main line ran from town to St. Sampson's and continued to L'Islet. From here a branch ran north across L'Ancresse Common to the coast—its course can still be seen as a levelled pathway crossing the golf course. The main line continued round the west coast from L'Islet to L'Erée. Traces may still be seen, for instance in the cutting back of a rocky spur at Albecq, and a cutting now used as a silage clamp at Le Catioroc. No attempt was made to extend the system to the more elevated south coast.

In Jersey the German railway system was more extensive. It followed the old Jersey Railway line from town to St. Aubin, then continued to Corbière, with a branch to Ronez Quarry on the north coast, the main source of stone for the fortifications.[9] From this branch another ran down to St. Ouen's Bay at Rue de la Marette; traces of it can be seen near the reservoir and where it crossed over the road at Bethesda Methodist church. A narrow gauge line ran the length of St. Ouen's Bay, from the quarries at L'Etacq to La Pulente. Another narrow gauge line followed the course of the Jersey Eastern Railway from St. Helier to Fort William in Grouville Bay. This left only the northern cliffs uncatered for.

The Alderney railway, the only line still running in the Channel Islands, was built for the purpose of transporting stone from Mannez Quarry to the breakwater, work on which began in 1847 and continued until 1864. The railway has continued in use until the present day, for the force of the waves is such that fresh stone has continually to be tipped over the seaward edge of the breakwater, to protect the foundations. The Germans used the railway for their construction work, and after the war the light engine, Molly II, continued to pull trucks of stone to the breakwater. Recently the railway has begun carrying summer visitors. From Mannez Quarry the line runs to White Gates, where it crosses the road by a level crossing. It continues past Battery Quarry and behind the houses of New Town to the depot at Fort Grosnez. The line runs along the breakwater on the upper, seaward level, so that the trucks can tip their stone directly over the edge.

Harbours, Lighthouses and Airports

Enough has been said in previous chapters to convey the fact that Channel Islanders have always been accomplished seamen, earning their living by fishing, trading, privateering, shipbuilding, or growing crops which have to be exported by sea. In all these activities the harbours have played a vital role. The harbours vary considerably, both in their siting and aspect, and because the economy of each island has developed differently. The common factors shared by them all are the extremely wide tide range, and the hard granite of which the piers are built.

The two main harbours of Guernsey provide an interesting comparison. St. Peter Port began as a completely open beach, transformed over some seven centuries into a vast artificial basin which now handles all the maritime traffic of the island except bulk cargoes. St. Sampson's Harbour began as a natural creek, nearly half a mile in length and forming the eastern entrance to the Braye du Valle. It was sheltered from almost every direction and merely had to be equipped with quays to facilitate the loading and unloading of vessels. It has always been assumed that St. Sampson's was the island's first harbour, but there is no concrete evidence for this, and the recent discovery of a wreck of Roman age in the roadstead of St. Peter Port causes one to suspect that the town harbour may be several centuries older than was previously thought. Certainly St. Peter Port Harbour existed in the 13th century, for in 1275 Edward I granted permission to levy a duty on all ships using the harbour, in order to build a new pier. The money seems to have gone astray, and it was not until 1590 that a pier was completed. This was the south pier, now covered by the Albert Pier; it sheltered the original harbour, now the Victoria Marina, from the worst seas, which come on this east-facing coast from the south-east. The harbour was converted into a basin of about four acres by a north pier, finished in 1750.

The west side of the basin was still a beach—the tall, gabled houses and cellars which still face the harbour stood on the beach, and at high tide the sea washed up the *vennelles* between the houses. By the beginning of the 19th century a quay had been built along the front, with an arch over Cow Lane, allowing sewage to flow into the harbour, and horses and carts to pass from the harbour bed into the town.

By now the harbour was totally inadequate, besides being dangerous when gales blew from the east. Throughout the first half of the 19th century there was increasing agitation to extend the harbour, but it was not until 1853 that work started in earnest. It was the relative prosperity of the sister isle, which had already built its harbour, that finally persuaded the reluctant States to put the work in hand. Numerous plans were considered and rejected, and even while the work was in progress the plans continued to be changed.[10] A new south pier was built out towards Castle Cornet; the broad Castle Emplacement where numerous boats are now laid up for the winter was intended for the ship-building yards which had been displaced by the harbour works at the landward end of the pier. The model yacht pond which covers much of the emplacement was built in 1887 to commemorate Victoria's jubilee. It was demolished in the First World War to make way for a French seaplane base, and in the Second World War it was used by the Germans as a park for their vehicles. Today there is pressure to abolish it for a third time to make way for cars.

A floating dock was originally intended between the Albert and the Castle Piers—the lock-gate would have been at the north-west corner of the Castle Emplacement. This was abandoned because of the nature of the bottom, but it accounts for the unfinished appearance of the wall at this point. The steam-packet berth was to have been at the north-eastern corner of the Emplacement, but again plans were changed. The decision to extend the St. Julian's breakwater as far as the White Rock was taken in 1862, and this eventually provided the berth for the steam-packets. The 'New Jetty', where today's car-ferries berth, was constructed of concrete piling in 1926. With this and other minor modifications the Victorian harbour, covering an area of some 80 acres, was adequate for Guernsey's needs for 100 years. It is only with the expansion of the locally-based fishing fleet and of the number of visiting yachts within the last decade that it has begun to be inadequate.

The dressed stone for the faces of the piers came from a variety of sources including Crevichon and, latterly, Les Vardes quarry. The infilling material was excavated from Les Terres and La Valette, where a promenade was constructed to take advantage of the view of Havelet Bay, Castle Cornet, Herm, Jethou, and Sark. This involved drilling two tunnels: the first, near the Bathing Places, collapsed, so that today the road passes through a cutting. The second, now occupied by an aquarium, affords from its far end a view over Soldier's Bay.

St. Sampson's, as we have seen, owes its existence as a modern harbour to the stone industry. As recently as 1800 it was a creek bounded by sandy bays to the north and south. The parish church was hard by the southern beach, and a breakwater at Mont Crevelt protected the haven from the south-east. The creek had a soft, muddy bottom on which ships were beached, to be loaded at low water. This mud must have been replaced from the Braye du Valle as fast as it was scoured away by the sea, for when the Bridge had been built and the Braye drained, the mud began to recede and boulders appeared in the bed of the harbour.[11] These became such a hazard that owners refused to allow their ships to put in at St. Sampson's. Accordingly in 1820 the first quay was built—the old North Pier which projects into the harbour from the north side. It was used at first largely for the export of oysters, but with the expansion of the stone trade it was soon inadequate. In 1841 the south quay was built straight across the sandy bay on which the church stood, the space between the church and the quay being filled with ships' ballast and quarry rubble. The north-facing arm at the seaward end was necessary as it was found that ships tied alongside thrashed about dangerously when a sea was running.

There followed a period when the harbour was badly neglected and there was even talk of building a railway to carry stone from the north to St. Peter Port for shipment. Finally a programme of improvements was carried out between 1860 and 1880 which resulted in the harbour we see today. The Bridge was incorporated into a quay. The North Quay was built across the northern bay, and again ships' ballast was used to fill in behind it. Today ships in need of ballast simply pump in water, but in the days of sail ships returning unladen had to carry solid ballast, often chalk or clay, and the disposal of this became a serious problem. When the North and South Sides had been filled in, an area of 11½ vergées was reclaimed from the sea below Vale Castle. This became the site of Griffith's stone-crushing plant. Ballast has been dumped in many other places around the northern shores of Guernsey; this accounts for many of the stones on the beaches that are obviously not of local origin.

With the decline in the stone trade St. Sampson's was faced with another period of stagnation, but since 1964 practically all Guernsey's bulk cargoes, such as oil, coal and timber, have been handled there, leaving St. Peter Port free for passenger traffic, tomatoes, containers, and yachts.

Jersey, though a far larger island, does not seem to have had a harbour suitable for ocean-going ships until 1700, when a pier was completed at St. Aubin's Tower. There were, however, several havens around the coast that were ideal for smaller vessels. Gorey, the natural port for the short run to Carteret on the adjacent coast of Normandy, is mentioned in a document of 1274. The present pier was built in the early part of the 19th century and owes its existence to a thriving oyster fishery which grew up at that time, exploiting an oyster bed not far from the shore. The cottages in Gorey Village were built to house the labour which was imported to fish, grade and pack the oysters, and Gouray church was built for them, since most were English-speaking and could not understand the services in the parish church. The oyster industry was destroyed by over-fishing in the 1860s and its place was taken by ship-building, until this, too, died with the passing of wooden ships.[12] Today the beautiful harbour and quay, in the shelter of Mont Orgueil Castle, is used mainly for tourism and pleasure.

The pier in Rozel Bay was built in 1829 to accommodate oyster boats which could not find room at Gorey; Bouley Bay was also used for this purpose. Two other north coast bays—Grève de Lecq, used once by small boats to Guernsey and Sark, and Bonne Nuit, said to have been a haunt of smugglers—were each equipped with a pier in 1872.

In the early 17th century Jersey's New World cod fishery, already referred to (p. 114), found the harbours of Jersey so inadequate that the fleet began to winter in St. Malo. For this reason, a pier was built at St. Aubin's Tower, projecting from the islet on which the tower stands. The pier was finished in 1700. The only approach to it was across the beach at low water, and it was not until 1754 that the present south pier of St. Aubin's Harbour was begun, followed by the north pier in 1819. The town, as we have seen, owes its existence to the harbour.

St. Helier, though a far older town than St. Aubin, was without a harbour for longer and its expansion was accordingly delayed. Imported goods had to be brought across the sands from St. Aubin until the first pier was built—this was the Old South Pier, begun in 1700, but not fit for use until the mid–18th century. Even then goods had to be carried half a mile, partly across the beach, to the centre of the town. The Old North Pier was begun in 1790; this was incorporated later into the New North Quay. When Le Quai des Marchands, in front of the Commercial Buildings, was finished in 1818, the inner harbour was complete, and at last the town had access to its harbour at any state of the tide.

The town now began to expand rapidly, and soon, as in Guernsey, a much larger harbour was needed. Unlike Guernsey, however, very little time was wasted and the first pier of the outer harbour, the Victoria Pier, was opened by the queen herself in 1846. The following year the Albert Pier, where today the car-ferries and hydrofoils berth, was begun. This gave an outer harbour twice the size of the inner, but it was still tidal and ships arriving at low water had to wait in the roads until there was enough water to enter. Several ambitious plans were put forward for a deep-water harbour; the one adopted, in 1871, was by Sir John Coode, who proposed a breakwater extending south-eastwards from Elizabeth Castle, and another, three-quarters of a mile long, projecting south-westwards from La Collette to meet it. The Castle Breakwater was built, though not according to plan, but work on La Collette Pier had to be abandoned after repeated storm damage, and only the base of it remains. Eventually the States contented themselves with deepening the harbour they already had, and in 1882 the dredgers moved in.

The magnificent Victorian harbours of Jersey and Guernsey have played a major part in the islands' history since they were built, and have been largely responsible for their prosperity. Although many passengers now travel by air, the roll-on roll-off car-ferries have brought renewed passenger traffic to the harbours, and bulk cargoes such as oil and timber still have to be imported by sea, as well as most consumer goods, now in containers. Pleasure boating has greatly increased in the last few years, and the visiting yachtsman is encouraged as a species of tourist which spends money in the islands and yet does not require a bed. The only way to accommodate the number of yachts that now come every summer is in marinas, but because of the considerable tide range these have to be constructed on the lines of a floating dock, which cannot be entered at low water. Mention has already been made of the marina at La Collette which has recently been provided as part of a land reclamation scheme. In Guernsey there is a private marina in a disused quarry at Beaucette, and the States have provided two in the town harbour. The Victoria Marina, for visiting yachts, is simply the old inner harbour, provided with pontoons and a sill to prevent the marina drying at low water. The Albert Marina, for local boats, occupies part of the Albert Dock, which was originally intended to be a floating dock. The marina is separated from the rest of the dock by an ugly concrete wall. Pressure is now building up in Guernsey for a fourth marina.

If the Victorian harbours, built with local money after considerable deliberation, have been an unqualified success the same cannot be said of the 'harbours of refuge', built after very much less deliberation with British taxpayers' money. In 1842 a Joint Services report recommended that 'harbours of refuge' should be built at Longis in Alderney, Fermain in Guernsey, and St. Catherine's Bay in Jersey. They were to be capable of accommodating a large fleet, and were ostensibly for shelter in bad weather, though in reality they would have been naval bases. Guernsey's harbour was dropped, and Alderney's was eventually begun at Braye, but Jersey's harbour at St. Catherine's went ahead, despite the almost universally held local opinion that it would immediately silt up. By 1847 work was in full swing at Braye and St. Catherine's.

The north arm of St. Catherine's harbour was built out from Verclut headland. The original plan had been to quarry away the headland to provide stone for the breakwater, but the officers of ordnance protested that they needed the headland to mount their guns to cover the harbour. Accordingly, quarrying took place further inland on both sides, isolating the headland and producing the curious horseshoe-shaped ravine through which the inner of the two roads passes. The south arm of the harbour was begun opposite Archirondel Tower and soon reached the islet on which the tower stands. The stone was to have come from the quarry on the coast just north of the tower, but this proved to be useless for the purpose and a quarry was opened in the valley below Rozel Manor, with a railway to carry the stone to Archirondel. The cottage, still named L'Hôpital, immediately to the north of the slipway in the centre of the bay, was used as a hospital by the contractors.

Work on the south pier was suddenly abandoned at a point only a few yards beyond Archirondel Tower. No explanation was ever given—it has been suggested that there was insufficient depth of water.[13] Work continued on the north breakwater, which was completed to its full length in 1855. After repeatedly refusing to buy it the States eventually accepted the breakwater, useless for anything except angling, as a gift.

Alderney's first harbour was almost certainly in Longis Bay, sheltered from westerly winds and defended first by the Nunnery and then by Essex Castle. In 1736 Henry Le Mesurier built the first stone jetty at Braye; this was the angled pier projecting into the bay from near the *Sea View* hotel. Henry used it for smuggling spirits, but his wife disliked Alderney so much that they retired to Guernsey. Henry's brother, John, who succeeded him as hereditary governor of Alderney, made a fortune privateering, bringing in many prizes to the jetty at Braye. The original jetty, built of large, rough boulders, was enlarged and strengthened in 1840 as the Douglas Quay. But the pier had altered the tidal flow and the sands of Braye accumulated in the Le Mesurier's harbour to such an extent that they eventually choked it.

The next harbour works in chronological order were the preparations for the 'harbour of refuge'. It was planned to convert the whole of Braye Bay into a gigantic harbour by building two great breakwaters, one from Grosnez Head and the other from some point to the east of the bay, which moved in stages, as the plans grew more and more extravagant, from Roselle Point to Chateau à l'Etoc. The western breakwater, the only one built, was begun in 1847. The most attractive inner harbour, though it has the appearance of being much older, was built for sheltering and loading the hopper barges which built up the bank on which the breakwater stands.

By 1856 the breakwater was 900 yards long. From here on, in much deeper water, the work was slower and constantly interrupted by storms, for nobody had appreciated the tremendous force of the seas that it would have to withstand. Nevertheless, the work continued, changing direction slightly to the north to accommodate the larger harbour that the Admiralty was by then demanding. Finally in 1864 the breakwater was completed to a length of 1,600 yards.[14] The last 600 yards sustained such repeated storm damage that it was abandoned, and all that is left today is a dangerous submerged bank, projecting beyond the breakwater, but slightly to the north of its present line. The remaining 1,000 yards were retained and are still kept in repair, using the railway line that was constructed for its building.

The foundation of the breakwater consists of a vast mound of rubble. On this are laid several courses of giant concrete blocks, with blocks of granite on the seaward side. The rest of the structure is of Mannez sandstone. It consists of two walls: the outer, facing the sea, is 14 feet higher than the inner, which forms the quay on the harbour side. At intervals niches in the vertical wall between the two levels provide shelter for those unfortunate enough to be caught on the breakwater when the sea begins to break over it.

Today the breakwater is maintained by the Department of the Environment. Though the 'harbour of refuge' came to nothing, the breakwater does provide the shelter without which the present harbour and jetty would be unusable. The jetty used today by cargo boats and hydrofoils was begun in 1895, after a long and bitter dispute over who should pay for it, and whether it was needed anyway. In the end the British government paid; in return the island undertook to contribute £100 per annum towards the cost of running the Crown offices, court house and prison. The jetty was lengthened in iron by the Germans. A start has been made at demolishing it, but the piles were embedded in concrete and wounds are at present being licked before the next attack is launched.

The original landing place in Sark was probably l'Eperquerie, which took its name from the poles or *perques* used for drying fish. Soon after the Elizabethan colonisation Helier de Carteret decided that the bay now called Creux Harbour would make an ideal haven, but first access would have to be provided from the land. This was not achieved until 1588, after Helier's death, when a tunnel was driven through the headland to the foot of the valley now called Harbour Hill. The name Creux, a cave or hole, refers to this tunnel. Creux Harbour must be one of the most beautiful in the world—of intimate size and surrounded by towering cliffs. The present outer wall dates from the 1880s. The harbour dries out at low spring tides, and with the increase in tourist traffic between the World Wars the need for a deep-water harbour became apparent. The new harbour of La Maseline, in the next bay to the north, was built in 1947.

The rocks and tides of Channel Island waters are notoriously treacherous, and lighthouses have played an important part in local maritime history. The first recorded light was on Maître Ile, part of Les Ecrehous reef between Jersey and Carteret. A small priory existed on the islet and a document of 1309 stated that the monks kept a light burning to warn shipping of the reef. The ruins of the priory are still to be seen. The most notorious reef, close to the Channel shipping lane and seven miles west of Alderney, are Les Casquets. The name means cascades, and certainly the worst seas the Channel Island ferries usually encounter are as they round the Casquets. Three lighthouses were built on the reef in 1785, lit first by coal, then oil. In 1877, when Trinity House accepted responsibility for them, one was improved and the other two were shortened and used for other purposes. They are still visible, painted white, from as far away as Guernsey.

The Hanois was, until a helicopter landing stage was built on its head, a classically-shaped lighthouse. The Hanois reef, a mile to the west of Pleinmont in Guernsey, had claimed many ships when Trinity House began the lighthouse in 1860. Cornish granite and Cornish masons were imported; the stone was dressed and fitted together on the newly-completed Castle Breakwater and towed from St. Peter Port to Les Hanois by barge.[15] The lighthouse keepers' cottages, on the road from the *Imperial* hotel to Les Pezeries, were built at the same time. The lighthouse is not visible from the cottages, but the wives used to signal to their husbands from La Varde Rock, the spur immediately to the west. It is still an excellent vantage point. When the Castle Breakwater was no longer required by the Cornish masons, the attractive battlemented lighthouse on the end of the breakwater was built in 1866 to the design of the local artist Peter Le Lièvre; the corbelled light on the White Rock was erected two years later.

La Corbière lighthouse, at the south-western extremity of Jersey, is interesting as one of the first ever to be built in concrete. It was first lit in 1874.

The lighthouses of Alderney and Sark are both on dry land and both were built in 1912. Alderney's light, of traditional design, but built of brick, stands near Quesnard Point at the north-east corner of the island. The Sark lighthouse stands halfway down the cliff on the headland to the north of La Maseline Harbour.

The first air services in the Channel Island have left no trace in the landscape as they used the beaches or, in the case of a brief flying-boat service to Southampton, St. Peter Port Harbour. The low-lying area at L'Erée in Guernsey, inland from the coast road as it rounds the bend past Fort Saumarez, was cleared of hazards and briefly used for flying in the 1930s. It is still known as L'Erée Aerodrome.

The first airport in the islands was opened in Alderney in 1935, using a flat, grassy stretch of the Blaye. The service operated only in summer, mainly for guests at the *Grand* hotel on Butes. After the Occupation it was re-opened, using Rapides. When the States took over the airport it was considerably extended and today the great majority of arrivals in Alderney are by air, using the Trilanders of Aurigny Air Services.

The States of Jersey airport at St. Peter was opened in 1937; the following year it handled 17,400 passengers. Since the war it has grown in stages as aircraft have become larger, and the number of passengers has increased. Further enlargement of the runway would be difficult as its western end has now reached the brink of the escarpment above St. Ouen's Bay, while its eastern end approaches a busy main road and built-up area.

The States of Guernsey airport at La Villiaze opened a few months before the outbreak of war in 1939. By modern standards it was comparatively modest in extent. Even so, it covered 126 acres and seven miles of hedgebank had to be demolished. Since the war the airport has been continually enlarged and updated. In 1959 it was extended considerably to the west and a concrete runway was laid. Since then there have been two major enlargements of the terminal building.

All three airports make use of the plateaux. In Alderney the open fields of the Blaye needed little modification, and in Jersey the airport was partly built on open fields. In Guernsey the whole area of the airport had been enclosed, but the removal of the hedges has produced a plateau landscape with distant views of sea and sky that probably approaches the landscape of the open fields, though there would certainly have been more trees beyond the fields.

Chapter Twelve

A LANDSCAPE TO ENJOY?

At one time any land of little or no agricultural value and useless for building development was derogatively termed waste land. It is now becoming more widely understood that some of this land, the sand dunes, the remaining marshy areas, the inland wooded côtils, the cliffs and the heathlands, are of immense importance.—Frances Le Sueur, 1976.

AS OFFSHORE ISLANDS of Continental Normandy which have for so many centuries been politically British, it is not surprising that the Channel Islands have a landscape unlike that to be found anywhere else. Parts of the Cotentin peninsula have similar rocks, vegetation and climate, but the history of the two areas since the political separation in 1204 has been very different, and this has been reflected in the landscape. The small fields of the Contentin, for instance, have a characteristic wooden gate of three horizontal bars and many vertical bars, with a hinge post taller than the rest of the gate, and a diagonal bar running from its head to the foot at the outer end. The islands have no traditional gate, since the cattle were tethered; the hedges were for shelter rather than for containing livestock, and openings are still commonly closed by a piece of old pipe or the ladder from a hay-cart. Where island fields are equipped with a proper gate, it is in tubular steel of the now universal English design. Again, the Cotentin fields nearly all have a standing stone in the centre. Whatever its origin (and folklorists would doubtless maintain it was to encourage the animals to breed) the function of the stone today is for scratching. This would be of no use in a field where the animals are tethered, and it is not found in the Channel Islands. Similarly there are differences in every other aspect of the scenery—the cattle in the fields, the road verges, the overhead wires, the houses and churches. Only in the wild scenery of the cliffs is the difference undetectable.

If we compare the islands with the United Kingdom the differences are even more marked. The only comparable areas in rural England are the granite regions of the South-West, and particularly the Lizard, but again the different histories have resulted in different buildings, roads and field patterns. In particular, the Channel Islands are mercifully protected by a difficult sea or air journey from the extreme tourist pressure to which Cornwall is subjected.

As this book has attempted to show, the islands reflect in their present-day landscape the physical features that were there before man arrived, to which has been added some legacy from every stage of man's history since he appeared on the scene. From Normandy they inherit the feudal remains, the laws of inheritance which have resulted in the fragmentation of properties, the hedges that sheltered the cider orchards, the characteristic varieties of elm, and the early architecture. From England they have taken their architecture, good and bad, from the 18th century onwards and to their position in the line of fire between England and France they owe their castles, fortifications and military roads.

The very accidents that produced the unique landscape of the Channel Islands are now threatening to destroy it. The independent status granted long ago by the kings of England has enabled the islands to order their affairs so that they are now tax havens. To their own growing population are added those who are escaping high taxation, those who work for firms based in the islands for the same reason, and those who came on holiday, liked what they saw, and decided to retire here. All require houses, and there is already a long waiting list of local people in the same position. All expect to run cars, and the roads and parking places are already saturated. Many expect to run boats, and the harbours and marinas are full. In the face of these and many other pressures, the task of conserving the Channel Islands' heritage is daunting indeed.

The first and overriding concern must be the preservation of the remaining open land. It is essential that no further development takes place on any land that is not already partially built up, and this applies as much to States departments as to private individuals. Coastal land is not at present at risk as it normally forms part of a 'green belt' which is recognised as such by the planning authority concerned. The risk here is from States departments acting for the 'public good'. An example is the Mare de Carteret, a low-lying area on the landward side of the coast road at Cobo in Guernsey. This was designated as green belt by the Island Development Committee, the intention being to plant trees and retain a green corridor between the developing built-up areas to north and south. Instead, the Education Council chose the site to build two large schools.

More at risk is ordinary agricultural land, and it is absolutely vital, for a number of reasons, to retain every remaining field. Although the islands are unlikely ever again to be self-supporting in food, every major industry depends, either directly or indirectly, on agricultural land. (The word agricultural is used here in the Jersey sense to include all land used for crops or livestock, including glasshouses—not in the restricted Guernsey sense of dairy farming only.) The export of early potatoes, broccoli, tomatoes and flowers, which still earns a major proportion of the islands' income, obviously requires land. The tourist industry depends on agricultural land because tourists would not be attracted to islands that were entirely built-up and industrialised, when they can already travel more cheaply to the Mediterranean or even to America; the *rentiers* who contribute to the exchequer by paying income tax would switch to the Isle of Man or the Bahamas for the same reason.

The other major sources of the islands' revenue, offshore finance, depends on agricultural land for a more subtle reason. Finance is an extremely fragile industry, in the sense that it could relatively easily move to some other tax haven at short notice. The great attraction that the islands offer the industry is their stable government. This is the result of a strong tradition in all the islands of unpaid public service, largely by self-employed people with roots in the soil. They and the electorate they serve are conservative (note the small 'c'), largely because of the long tradition, unbroken since feudal times, of identifying with the land and working it as a family concern. If they do not farm themselves they own the odd field, or have inherited a *rente* on one. Without the land, besides the loss of their beauty, the islands would be subjected to the tensions that go with industrialised societies everywhere, and offshore finance would go elsewhere.

Dairy farming brings little money into the islands directly, since most of its products are consumed locally. It does save the expense of importing milk, but of more importance than this is the immense scenic value of the dairy land. Visitors like to see green fields grazed by cattle of the appropriate breed. The hedgebanks bordering the many miles of lanes are trimmed, at no expense to the public, by the farmers. Most important of all, the fields, with their tree-lined hedges, give a deceptively rural appearance to these heavily populated islands, which would otherwise be pure suburbia from coast to coast. Guernsey's Outline Development Plan of 1967[1] designates corridors of agricultural land that weave between the built-up areas, so that as one moves around the island from one built-up zone to the next, one periodically passes between green fields with hedges and trees.

Both islands recognise the importance of dairy farming beyond the actual production of milk, and support the industry in various ways. One method, used with slight differences in both Jersey and Guernsey, is to pay a bonus based on the yield of each cow. But the authorities must also support the industry by ensuring that no more land is lost to it.

The glasshouses of Guernsey present a special problem. Because of the scattered pattern of glasshouse development in Guernsey, it is important to regard greenhouse land as agricultural, and not development land. It used to be fairly easy to obtain permission to build a house on the site of old glass, and since the original siting of the glass was subject to no planning restrictions whatever, this has resulted in a rash of badly-sited housing that makes some parts of the island resemble a bad case of measles. With the tomato industry at present in financial difficulties there is much glass, new and old, on the market, and the owners would naturally like to be able to sell their properties as building land, with the high prices that this commands. There is no financial incentive to demolish the glass and restore the land to a more extensive form of husbandry, yet this would be in the best long-term interest of the island.

Hedges are still an extremely important element in the landscapes of Jersey, Guernsey and Sark. They vary from island to island, and within each island from parish to parish, and are largely responsible for the special atmosphere, so strong and yet so difficult to define, that distinguishes one parish from another. The network of hedges bounding numerous small fields also give the islands the appearance of being larger than they really are; visually, they make the most of a small space. There is a tendency for farmers to demolish hedges to create larger fields in which machinery can work more efficiently, and to reduce labour costs. Apart from Jersey's wooded valleys, nearly all the surviving trees of the islands are in hedgerows, which are now the main reservoir, not only of trees, but also of woodland plants, birds, insects and mammals. Thus if an appreciable number of hedges were lost, not only would the islands lose their deceptively wooded appearance, but also much of their wild life. The alternative would be to plant clumps of trees, though this would alter the character of the landscape. It could be argued that by removing hedges, we are returning to the landscape of the open fields. The difference is that the medieval open fields were surrounded by wilderness, with abundant woodland, heath and scrub providing fuel and sheltering wild life. Today's open fields would be surrounded by nothing but houses, standing starkly above the line of the plateau and finally destroying the rural appearance which the islands have incredibly managed to retain despite their heavy density of development.

A major threat to the landscape, which is being treated very seriously by both States, is the lethal strain of Dutch elm disease which was first noticed in Jersey in 1974, and reached Guernsey three years later. The importance of elms in the landscape has already been stressed (p. 30). Both islands are rightly spending a great deal of money annually in felling and burning diseased trees. Although there is at present no chance of eradicating the disease, the felling policy is successfully checking its spread; in Guernsey 7,000 elms have been felled in the first four years of the campaign, which represents only three and a half per cent. of the total elm population. Meanwhile young trees of other species are being planted, and there is always hope that either the disease will lose its virulence, or an effective treatment will be found.

Where elms are replaced by other trees the choice of suitable species is surprisingly difficult. The elm was ideally suited to the island conditions in its habit of growth, its late opening and its small, wind-resistant leaves. Perhaps the nearest in these respects would be some of the species of southern beech (*Nothofagus*) from the southern hemisphere, but these have not yet been sufficiently well tried locally. It is tempting to plant fast-growing trees such as poplar hybrids, but these are unable to withstand the gales and soon become broken and ragged. Evergreens such as *Cupressus leylandii* have been much planted, but they are alien to the character of the rural parts of the islands; like flowering cherries, they look best in the suburbs. The safest rule would be to plant native species, preferably those with small leaves, even if they are slow-growing. Examples would be English oak, ash, hawthorn, lime, and the occasional holly.

Scale, though an exceedingly abstract concept, is of enormous importance in the landscape. The islands are in reality extremely small, yet the intricate detail of fields, hedges, valleys and narrow lanes creates an illusion of space which enables islanders to live together in comparative peace without feeling overcrowded. This illusion is very easily broken. The steep-sided valleys, which are among the most attractive features of all the islands, illustrate this point. Such a valley typically has a narrow strip of meadow in its floor, grazed perhaps by heifers, with a stream running through it. The steeper slopes are clothed by bracken and the skyline on each side is bounded by trees. In absolute terms the valley may be no more than 100 yards across from shoulder to shoulder, yet it is a world unto itself. The compactness of the hawthorn and blackthorn bushes, the curve of the valley which conceals the ends, the absence of hard lines conspire to abolish scale and create an illusion of distance. If now a clearing is made on one side of the valley and a bungalow is built, the illusion is shattered. The bungalow may be of modest size, but its hard, definable lines have destroyed the scale of the valley.

The greatest glory of the Channel Islands is its coastal scenery. Its importance to tourism is fully recognised and it is unlikely to be harmed by any development other than a badly-sited public lavatory. The threat to the coast is from the sheer pressure of wheels and feet. The steep cliffs—the only truly wild scenery in the islands—are mostly accessible only on foot, and are therefore visited by comparatively few people. Where there is a cliff-top car park, as at Icart in Guernsey, the damage to the turf by trampling only extends some 50 yards in each direction. The provision of a cliff path, which need be only three or four feet wide, provides access to many miles of remote and breathtakingly beautiful scenery for those who are prepared to walk.

The low-lying sandy coasts are a more delicate habitat, as well as having the bays that attract most of the visitors. Here the short turf, rich in wild plants and vital for retaining the sand beneath, is being worn away by those who come to enjoy it. If restriction is necessary it seems reasonable to restrict cars rather than people. Much can be done by providing well-defined car parks.

Inland from the low-lying coasts are considerable areas that are now built up, but which were once meadowland. In winter the meadows were too wet for grazing, but in summer a crop of hay was taken and the aftermath was grazed. These low-lying meadows are becoming rare and those that remain are well worthy of conservation. In early summer, before the hay is mown, they produce a brilliant display of wild flowers, particularly the claret-coloured Jersey orchid. In late summer they provide useful grazing at a time when the grass on the drier land has stopped growing. They need to be managed in the traditional way, for without grazing and mowing, water dropwort and other weeds rapidly take over.

Passing from the natural to the architectural landscape, here again the Channel Islands are unique. The vernacular architecture has affinities with other granite areas, particularly of the adjacent coasts of France, but the remarkably uniform and symmetrical Channel Island house has a character that is entirely its own. In the 18th century English architecture was enthusiastically adopted, but with adaptations to suit local materials and conditions. In Victoria's reign the prevailing architectural taste was well suited to local stone and masonry reached the height of technical excellence. Only in the present century have materials and design been at variance with local conditions. This is well illustrated by school buildings.

There have been two great waves of school building in the islands: the late 19th century, when education became universal, and the late 20th century, when the post-war increase in population and the demand for more facilities made it necessary to build more and larger schools. The Victorian schools were solidly built of granite with steeply-pitched slate roofs, large echoing classrooms with high ceilings, and high windows, so that the children would not be distracted by what was going on outside, and a minimum of other facilities. They were difficult to heat, and every sound reverberated. The post-war schools were flat-roofed and flimsily built of imported materials to an imported design. The classrooms were smaller and easier to heat, with large, low windows and a multitude of other facilities, but the materials and design did not suit local conditions. Soon the paint began to peel, the woodwork to rot, and the roofs to leak, and this has continued despite repeated repairs. More recently some extensions to Victorian schools have been made in both Jersey and Guernsey in the traditional style, with pitched roofs and stone walls. Besides looking far more comfortable next to the old buildings, these will need less maintenance.

Commercial architecture provides many examples of alien styles which ignore the environment both in design and materials. An interesting juxtaposition may be seen in the South Esplanade of St. Peter Port. Until 20 years ago most of the buildings between the Picquet House and the B.E.A. office were grey granite warehouses of the 19th century. Although they were of no great age, they were built of local materials and in the local idiom. In recent years most of the warehouses have either been converted to, or replaced by, offices and shops. The building on the right is the Albany, built in 1960 to the designs of a London partnership. In design and material it is wholly alien—the only acknowledgement that the building makes to the fact that it is in Guernsey is a gimmicky panel of granite, surrounded by concrete. The emphasis is horizontal rather than vertical and the roofline, though broken, is flat. To the left, clustered around the *Yacht* hotel, is a group of converted warehouses. Within they have been rebuilt, but their gabled facades have been retained and in all the details such as sash windows with their vertical emphasis, due regard has been given to the history and character of the waterfront site. Credit must be given both to the architects, well versed in local materials and design, and to the Island Development Committee, who were not prepared to allow a repetition of the Albany mistake.

The conversion of old buildings into flats saves considerable land, as well as producing dwellings of great character. Some extremely imaginative conversions of Victorian buildings have been accomplished in recent years. The parish arsenals lend themselves particularly well to sub-division in this way. That of St. Laurence in Jersey is one of a line of four buildings of which the parish is justly proud—from south to north they are the parish church, the parish hall, the parish arsenal, and the parish school. The arsenal has been sympathetically converted into dwellings, and the school has recently been extended, in each case without destroying the character of the old building. In Guernsey, St. Peter's School, made redundant when the primary schools of two parishes were amalgamated, has similarly been divided into dwellings of character; the Housing Authority has also renovated and sub-divided a number of large derelict houses.

Planning Authorities and Amenity Societies

The Channel Islander has always been independent, resenting bureaucratic interference, but the pressures on the islands, mainly from outside, are now so enormous that rigid control of development is vital.

At the beginning of the present century the amount of land available for development must have seemed limitless. Improved roads and motor transport were giving access to the whole countryside, and planning controls were negligible. As recently as 1927 in Guernsey a man could build anything he liked on his own land anywhere in the island, subject only to a *bornement* (consent of the parish authorities) if it was to be within 30 feet of a road.[2] A very considerable amount of building took place in Guernsey between the two World Wars; hundreds of houses and bungalows were built, extending into the countryside the ribbon development which had previously been confined to the outskirts of the towns. Examples of this ribbon development are to be seen along the Forest Road and much of the west coast. In 1927 action was at last taken to protect some of the remaining natural beauty; a law was passed which prohibited building in a strip along the south coast and on certain headlands, without permission. From 1929, when the Preservation of Natural Beauty Law took effect, some control was exercised over the siting and appearance of buildings, but only in areas where natural beauty might be affected. It was not until 1959 that the control of agricultural land was added to the law, and it became possible to control buildings, other than glasshouses, on agricultural land. The exclusion of glasshouses from the law accounts, as we have seen, for the scatter of housing in rural areas, for it was impossible under the 1959 law to prevent old vineries from being sold as building plots.

In 1967 the Preservation of Natural Beauty and Control of Agricultural Land Committee became the Island Development Committee, and in the same year the Committee presented its Outline Development Plan, which was unanimously accepted by the States. The plan, published by the Greffe as *Billet d'Etat XIV* of 1967, includes as an appendix a 'Survey of Cause and Effect in the Development of Guernsey' which amounts to an exhaustive study in regional geography. The effect of the plan is to divide the island into zones of various categories, in which either no development, or development of specified types, may take place. Being an outline plan, the boundaries are not precisely drawn and more detailed plans, covering limited areas, are gradually being produced. The Outline Development Plan, or Detailed Development Plans where these are available, have formed the basis for all planning decisions since 1967.

In Jersey, too, a great deal of sub-standard housing was built between the wars, particularly on the eastern outskirts of the town, and around the coast. Immediately after the Second World War the States set up a Natural Beauties Committee, with powers to prevent building on agricultural land, or in any other place where the natural beauty of the island would be affected. Pressure was enormous and it soon became clear that the island would have to be zoned. Mr. William Barrett was invited to draw up a plan; this was completed in 1962, accepted by the States and incorporated into the Island Development Plan of 1963. The Barrett Plan defined a green belt of coastal land and certain inland areas where no building would be permitted, and designated other areas, particularly round the parish centres, for development.

The Natural Beauties Committee, re-named the Island Development Committee, has jealously guarded the green belt, but pressure is so immense to develop every corner of Jersey that some unfortunate decisions have inevitably been made. In some parishes the 'village developments' have taken place as envisaged in the Barrett Plan. In some other areas development has been more piecemeal. There is a particularly large and sprawling complex of housing estates—some of States houses, and some built privately, assisted by States loans—at Red Houses in the parish of St. Brelade. It does, however, house a substantial proportion of the population of the island.

Jersey's housing shortage was aggravated by the rapid post-war expansion of tourism. In 1965 it was realised that houses were becoming guest-houses so fast that the stock of housing for local people was becoming seriously depleted. Accordingly the expansion of tourism was brought under control and the emphasis now is on quality rather than quantity.

The present policy of the Jersey States is for new dwellings to be built on run-down industrial sites; the countryside is recognised as an asset which must not be used for housing.

By 1960 even the fiercely independent island of Sark found it necessary to appoint a Committee for the Preservation of Natural Amenities, with powers to control all future development. The committee found its task so daunting that it appointed Mr. G. A. Jellicoe, author of *A Landscape Charter for the Isles of Scilly,* to draw up a plan for Sark. In *A Landscape Plan for Sark*[3] Mr. Jellicoe urged that fewer houses should be built, and that those which were built should be of better quality, and exclusively for Sark people. All future development should be concentrated in a few well-defined areas which would be screened by trees, and certain agricultural fields should be earmarked as overspill for future development. The people of Sark regarded all this as an infringement of their ancient liberties, and the Jellicoe Plan was rejected in 1968.

In Alderney there is a particularly sharp contrast between the old houses, built of local materials in the distinctive local idiom, and the English suburban houses built by the newcomers to the island since the war. For many years a green belt has been recognised on which development is not allowed, but elsewhere decisions have been made on an *ad hoc* basis. Recognising the need for an overall plan, in 1967 the States of Alderney commissioned W. R. Davidge and Partners to produce a report. The Davidge Report advised the retention of the green belt, with future development limited to certain areas, such as Platte Saline and Valongis, where there are already numerous buildings, but also plenty of room for infilling. Some open spaces would be retained even within the development areas.

Though the Davidge Report was not rejected when it was considered by the States in 1969, it has never been fully implemented. Also, Alderney has no legislation that recognises buildings of architectural or historic interest. A draft law which would have empowered the Building and Development Control Committee to schedule such buildings, and to designate a conservation area in which special vigilance should be maintained, was rejected by the States in 1975. To complement the proposed law, the Alderney Society had invited the architectural historian, Mr. C. E. B. Brett, to prepare a survey of the buildings of the island. This was published in 1976.[4] Mr. Brett recommended that the conservation area should include the whole town of St. Anne, and extend down La Route de Braye to include the warehouses of Braye Street and the old jetty.

It is to be hoped that the Davidge Report, or a similar overall plan, will be fully implemented before it is too late, and also that the unique town of St. Anne will be designated a conservation area. In the meantime, Alderney's planning decisions continue to be made on an *ad hoc* basis.

It will be seen from the foregoing that, while restrictions become inevitable with the increase in population, they are fiercely resisted, and in many cases only accepted after the damage has been done. A sign of the increasing concern shown by many islanders for the preservation of their environment is the strength of the amenity societies, and also of the 'learned societies' which, although their main object is local research, become politically active when they feel that some aspect of their particular island's heritage is being threatened. The senior society is the Société Jersiaise, founded in 1873, and concerned with the study of the history, archaeology, geology and natural history of Jersey. Papers on these subjects are published in an *Annual Bulletin*. The society's headquarters are at 9 Pier Road, St. Helier, where there is a comprehensive museum, library and art gallery. The society also owns many of the prehistoric remains of Jersey, including La Hougue Bie, where there are further specialised museums, and it co-operates with the National Trust for Jersey in running nature reserves.

La Société Guernesiaise was founded in 1882 and covers the Bailiwick of Guernsey. It is at present without a permanent headquarters, but its sections are active in the various branches of natural history, archaeology and local history, and papers are published annually in the *Report and Transactions*. The run of *Bulletins* and *Transactions* of these two societies constitute the main source of material on local studies, and may be consulted in the main public libraries, both in the islands and the United Kingdom.

The two bodies primarily concerned with the environment are the National Trusts of the two main islands. Although their aims are similar to those of the National Trust in England, both are independent bodies. The National Trust for Jersey was founded in 1936 by a group of islanders who were concerned at the despoliation of the island by uncontrolled building. Its first property, Le Don Le Gallais, was a wooded côtil in La Vallée des Vaux, immediately to the north of St. Helier. Many other properties have followed, either by gift or purchase, including other côtils in the same valley, Quetival Mill and a chain of côtils in St. Peter's Valley, more côtils in Queen's Valley, Le Rât Cottage and Morel Farm to the west of St. Laurence's church, the *colombier* behind Longueville Manor, Grève de Lecq Barracks, and some magnificent stretches of cliff at Le Col de la

Rocque in St. Mary's parish. Here the experiment has been tried of providing two cliff paths, one for pedestrians and one for horses.

Further along the coast in the parish of St. John the Trust owns La Vallette, a farm between Mont Mado and Bonne Nuit Bay, and several pieces of land bordering the road leading up from the bay to the east. It owns The Elms, a magnificent farm near the head of a valley to the south-east of St. Mary's church—the substantial enclosed farmyard is of the traditional Jersey type, with access by two large arches. In St. Ouen's Bay the Trust owns several sand pits and meadows, and through the Benjamin Meaker Trust it has been able to buy St. Ouen's Pond, to secure its future as an important nature reserve.

The National Trust of Guernsey was founded in 1960 with similar aims. Its first property was a wooded valley, Le Vau de Monel, at Pleinmont. A house existed here before the war and from the terrace, and the paths around the perimeter of the property, are magnificent views over Rocquaine Bay. Other Trust properties are in the Talbot Valley, on the south cliffs, and at Le Catioroc, where the Trust owns the land on the south side of Le Chemin Le Roi, once the King's Highway, but now a cart track on the spine of the ridge above the dolmen. The Trust also runs, in collaboration with La Société Guernesiaise, a folk museum at Saumarez Park.

Much of Guernsey's coastal land is owned by the States and there is little danger at present of it being developed, but States policies change with time, while the Trust properties are held in perpetuity for the benefit of the people of the island. Most of the land belonging to the National Trusts in both islands is open free of charge to the public, who are simply asked not to damage the properties or leave litter.

The Alderney Society, founded in 1966, takes an interest in all aspects of local research, runs an excellent museum in the Old School, High Street, and works in many ways to preserve the Alderney heritage. Finally, La Société Sercquiaise was founded, with similar aims, in 1975.

In 1974 the National Trust of Guernsey, wishing to make both the States and the public more aware of the architectural heritage of the island, invited Mr. C. E. B. Brett to produce a survey of the buildings of St. Peter Port, on the lines of the surveys he had already undertaken for the Ulster Architectural Heritage Society. With help from a team of local researchers, Mr. Brett's list was published in 1975.[5] It was so successful that he was immediately invited by the Alderney Society to compile a similar list of the buildings of Alderney. The list, already referred to in this chapter, was published in 1976 and was followed a year later by a survey of St. Helier, compiled at the invitation of the National Trust for Jersey.[6]

These three lists, published in Belfast in the same format as the lists compiled by Mr. Brett for the Ulster Architectural Heritage Society, have done more than anything else to open our eyes to the richness of the islands' architectural heritage.

*   *   *   *   *   *

One thing that has impressed me particularly while writing this book is the enormous amount of work that remains to be done, despite the formidable literature that already exists. Repeatedly I came across problems which I would dearly have liked to pursue further, but which were too detailed to include in a general survey such as this. A rewarding line of study would be to undertake a detailed analysis of the landscape of a small area—a single parish, or even a valley, a bay or a settlement. The more restricted studies could be undertaken by individuals, either as a school or university project, or simply for the satisfaction of becoming better acquainted with the environment. Parish surveys might be undertaken by groups such as the 'learned societies' or schools with sixth forms.

Subjects for investigation would include the reason for the line of each road, how it came to be the width it is, and the type of hedge or wall bounding it; the name and origin of each field and the reason for its shape; the age of every house and the reason for its siting. Some work has already been done, but is unpublished; the most scholarly contribution is a study of the place-names of Jersey, largely by the late Charles Stevens. Plans are in hand to publish this important work, and in the meantime it may be consulted in typescript in the library of the Société Jersiaise.

The study of the landscape is of more than academic interest. Beside the heightened pleasure that a knowledge of one's surroundings gives, a proper understanding of the reasons for the present state of affairs is essential if sound decisions are to be made when planning for the future. Sir John Coode, who designed the abortive outer harbour of St. Helier, was the leading harbour architect of his day; a more eminent expert could not have been found. Yet he lacked local knowledge and one of his breakwaters was washed away. The designers of the even more abortive 'harbours of refuge' had no local knowledge whatever. The successful harbour works have been those that evolved gradually, using the accumulated experience of the men on the spot.

So it is with every form of development. The building that looks right and lasts is the one that has due regard for the landscape of which it forms part.

The landscape of the Channel Islands is unique. In no other part of the world has the same history reacted with the same rocks and climate to produce the beautiful and immensely complex scenery of the islands. Those who are fortunate enough to live in it must never allow themselves to forget what a unique landscape it is.

REFERENCES

Chapter One

1. Renouf, J., 'Geology', in Coysh, V. (ed.), *The Channel Islands a New Study* (Newton Abbot, 1977), p. 19.
2. Roach, R. A., 'An Outline of the Evolution of the Rocks of Guernsey', *Trans. Soc. Guernesiaise*, 1972, p. 142.
3. Pudsey, C. J., 'Geologica Ridunae', *Trans. Soc. Guernesiaise*, 1977, p. 259.
4. Mourant, A. E., 'The Use of Fort Regent Granite in Megalithic Monuments in Jersey', *Bull. Soc. Jersiaise*, 1977, p. 41.
5. Renouf, J., *The Channel Islands a New Study*, p. 26.
6. George, P. K., 'The Quaternary on Guernsey', *Trans. Soc. Guernesiaise*, 1972, p. 161.
7. Zeuner, F. E., *The Pleistocene Period*, 1959, p. 287.
8. Mourant, A. E., The Raised Beaches and Other Terraces of the Channel Islands, *Geol. Mag. Lond.*, 70, 1933, p. 58.
9. Zeuner, F. E., 'A New Subspecies of Red Deer from the Upper Pleistocene of Jersey', *Bull. Soc. Jersiaise*, 1940, p. 27.
10. Renouf, J., *et al., Provisional Notes on the Geology of Alderney*, Alderney, 1972.
11. Keen, D. H., 'Two Aspects of the Last Interglacial in Jersey', *Bull. Soc. Jersiaise*, 1975, p. 393.
12. Sinel, J., 'The Submerged Peat and Forest Beds of the Channel Islands', *Trans. Soc. Guernesiaise*, 1909, p. 25.
13. Sinel, J., 'The Relative Ages of the Channel Islands', *Bull. Soc. Jersiaise*, 1909, p. 442.
14. George, P. K., 'The Quaternary on Guernsey', *Trans. Soc. Guernesiaise*, 1972, p. 179.
15. Girard, P. J., and Elhai, H., 'Notes on the Quaternary in Guernsey', *Trans. Soc. Guernesiaise*, 1964, p. 597.
16. Balleine, G. R., *The Bailiwick of Jersey* (London, 1951), p. 4.
17. Ansted, D. T., and Latham, R. G., *The Channel Islands*, 1862.
18. Wilson, K., in Lucas, A. H. S. (ed.), *An Alderney Scrapbook*, Alderney, 1972, p. 61

Chapter Two

1. Dury, G., 'The Channel Islands', in *The Land of Britain*. Report of the Land Utilisation Survey of Britain, 1951.
2. Girard, P. J., and Elhai, H., 'Notes on the Quaternary in Guernsey', *Trans. Soc. Guernesiaise*, 1964, p. 607.
3. Ranwell, D. S., 'The Dunes of St. Ouen's Bay, Jersey', *Bull. Soc. Jersiaise*, 1975, p. 385.
4. Le Sueur, F., *A Natural History of Jersey*, 1976, p. 30.
5. Richens, R. H., Private communication; Le Sueur, F., *A Natural History of Jersey*, p. 30.
6. Le Maistre, F., *Dictionnaire Jersiais-Francais*, 1966, 'geon', p. 267
7. Carey, E. F., *Essays on Guernsey History*, Guernsey, 1936, p. 25.
8. Le Sueur, F., *A Natural History of Jersey*, p. 90.
9. Pollard, E., *et al., Hedges*, 1974, p. 133.
10. Le Sueur, F., 'Changes in the Flora of Jersey, 1873–1973', *Centenary Bulletin Soc. Jersiaise*, 1973, p. 36.
11. Le Sueur, F., *op. cit.*, p. 37.
12. Le Sueur, F., *op. cit.*, p. 36.

Chapter Three

1. Johnston, D. E., 'Prehistory and Archaeology', in Coysh, V. (ed.), *The Channel Islands a New Study* (Newton Abbot, 1977), p. 43.
2. Johnston, D. E., *op. cit.*, p. 53.
3. Hawkes, J., *The Archaeology of the Channel Islands*, Vol. II (Jersey, 1938), p. 258.
4. Kendrick, T. D., *The Archaeology of the Channel Islands*, Vol. I (London, 1928), p. 107.
5. de Garis, M., *The Folklore of Guernsey* (Guernsey, 1975), p. 234.
6. Kendrick, T. D., *op. cit.*, p. 26.
7. Kendrick, T. D., *op. cit.*, p. 198.
8. Cachemaille, J. L. V., *The Island of Sark* (1874-6, reprinted London, 1928).
9. Hawkes, K., *Sark* (Newton Abbot, 1977), p. 89.
10. de Guerin, T. W. M., 'List of Dolmens, Menhirs and Sacred Rocks' *Trans. Soc. Guernesiaise*, 1921, p. 30.
11. Hawkes, J., *op. cit.*, p. 133.
12. Burns, R. B., 'The Late Iron Age Site at the Tranquesous' *Trans. Soc. Guernesiaise*, 1977, p. 188.
13. Kendrick, T. D., *op. cit.*, p. 257.
14. Stevens, J., *Old Jersey Houses*, Vol. I (Jersey, 1965), p. 22.
15. Stevens, C. G., *et al.* 'The Roman Pillar in St. Laurence's Church', *Bull. Soc. Jersiaise*, 1975, p. 343.
16. de Gruchy, G. F. B., *Medieval Land Tenures in Jersey* (Jersey, 1957), p. 201.

Chapter Four

1. Ewen, A. H., 'The Fiefs of the Island of Guernsey', *Trans. Soc. Guernesiaise*, 1961, p. 173.
2. Lemprière, R., *The Customs, Ceremonies and Traditions of the Channel Islands* (London, 1976), p. 67.
3. de Gruchy, G. F. B., *Medieval Land Tenures in Jersey* (Jersey, 1957), p. 28.
4. Stevens, J., *Old Jersey Houses*, Vol. II (Chichester, 1977), back end paper.
5. Ewen, A. H., and de Carteret, A. R., *The Fief of Sark* (Guernsey, 1969), p. 38.
6. de Gruchy, G. F. B., *op. cit.*, p. 170.
7. Ewen and de Carteret, *op. cit.*, p. 39.

Chapter Five

1. Ransom M. E., Report on samples from Vazon Bay, Guernsey, *Trans. Soc. Guernesiaise*, 1966, p. 33. A further report appears in the *Trans.* for 1967, p. 146.
2. Ewen, A. H., 'Origins and Early Development of Agriculture in Guernsey', *Trans. Soc. Guernesiaise*, 1962, p. 333.
3. Ewen, A. H., 'Field systems and Island History', *Trans. Soc. Guernesiaise*, 1959, p. 424.
4. Ewen, A. H., *op. cit.*, p. 417.
5. Le Huray, C. P., 'Some Notes on the Open Field System and Enclosure Movement in Guernsey', *Trans. Soc. Guernesiaise*, 1952, p. 186.
6. de Gruchy, G. F. B., *Medieval Land Tenures in Jersey* (Jersey, 1957), p. 120.
7. Stevens, J., *Old Jersey Houses*, Vol. I (Jersey, 1965), p. 78.
8. *Acts des Etats*, Vol. I (Guernsey), p. 362.
9. de Gruchy, G. F. B., *op. cit.*, p. 165.
10. de Gruchy, G. F. B., *op. cit.*, p. 166.
11. Dury, G. H., 'Some Land Use Statistics for Jersey in the late 18th Century', *Bull. Soc. Jersiaise*, 1952, p. 439.
12. Dury, G. H., 'Some Land Use Statistics for Guernsey in the late 18th Century', *Trans. Soc. Guernesiaise*, 1953, p. 258.

13. Warren, J. P., 'Partage des Communes de la Forêt' *Trans. Soc. Guernesiaise*, 1952, p. 193.

14. Pollard, E., Hooper, M. D., and Moore, N. W., *Hedges* (London, 1974), p. 79.

15. Stevens, J., *Old Jersey Houses*, Vol. I, p. 27.

Chapter Six

1. Stevens, J., *Victorian Voices* (Jersey, 1969), p. 210

2. *Agricultural Statistics*, compiled annually by the Agriculture and Fisheries Committee. States Greffe, Jersey.

3. *Jersey and the E.E.C.*, Report of Special Committee of the States of Jersey (Jersey, 1967), p. 138.

4. Girard, P. J., 'Development of the Bulb and Flower Industry in Guernsey', *Trans. Soc. Guernesiaise*, 1939, p. 284.

5. Jacob, J., *Annals of the British Norman Isles*, Part I (Paris, 1830), p. 199.

6. Girard, P. J., 'The Guernsey Grape Industry', *Trans. Soc. Guernesiaise*, 1951, p. 126.

7. Wheadon, E. A., 'The History and Cultivation of the Tomato in Guernsey', *Trans. Soc. Guernesiaise*, 1935, p. 337.

8. Girard, P. J., 'Survey of the Development of Glasshouses in an area from Vazon Bay to Cobo Road', *Trans. Soc. Guernesiaise*, 1959, p. 438.

9. Island Development Committee, *Outline Development Plan*, States of Guernsey, 1967, p. 448.

Chapter Seven

1. St. Mary's church pamphlet. Anonymous, but in the style of Joan Stevens.

2. Curtis, S. C., 'The Evolution of the Country Churches', *Trans. Soc. Guernesiaise*, 1919, p. 199.

3. Leapingwell, E. J., 'Architecture in Jersey' in *The Channel Islands: A New Study*, ed. Coysh, V. (Newton Abbot, 1977), p. 138.

4. Stevens, J., *Old Jersey Houses*, Vol. I, p. 22.

5. de Guérin, T. W. M., 'Guernsey Crosses', *Trans. Soc. Guernesiaise*, 1907, p. 358.

6. Stevens, J., *Old Jersey Houses*, Vol. I, p. 58. [In a personal communication of 23 August, 1980, Mrs. Stevens tells me she now suspects that a few buildings, such as Leoville Farm, St. Ouen, may date from before 1500.]

7. Meirion-Jones, G. I., 'The Long-House in Brittany—A Provisional Assessment', *Post-Medieval Archaeology*, Vol. 7, 1973, p. 1.

8. *The Guernsey Farmhouse* (London, 1963). 'By members of the Guernsey Society', but written in the style of T. F. Priaulx, p. 92.

9. *op. cit.*, p. 26.

10. A map of the world distribution of pantiles will be found in Robinson, G. W. S., *Guernsey* (Newton Abbot, 1977), p. 39.

11. Ewen, A. H. and de Carteret, A. R., *The Fief of Sark* (Guernsey, 1969), p. 116.

12. Stevens, J., *Old Jersey Houses*, Vol. I, p. 87.

Chapter Eight

1. Nicolle, E. T., *The Town of St. Helier* (Jersey, 1931), p. 10.

2. Stevens, J., *Old Jersey Houses*, Vol. II, p. 138.

3. Carey, E. F., *Essays on Guernsey History* (Guernsey, 1936), p. 10.

4. Stevens, J., *Old Jersey Houses*, Vol. II, p. 106.

5. Brett, C. E. B., *Buildings of the Island of Alderney* (Belfast, 1976), p. 42.

6. Brett, C. E. B., *Buildings in the Town and Parish of St. Peter Port* (Belfast, 1975), p. 14.

7. Leapingwell, E. J., 'Architecture in Jersey', in *The Channel Islands: A New Study*, ed. Coysh, V. (Newton Abbot, 1977), p. 146.

8. Stevens, J., *Old Jersey Houses*, Vol. II, p. 90.

9. Brett, C. E. B., *Buildings in the Town and Parish of St. Peter Port* (Belfast, 1975), p. 68.

10. Brett, C. E. B., *op. cit.*, p. 33.

11. Little, B., *St. Peter Port, its Story and its Buildings* (Guernsey, 1963), p. 13.

12. Brett, C. E. B., *Buildings in the Town and Parish of St. Helier* (Belfast, 1977), p. 34.

13. Hampton, R., 'The Pre-Raphaelite Window in St. Aubin's Church', *Bull. Soc. Jersiaise*, 1979, p. 301.

14. Lemprière, R., *Buildings and Memorials of the Channel Islands* (London, 1980), p. 99.

Chapter Nine

1. Barton, K. J., 'Fortifications of the Channel Islands', *Review Guernsey Soc.*, Spring 1980, p. 7.

2. Le Patourel, J., *The Building of Castle Cornet* (Guernsey, 1958).

3. O'Neil, B. H. St. J., *Castle Cornet* (Guernsey, 11th edition, 1970).

4. Ewen, A. J., and de Carteret, A. R., *The Fief of Sark* (Guernsey, 1969), p. 44.

5. Stevens, J., *Old Jersey Houses*, Vol. I (Jersey, 1965), p. 143.

6. Pocock, H. R. S., 'Jersey's Martello Towers', *Bull. Soc. Jersiaise*, 1971, p. 289.

7. Lemprière, R., *Buildings and Memorials of the Channel Islands* (London, 1980), 118.

8. Ouseley, M. H., 'The Decision to build the Forts of Alderney', *Review Guernsey Soc.*, Winter, 1977, p. 82.

9. Brett, C. E. B., *Buildings of the Island of Alderney* (Belfast, 1967), p. 10.

10. Gen. Hans Spiegel, quoted in *An Alderney Scrapbook* (Guernsey, 1972), p. 40.

11. Cruickshank, C., *The German Occupation of the Channel Islands* (Guernsey, 1975), p. 187.

Chapter Ten

1. Stevens, J., *Old Jersey Houses*, Vol. I (Jersey, 1965), p. 40.

2. Marshall, M., 'History of the Water Mills at Petit Bôt', *Trans. Soc. Guernesiaise*, 1964, p. 583.

3. Winkworth, J. W., 'The Watermill', in A. H. S. Lucas (ed.) *An Alderney Scrapbook* (Alderney, 1972), p. 105.

4. Robinson, G. W. S., *Guernsey* (Newton Abbot, 1977), p. 78.

5. Kellet Smith, S. K., 'Quarrying and Mining on Herm and Jethou', *Trans. Soc. Guernesiaise*, 1961, p. 246.

6. Mourant, A. E., and Warren, J. P., 'Minerals and Mining in the Channel Islands', *Trans Soc. Guernesiaise*, 1933, p. 73.

7. Balleine, G. R., *The Bailiwick of Jersey* (London, 1951), p. 20.

8. Rutherford, W., *Jersey* (Newton Abbot, 1976), p. 142

Chapter Eleven

1. Carey, E. F., 'The Chevauchée de St. Michel' *Trans. Soc. Guernesiaise*, 1915, p. 248, quoting the Assize Roll of 1309.

2. de Gruchy, G. F. B., *Medieval Land Tenures in Jersey* (Jersey, 1957), p. 116.

3. Stevens, J., *Old Jersey Houses*, Vol. I, p. 26.

4. Archives Section Report, *Bull. Soc. Jersiaise*, 1980, p. 364.

5. A map of Don's roads and the fortifications of Jersey will be found as the front end-paper of Joan Stevens' *Old Jersey Houses*, Vol. II.

6. Berry, W., *History of the Island of Guernsey* (London, 1815), p. 218. (This work includes a fold-out map, dated 1814, which shows the approximate courses of the military roads completed by that date.)

7. *Actes des Etats*, Tome 3, 1780–1815 (Guernsey, 1910), p. 255.

8. Stevens, J., *Victorian Voices* (Jersey, 1969), p. 76.

9. Cruikshank, C., *The German Occupation of the Channel Islands* (Guernsey, 1975), p. 188.

10. Sharp, E. W., 'The Evolution of St. Peter Port Harbour', *Trans. Soc. Guernesiaise*, 1967, p. 226.

11. Sharp, E. W., 'The Evolution of St. Sampson's Harbour', *Trans. Soc. Guernesiaise*, 1968, p. 304.

12. Balleine, G. R., *The Bailiwick of Jersey* (London, 1951), p. 20.

13. Davies, W., 'What a Series of Blunders these Admiralty Harbours have been', *Bull. Soc. Jersiaise*, 1979, p. 295.

14. Brett, C. E. B., *Buildings of the Island of Alderney* (Belfast, 1976), p. 43.

15. David, J. M., 'The Early History of the Hanois Lighthouse', *Trans. Soc. Guernesiaise*, 1960, p. 53.

Chapter Twelve

1. Island Development Committee, Guernsey, 'Outline Development Plan', *Billet d'Etat XIV* of 1967.

2. *Ibid.*, p. 442.

3. Jellicoe, G. A., *A Landscape Plan for Sark* (Sark, 1967).

4. Brett, C. E. B., *Buildings of the Island of Alderney* (Belfast, 1976).

5. Brett, C. E. B., *Buildings in the Town and Parish of St. Peter Port* (Belfast, 1975).

6. Brett, C. E. B., *Buildings in the Town and Parish of Saint Helier* (Belfast, 1977).

SELECT BIBLIOGRAPHY

The main sources of information on local studies in the Channel Islands are the *Annual Bulletin* of the Société Jersiaise, published annually since 1875, and the *Report and Transactions* of La Société Guernesiaise, published annually since 1888. Numerous papers from these journals are referred to in the text; the references are given by chapters, beginning on page 184. The journals may be consulted in the island libraries, and in the larger universities and municipal libraries elsewhere.

A few suggestions of subjects for further study will be found on pages 59, 73, 74, 89, 116, 157 and 183.

Although virtually nothing has been written on the Channel Islands' landscape as such, the following selection of books contain relevant material:

Ansted, T. D., and Latham, R. G., *The Channel Islands* (London, 1862).
Balleine, G. R., *The Bailiwick of Jersey* (London, 1951).
Berry, W., *History of the Island of Guernsey* (London, 1915).
Brett, C. E. B., *Buildings in the Town and Parish of St. Peter Port* (Belfast, 1975).
Brett, C. E. B., *Buildings in the Island of Alderney* (Belfast, 1976).
Brett, C. E. B., *Buildings in the Town and Parish of St. Helier* (Belfast, 1977).
Carey, E. F., *Essays on Guernsey History* (Guernsey, 1936).
Coysh, V., *Alderney* (Newton Abbot, 1974).
Coysh, V. (editor), *The Channel Islands—a New Study* (Newton Abbot, 1977).
Cruikshank, C., *The German Occupation of the Channel Islands* (Guernsey, 1975).
De Garis, M., *Dictiounnaire Angllais-Guernesiais* (Chichester, 1982).
de Gruchy, G. F. B., *Medieval Land Tenures in Jersey* (Jersey, 1957).
Dury, G., 'The Channel Islands' in *The Land of Britain.* (Report of the Land Utilisation Survey of Britain, 1951.)
Ewen, A. H., and de Carteret, A. R., *The Fief of Sark* (Guernsey, 1969).
Fleure, H. J., *British Landscape through Maps—Guernsey* (Sheffield, 1961).
Guernsey Society, *The Guernsey Farmhouse* (London, 1963).
Hawkes, J., *The Archaeology of the Channel Islands,* Vol. II (Jersey, 1938).
Hawkes, K., *Sark* (Newton Abbott, 1977).
Hoskins, W. G., *The Making of the English Landscape* (London, 1955).
Island Development Committee, Guernsey. *Outline Development Plan* (States of Guernsey, 1967).
Jacob, J., *Annals of the British Norman Isles* (Paris, 1830).
Jee, N., *Guernsey's Natural History* (Guernsey, 1967 and 1972).
Jellicoe, G. A., *A Landscape Plan for Sark* (Sark, 1967).
Johnston, D. E., *The Channel Islands: An Archaeological Guide* (Chichester, 1981).
Kendrick, T. D., *The Archaeology of the Channel Islands,* Vol. I (London, 1928).
Le Huray, C. P., *The Bailiwick of Guernsey* (London, 1952 and 1962).
Lemprière, R., *Portrait of the Channel Islands* (London, 1970).
Lemprière, R., *History of the Channel Islands* (London, 1974).
Lemprière, R., *Customs, Ceremonies and Traditions of the Channel Islands* (London, 1976).
Lemprière, R., *Buildings and Memorials of the Channel Islands* (London, 1980).
Le Sueur, F., *A Natural History of Jersey* (Chichester, 1976).
Lucas, A. H. S. (editor), *An Alderney Scrapbook* (Alderney, 1972).
McCormack, J., *The Guernsey House* (Chichester, 1980).

Nicolle, E. T., *A Chronology of Jersey* (Jersey, revised 1935).
Nicolle, E. T., *The Town of St. Helier* (Jersey, 1931).
Pollard, Hooper and Moore, *Hedges* (London, 1974).
Robinson, G. W. S., *Guernsey* (Newton Abbot, 1977).
Rutherford, W., *Jersey* (Newton Abbot, 1976).
Stamp, L. D., *Man and the Land* (London, 1955).
Stevens, J., *Old Jersey Houses*, Vol. I (Jersey, 1965; revised edition, Chichester, 1980).
Stevens, J., *Old Jersey Houses*, Vol. II (Chichester, 1977).
Stevens, J., *Victorian Voices* (Jersey, 1969).
Sutcliffe, S., *Martello Towers* (Newton Abbot, 1972).
*Syvret and Stevens, *Balleine's History of Jersey* (Chichester, 1981).
Taylor, C., *Fields in the English Landscape* (London, 1975).
Zeuner, F. E., *The Pleistocene Period* (London, 1959).

*This important work was published too late to be referred to in the main text.

INDEX